EVENT-CITIES 3

MIT Press books may be purchased at special quantity discounts for business or sales promotional use. For information, please email special_sales@mitpress.mit.edu or write to Special Sales Department, The MIT Press, 5 Cambridge Center, Cambridge, MA 02142.

Event-Cities, published in 1994 on the occasion of Bernard Tschumi's exhibition at The Museum of Modern Art in New York, was an expanded version of *Praxis Villes-Événements* (Le Fresnoy and Massimo Riposati, Editeurs, Paris). *Event-Cities 2* included work done from 1994 to 1999. *Event-Cities 3* gathers together projects developed by Bernard Tschumi from 1999 to 2004.

Book design and production: Bernard Tschumi and Irene Cheng, with David Benjamin, Adam Marcus, Elizabeth Hodges, and Meredith Collins
Copy editor: Stephanie Salomon
Printer: Massimo Riposati, Edizioni Carte Segrete, Rome - Italy

Library of Congress Cataloging-in-Publication Data

Tschumi, Bernard, 1944–
   Event-cities 3 / Bernard Tschumi.
   640 p.   23 x 16,5 cm
   Includes bibliographical references.
   ISBN 0-262-70110-3 (pbk.: alk. paper)
     1. Tschumi, Bernard, 1944– 2. Architecture, Modern—21st century.
     3. Architecture, Modern—20th century. 4. Architecture—Philosophy.
     I. Title: Event-cities three. II. Title.
NA1353.T78A35 2005
724'.7—dc22   2004056686

Printed and bound in Italy - Grafica Ripoli for Edizioni Carte Segrete, Rome
riposati@cartesegrete.com

BERNARD TSCHUMI

EVENT-CITIES 3
Concept vs. Context vs. Content

The MIT Press
Cambridge, Massachusetts
London, England

Acknowledgments

Many individuals affiliated with Bernard Tschumi Architects have been essential to the development of the projects in this book. I would like to thank, in particular, Véronique Descharrières in the Paris office and Kim Starr, Anne Save de Beaurecueil, and Joel Rutten in the New York office. The following also deserve special thanks: in New York, Valentin Bontjes van Beek, Jon Chace, Chong-zi Chen, Irene Cheng, Andrea Day, Adam Dayem, William Feuerman, Thomas Goodwill, Ludovic Ghirardi, Phu Hoang, Elizabeth Hodges, Robert Holton, Daniel Holguin, Matthew Hufft, Sarrah Khan, Liz Kim, Jane Kim, Dominic Leong, Nicolas Martin, Michaela Metcalfe, Johanne Riegels Oestergaard, and Eva Sopeoglou; and in Paris, Sylviane Brossard, Cristina Devizzi, Jean-Jacques Hubert, Antoine Santiard, Matteo Vigano, and Alex Reid, whose construction experience has been invaluable on European sites.

In locations away from our usual bases of operation, Art Hupp of Glaserworks and Michael Photiadis of ARSY played major roles in our buildings in Cincinnati and Athens, respectively. Several structural and mechanical engineers, as well as other consultants, helped us to formulate some of the concepts developed in these projects, especially Hugh Dutton of Hugh Dutton Associates in Paris; Leo Argiris, Nigel Tonks, Matt King, Patrick McCafferty, and Brian Streby of ARUP New York; William Faschan of Leslie E. Robertson Associates, New York; and Israel Berger of Israel Berger & Associates.

I would also like to thank the students and faculty of the School of Architecture at Columbia University for their feedback, particularly on projects that were discussed in lectures and forums at the School. In addition I am grateful to the university's administration—first, President George Rupp and Provost Jonathan Cole, and later, President Lee Bollinger and Provost Alan Brinkley—for their support.

Event-Cities 3 could not have been completed without the perspectives and critical outlook of Irene Cheng, who oversaw its editing and production, and Roger Conover at The MIT Press, whose constant support has been instrumental in helping define the format of this series. Finally, I want to thank Kate Linker, whose involvement in so many aspects of these projects makes her a major figure in our enterprise.

Contents

CON<del>T</del>EXT(s)

Concept, Context, Content

Concept versus Context(s)

There is no architecture without a concept—an overarching idea, diagram, or *parti* that gives coherence and identity to a building. Concept, not form, is what distinguishes architecture from mere building. However, there is also no architecture without context (except in utopia). A work of architecture is always in situ, or "in situation," located on a site and within a setting. The context may be historical, geographical, cultural, political, or economic. It is never solely a matter of its visual dimension, or what in the 1980s and 1990s was termed "contextualism," with an implied aesthetic conservatism.

Within architecture, concept and context are inseparable. Frequently, they also conflict. The concept may negate or ignore the circumstances that surround it, while the context may blur or dampen the precision of an architectural idea.

Should one of these two terms take precedence over the other? The history of architecture abounds in debates between the partisans of tabula rasa (concept) and those of genius loci (context), or between generic concepts and specific contexts. The answer may lie not in the triumph of one over the other, but in the exploration of the relationship between concept and context. As a starting point, it is useful to look at three basic ways in which concept and context may relate:

1. Indifference, whereby the idea and its siting are superbly ignorant of one another—a kind of accidental collage in which both coexist but do not interact. Poetic juxtapositions or irresponsible impositions may result.

2. Reciprocity, whereby the architectural concept and its context interact closely with one another, in a complementary way, so that they seem to merge seamlessly into a single continuous entity.

3. Conflict, whereby the architectural concept is strategically made to clash with its context, in a battle of opposites in which both protagonists may need to negotiate their own survival.

These three strategies—indifference, reciprocity, and conflict—are all valid architectural approaches. Selecting the appropriate strategy for a given project is part of the concept.

If we agree that concept and context invariably are engaged in some sort of relationship, the question arises: can a concept be contextualized, or a context conceptualized? Contextualizing a concept means adapting it to the circumstances of a particular site or political situation. Conceptualizing a context means turning the idiosyncrasies and constraints of a context into the driving force behind the development of an architectural idea or concept, not unlike the tactic of a judo player who uses the strength of his opponent to his own advantage.

Concept versus Content

What about content then? There is no architectural space without something that happens in it, no space without content. Most architects begin with a program, that is, a list of users' requirements describing the intended purpose of the building. At various moments in architectural history, it has been claimed that program or function can be the generator of form, that "form follows function," or perhaps that "form follows content." In order to avoid engaging in a discourse of form per se or of form versus content, the word "form" is replaced here with the word "concept." Can one therefore substitute "form follows function" with an alternative formulation, namely, "concept follows content"?

The concept of a building, however, can precede the insertion of a program or content, since a neutral container can house any number of activities. Conversely, a given programmatic element can be exacerbated or thematized to such an extent that it becomes the concept of the building. For example, in the Solomon R. Guggenheim Museum, Frank Lloyd Wright takes one implicit element of the program—the movement through a building in a linear fashion from entrance to exit—and conceptualizes it in the form of a continuous ramp that ultimately characterizes the museum. The fact that the ramp configuration may or may not derive from a parking-garage typology is secondary to the determination of the building's overall concept.

The above example suggests that the relationship between content and concept, like that between context and concept, can be one of indifference, reciprocity, or conflict as well. For instance, one may cook in the open (indifference), in the kitchen (reciprocity), or in the bedroom (conflict). Or, to use a less domestic example, one can choose to bicycle in a plaza (indifference), a velodrome (reciprocity), or in a concert hall (conflict).

A program or content can also be utilitarian or symbolic. The relationships of indifference, reciprocity, or conflict apply in either case. For example, a memorial can be made of water, trees, and light, or it can consist of a night club, dancing bodies, and blaring sounds. Consequently, content can qualify or disqualify concepts.

Content versus Context(s)

What about the relationship between context and content? Debates about the uses appropriate to a given place generally occur outside architecture, namely, within society at large. The construction of an airport within a nature preserve or a shopping center in a historical district are familiar examples of polemical juxtapositions of context and content. Yet such oppositions can lead to challenging architectural or social concepts, as exemplified by the military landing strips built inside tunnels in the Swiss Alps during World War II, or the major shopping mall constructed underneath the Louvre in Paris. In other words, a bird sanctuary may or may not be located in a park, a store in a shopping mall, or a swimming pool in the ocean. The relationship between content and context can also be one of indifference, reciprocity, or conflict.

Fact versus Interpretation

Although architects generally make a clear distinction between what is given (context) and what is to be conceived (concept), the relationship is not so simple. Rather than a given, context is something defined by the observer, in the same way that a scientific fact is influenced by the observation of the scientist. Contexts are framed and defined by concepts, just as the reverse is true. Context is not a fact; it is always a matter of interpretation. The context for a preservationist is not necessarily the same as that for an industrialist. The preservationist sees a natural habitat for fish where the industrialist envisions water turbines providing energy for thousands. Context is often ideological and hence, may be qualified or disqualified by concepts.

A Genealogy of Concepts

The history of architecture is not so different from the history of science. It is a history of forms of conceptualization. Elaborating a concept means beginning with a question or problem that often builds upon previous concepts, but that does not presuppose the existence of a specific answer or solution.

Throughout this history, architects have been fascinated by the temptations of utopia and universality, namely, by concepts that can be applied, unaltered, to all situations and cultures. Hence our obsession with ideal geometries, mathematical models, and social archetypes. This applies as much to the digital as it does to the analog era. If one was to try to reconstitute a genealogy of architectural concepts, one would no doubt find that architecture is filled with unquestioned presuppositions, including those preconceived ideas that dissimulate unauthorized, forbidden territories, precluding new inventions or discoveries. Such a genealogy would list general concepts such as order, structure, form, hierarchy, and specific ones such as base-middle-top, or *plan-libre*. Most importantly, it might also uncover another history, in which concepts simply derive from the very contexts they have to address. It would also show that concepts evolve through their confrontation with context and/or content.

Without the generic overview imparted by concepts, no objective knowledge would be possible; yet, without the specificity imposed by contexts and contents, the world would be reduced to the rigid and predictable rule of a conceptual framework. A genealogy of concepts might therefore show a record of contaminations of the purity of concepts by the messiness of their contexts, in which concepts and contexts collide in apparently unpredictable and yet strategic ways.

EVENT-CITIES 3

The projects in *Event-Cities 3* explore several of the issues outlined above. In the making of these works, rarely were there set recipes. At times, a project developed out of a specific conceptual idea or strategy. At other times, the strategy took shape while we struggled with the complex functional or site-related issues surrounding a particular design question. Through working on these diverse projects, we found that concepts could qualify or disqualify contexts, as often as contexts could qualify or disqualify concepts. *Event-Cities 3* documents our explorations and occasional discoveries, organizing the projects into six categories that describe different relationships among concept, context, and content.

The introductory project, the Urban Glass House, is sited on the rooftops of Manhattan. In this project, concept and context are at once equally weighted, totally indifferent, and yet easily compatible.

Part A Tactical Indifference

Part A presents three projects that originate with a concept in which the surrounding generic context plays almost no role. Instead, the concepts of these buildings all explore the potential of architecture as envelope, de-emphasizing compositional notions of facades or articulations, while keeping the relationship between concept and context tactically indifferent. The projects in Angoulême, Geneva, and Strasbourg all adopt a similar approach: bending a two-dimensional sheet to provide shelter for a variety of unrelated activities. All are freestanding objects unencumbered by their settings.

Part B Reciprocity and Conflict

In Part B, the concept of the autonomous envelope remains the primary force propelling the projects, but the concept is made to interact with context in calculated ways. The relationship between the envelope and its context can sometimes be reciprocal, as in our Zenith Concert Hall in Limoges, or it may seem contradictory, as in the Carnegie Science Center in Pittsburgh. At Limoges, reciprocity is achieved by taking the concept of the Rouen Concert Hall, a curved double envelope, and transforming its materials in response to a new location: a forest ecology. For the sports center in Vendée, France, the abstract envelope mediates between context and content, in that content must combine opera house and velodrome while context intersects nature and a major highway. In the case of the Carnegie Science Center, where old and new are superimposed in a condition reminiscent of our contemporary art center for Le Fresnoy (described in *Event-Cities 1*), the creation of an "in-between space" changes the apparently contradictory relationship between concept and context into an unexpected reciprocity.

Part C Contextualizing Concept

In Part C, the strategy is to contextualize an architectural concept. An a priori idea is adapted to a specific environment. For instance, in the Rome office building and Antwerp museum projects, the explorations of fractal geometries are adjusted according to programmatic requirements and site specificities. Even more extreme is the case of the Electronic Media and Performing Arts Center in Troy, New York, where a decisive concept, the idea of a minimalist double envelope enclosing an intricate program and circulation, is maximized by taking advantage of its context, a steep slope. Similarly, in São Paulo, the hybrid curvilinear geometry of the new museum tower responds to the project's particular site conditions.

Part D Conceptualizing Context

Part D reverses the proposition of Part C: Here, context takes over. The overriding complexities of the site and program demand that context and content be understood and tamed. As the context cannot be bypassed, ignored, or circumvented, it must be conceptualized. The concept therefore directly addresses the contextual constraints and turns them to an advantage. For example, in the design for the Museum for African Art, located in New York's Special Park Improvement District, the zoning requirements are pushed to the extreme. The result is a code-compliant glass box that houses an irregular geometry otherwise strictly forbidden by the local New York code. The Athletic Center in Cincinnati turns site constraints to conceptual advantage by positing the notion of a conceptual infill or a contextual free form. The context of the New Acropolis Museum in Athens includes the Parthenon above, archaeological ruins below, and the Elgin or Parthenon marbles within, as well as stringent local zoning rules. Here, the preexisting complexities are unraveled and turned into a concise argument. For all these projects, conceptualizing the context(s) is the dominant strategy.

Part E Context Becoming Concept

In the campus for Nice, context is conceptualized to an extreme: the project literally transplants the "natural" surroundings onto the facades of the buildings, adopting a strategy of camouflage. The context is transformed into the project's concept. Or is it the other way around? In Nice, concept and context become interchangeable.

Part F Large Scale: Concepts Becoming Contexts

Part F explores four large-scale urban projects. By its very scale, any urban concept becomes its own context. Yet in these projects, the original context often provided the impetus for the choice of concept. A master plan concept for an international exposition, Expo 2004, on the outskirts of Paris was intended to become the context for a future campus housing start-up technology firms. For the Downsview Park project in Toronto, designing another park after La Villette was challenging in terms of creating something new, so we took the original La Villette propositions and inverted each of them. While the investigation for New York's Ground Zero undoubtedly was influenced by the emotions surrounding the events of 9/11, here too the project started with an urban concept: the idea that density and dynamism are fundamental constituents of the 21st-century city. In the project for Factory 798 in Beijing, the concept is a polemic about the context. The new development hovers above the old city, allowing the existing neighborhood to be preserved.

Theory, Practice, and the City

The projects collected in this volume suggest that the activity of architecture is less about the making of forms than an investigation of concepts and their subsequent materialization. As society evolves, its architecture announces or responds to these evolutions by generating new concepts while questioning and replacing ancient, obsolete ones. In this process, it might be beneficial, though not easy, for architects to reject predetermined methods, a priori dogmas, academic canons, and historicist typologies. Architectural thought has little to do with religion; it is not about imposing belief systems, as seems to have been the case during much of the 20th century.

Architecture resembles a large contemporary city, in which no overriding system predominates over all the others, but, on the contrary, the inherent tensions and differences lead to alternatives and sometimes new modes of action. The investigations in *Event-Cities 3* suggest that conflicts, confrontations, and contaminations between concept, context, and content are part of the definition of contemporary urban culture, and therefore of architecture. Theory is a practice, a practice of concepts. Practice is a theory, a theory of contexts.

Prologue

At the end of 1999, *Time* magazine asked us to design a house for the 21st century. To project into the future required analyzing the present—specifically, the conditions and experiences that make up the contemporary metropolis. For this we looked no further than our immediate surroundings in Manhattan. A house in the city must provide refuge from, but at the same time can never fully escape the heady rush of the metropolis. Like the modern city dweller, it must exist in a state of absorbed distraction—immersed and yet indifferent to its surroundings. The concept of the house is therefore the paradoxical relationship of its content to its urban context.

New York, Urban Glass House, 2000

Vision Glass

The proposed house responds to a contemporary desire for infinite space in the dense metropolis. It is a reaction against the recurring dream of suburbia; rather than abandoning the city and recreating an artificial urban experience outside of it, the house addresses the city by existing both within and above it.

Celebrating domesticity and everyday life

The House in the City

In Lower Manhattan, as elsewhere in New York, numerous penthouses on top of low warehouses and manufacturing buildings have been converted to residential use. Multiplied, these have the potential to become dynamic additions to the city skyline and to urban life. With minimal adjustments to the roofs of host buildings, the proposed urban glass house can be located on high- and low-rise buildings, on brownstones as well as mega-blocks. It would act as an illuminated beacon, elevating domesticity and everyday life to the status of ephemeral monuments. In a fitting counterpoint to the Internet, which privatizes public life, the house publicizes private life. It also makes a striking observation point from which to view the spectacle of the city below.

The inhabitants of the house can be anyone—singles, couples, and trios of any age or gender, or small nuclear families. The house can used as a residence, pied-à-terre, or even as a hotel for temporary stays.

Architecture of the House

The architecture of this glass house in the sky plays on the opposition between its industrial-looking rectangular envelope and the lush curvature of its inner volumes. The strict glass-and-steel detailing of its exterior contrasts with the soft velvet or silk curtains, rounded and polished marble, curved translucent glass, and exotic wood veneers of the interiors.

The services and circulation are contained in an undulating sandwich wall that also helps define the living spaces. The wall expands and folds back on itself, enclosing spaces for privacy and opening to allow rooms and corridors to flow continuously into one another. It acts as the subconscious of the house, adjusting to the specific desires of the user.

Bathrooms are contained in a large "liquid" or "wet" wall that extends through the house. This "wet" wall surface, made of a glass and resin composite, changes from transparent to translucent to opaque. Its other side is a "digital" wall. If the house's occupants are so inclined, this curved digital wall can function as a projection screen displaying enlargements of the most intimate moments of their everyday life. Should they prefer anonymity, other messages can be projected, from advertising slogans to exhibitions of their video art collection. The digital wall appears as a media installation of soft, pliable electronic images.

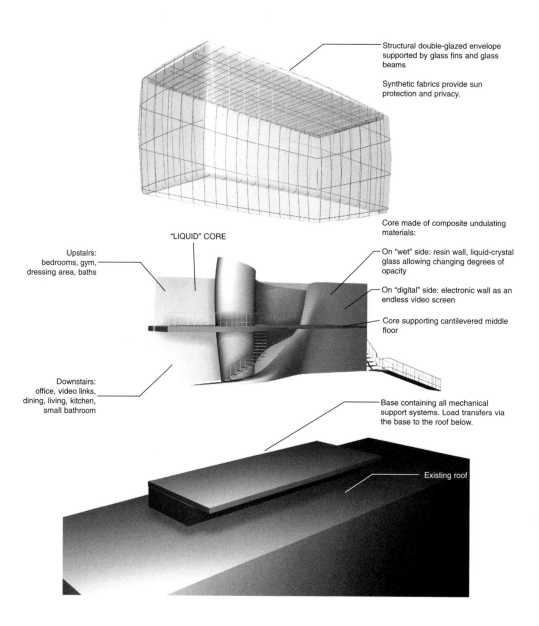

Structural double-glazed envelope supported by glass fins and glass beams

Synthetic fabrics provide sun protection and privacy.

"LIQUID" CORE

Upstairs: bedrooms, gym, dressing area, baths

Core made of composite undulating materials:

On "wet" side: resin wall, liquid-crystal glass allowing changing degrees of opacity

On "digital" side: electronic wall as an endless video screen

Core supporting cantilevered middle floor

Downstairs: office, video links, dining, living, kitchen, small bathroom

Base containing all mechanical support systems. Load transfers via the base to the roof below.

Existing roof

A glass envelope over a curved, pliable solid

Concept and context are equally weighted, totally indifferent, and yet easily compatible.

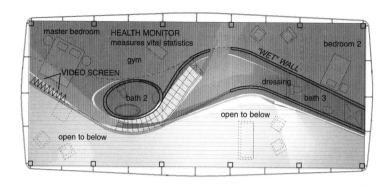

master bedroom HEALTH MONITOR
measures vital statistics

bedroom 2

gym

"WET" WALL

VIDEO SCREEN

dressing

bath 2

bath 3

open to below

open to below

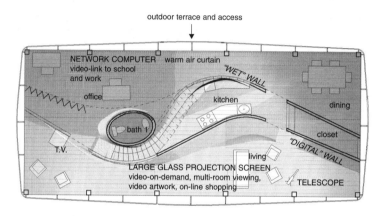

outdoor terrace and access

NETWORK COMPUTER warm air curtain
video-link to school
and work

"WET" WALL

office

kitchen

dining

bath 1

closet

T.V.

"DIGITAL" WALL

LARGE GLASS PROJECTION SCREEN
video-on-demand, multi-room viewing,
video artwork, on-line shopping

living

TELESCOPE

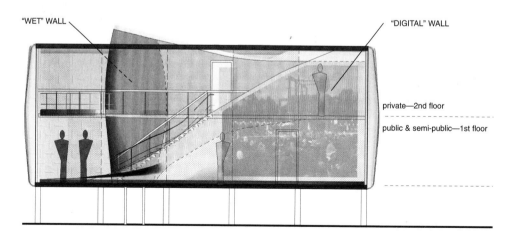

"WET" WALL

"DIGITAL" WALL

private—2nd floor

public & semi-public—1st floor

Second floor plan, first floor plan, and section

The occupants of the glass house become players in a shadow theater.
An undulating wall acts as the subconscious of the house.

A.
Tactical Indifference

While every project has a context—geographic, cultural, social, and political—not all contexts are equal, or equally interesting. What if the context is relatively banal, for example, an empty field beside a highway? One can try to conceptualize banality, but this can prove laborious, if not futile. Sometimes the ordinary is just ordinary. In these situations, it may be more fruitful to take advantage of near tabula-rasa conditions to distill a concept to its clearest manifestation. The three projects in this section begin with a simple and elemental concept—a two-dimensional sheet, which is bent or folded to create an all-encompassing monolithic envelope. Each project emphasizes the relationship of the envelope to what happens inside rather than to conditions outside. The envelope provides an umbrella, both literal and metaphorical, under which a multiplicity of activities coexist and coincide. Tactically indifferent to their surroundings, these buildings rely on the strength and singularity of the envelope's concept to generate dynamic spatial effects.

Angoulême, Exhibition Center, 2000

Concept Decontextualized

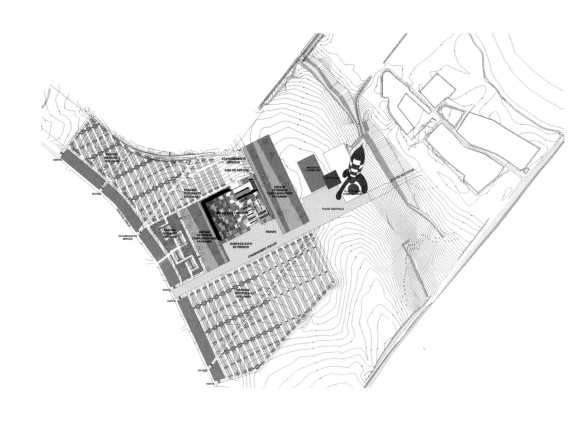

Located in a wooded area near the city of Angoulême in southwestern France, the new Exhibition Center consists of a large 6,500-square-meter hall that can accommodate exhibitions, trade fairs, concerts, and spectacles for up to 5,000 visitors. The proposal would encompass all of the center's activities within a metal envelope curved in one direction. The two ends of the hall are closed by wood-framed curtain walls.

The metal sheet also works as an awning to protect visitors from the sun and rain. A large, double-height lobby acts as a pivot for the different activities: exhibitions and spectacles to the west and a smaller 900-seat hall and meeting rooms to the east. All materials are deployed in their natural colors. Acoustical requirements are met by giving each material a specific texture or porosity.

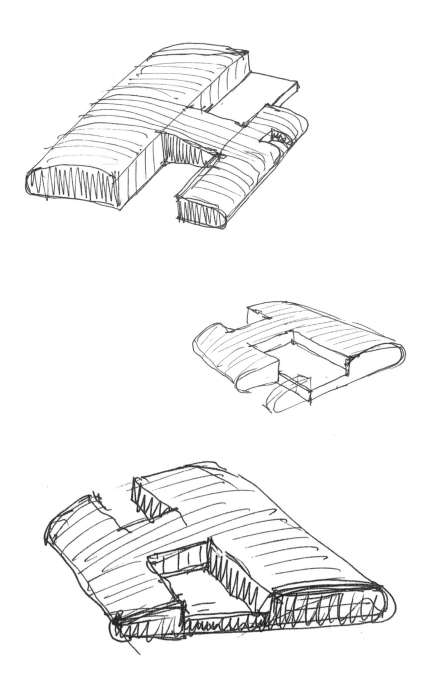

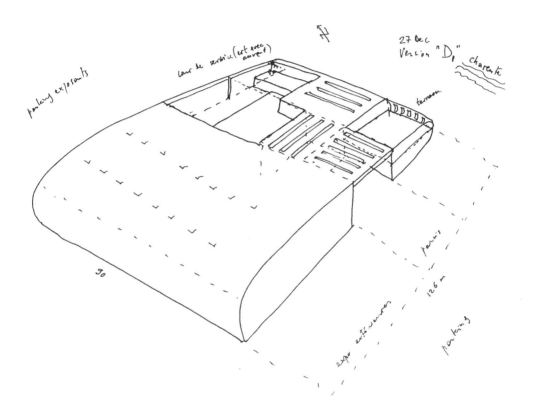

parking exposants

cour de service (ert avec auvent)

27 Dec
Version "D" charente

terrasse

go

parvis

126 m

expo exterieur

parking

Preliminary conceptual sketches

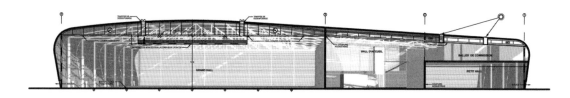

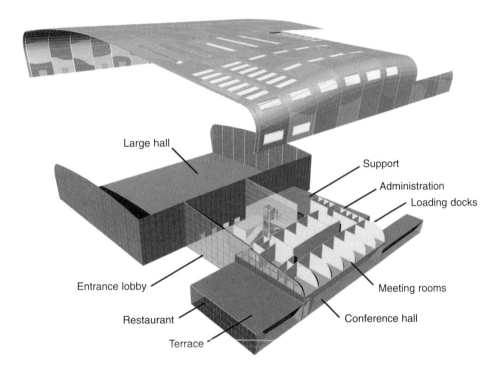

Large hall

Support

Administration

Loading docks

Entrance lobby

Meeting rooms

Restaurant

Conference hall

Terrace

A curved metal sheet encloses all the activities of the Center.
A large double-height lobby acts as a pivot point for the two sides of the building.

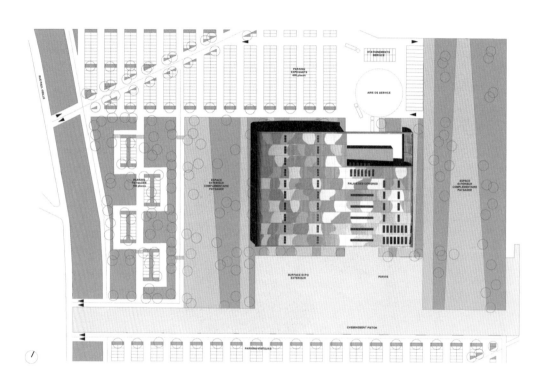

Site plan

Keeping the relationship between concept and context tactically indifferent

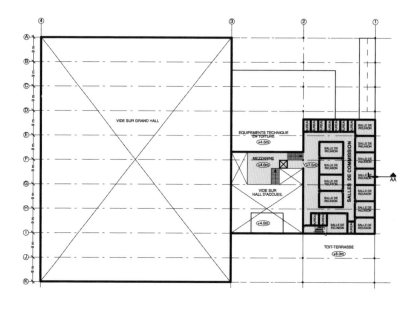

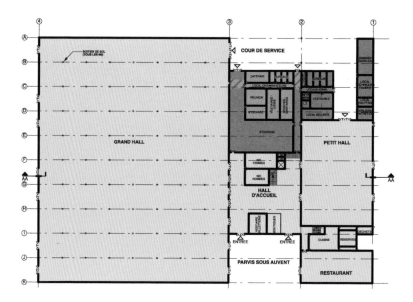

Upper level: meeting rooms
Lower level: lobby flanked by an exhibition space on the west and a smaller hall on the east

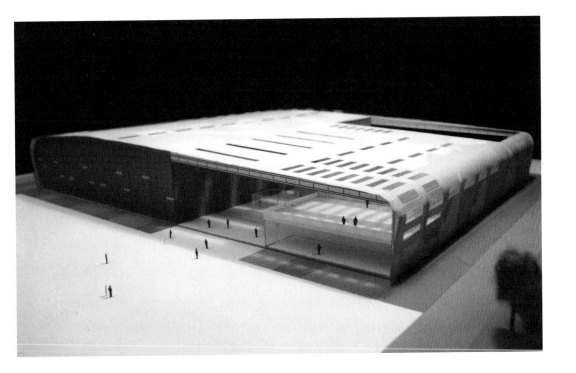

The envelope can be opaque, translucent, transparent, or a combination of all three.
Punctured areas are glazed and bring daylight to the interior.

Geneva, Vacheron Constantin Headquarters,
2001–04

Manufacturing Time

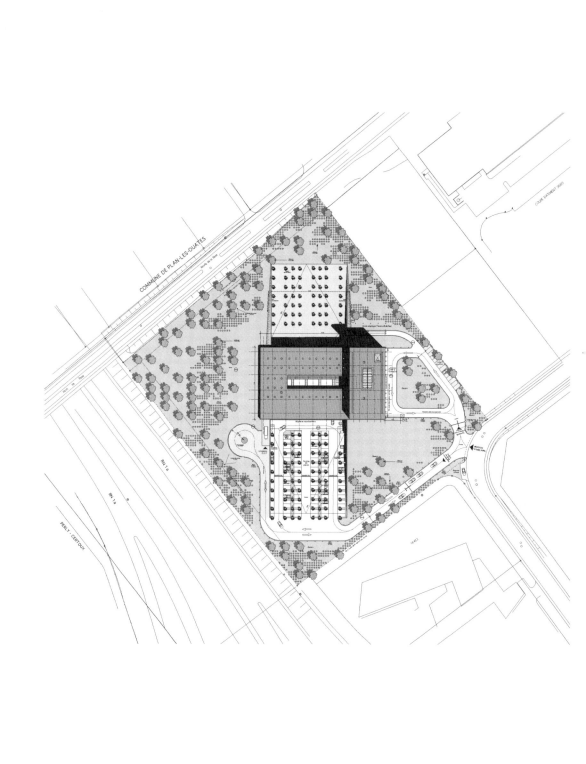

This building serves as the manufacturing and administrative headquarters of Switzerland's oldest watchmaking company. The concept for the project is based on the idea of a thin, flexible envelope. The exterior surface is formed from a metallic sheet that unrolls over the structure's geometry, lifting to create a larger multistory portion of the building. The interior is clad with a wood veneer. The resulting space is sleek and precise outside, warm and inviting inside. The logic of unrolling makes the building appear almost unenclosed. The envelope opens to welcome workers and visitors, admitting ample direct light on the north side and filtered light on the south.

In contrast to the wood-and-metal envelope, major movement vectors are made of glass. For example, in the multistory part of the building, a glass atrium contains several circulation elements—such as walkways, stairs, and an elevator—all made of glass. The building rests on an artificial dip in the landscape that houses a naturally lit parking garage. Above the garage, in the lower, flat section of the envelope, a tranquil, airy courtyard extends through the building from east to west. The continuity of the monolithic metal cladding lends the building a visual and functional coherence, and suggests a fluid relationship between management, design, and production in the company's operations.

β→V   Vacheron, 8 mai

club
fitness

←extension

←SOMBRERO

Preliminary conceptual sketches

12 May 2

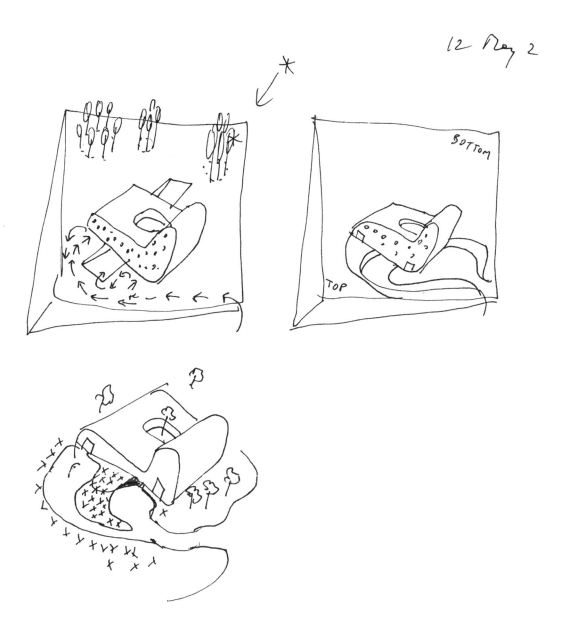

BOTTOM

TOP

12 Juin

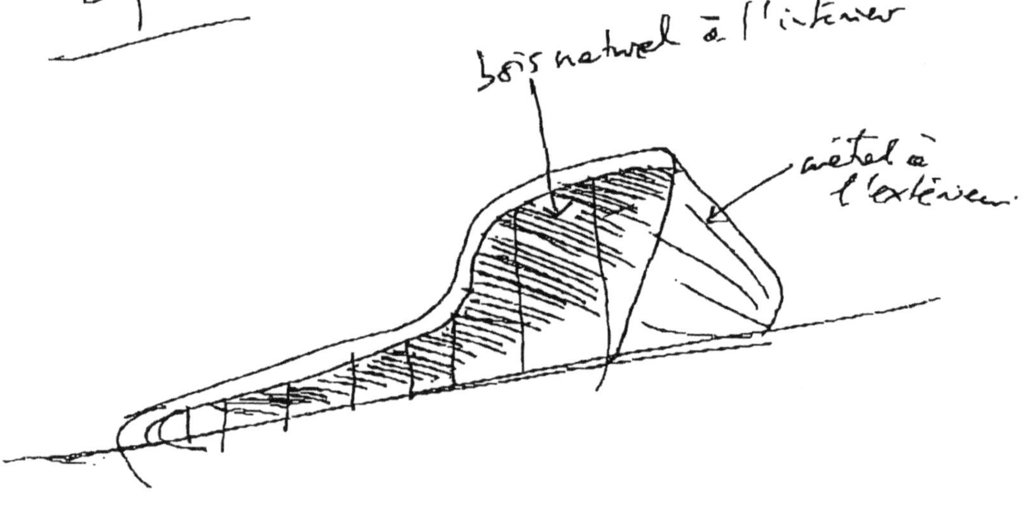

bois naturel à l'intérieur

métal à l'extérieur.

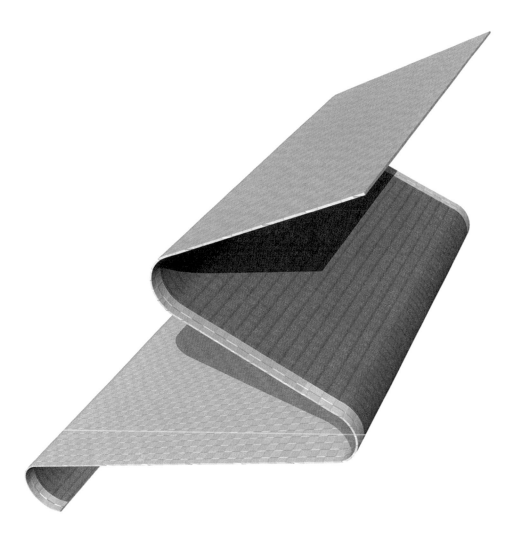

A thin, flexible double envelope

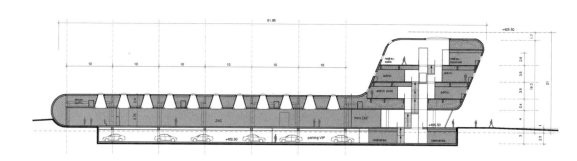

The logic of unrolling makes the building appear almost unenclosed.

A concept in which the generic context plays almost no role

The potential of architecture as envelope, de-emphasizing facade composition

The curve was changed at the client's request.

Bending a two-dimensional sheet to provide shelter for a variety of unrelated activities

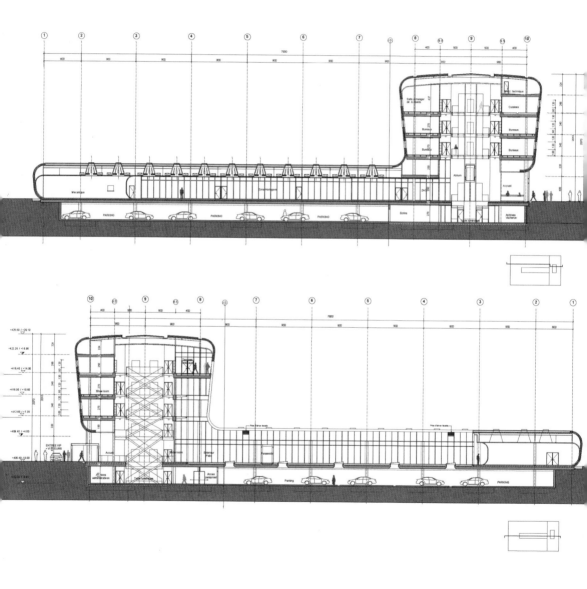

Longitudinal sections through offices, factory, and garage

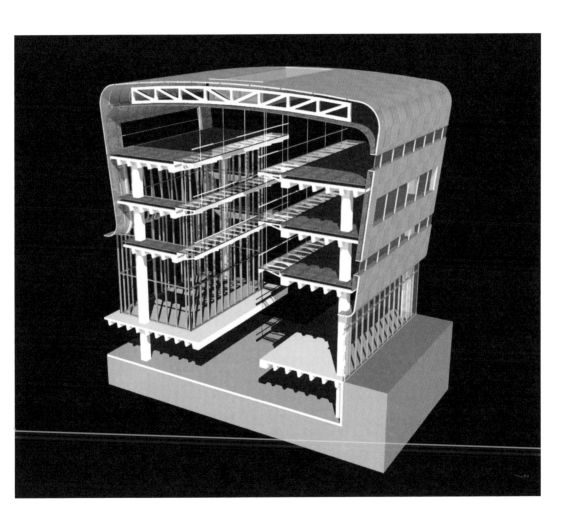

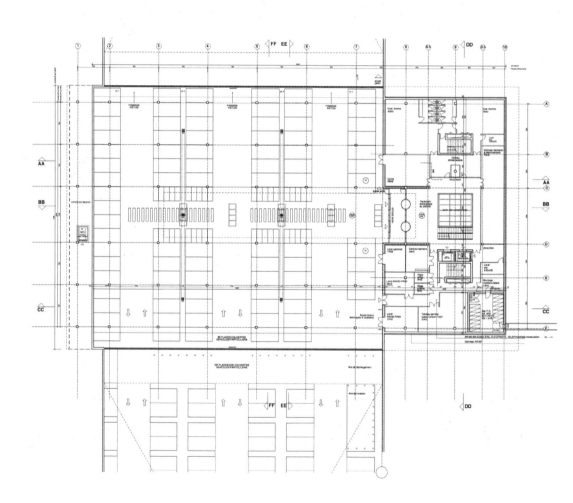

Ground level

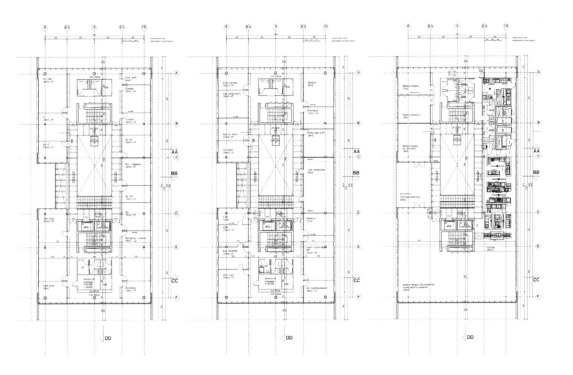

Levels 1, 2, and 3

architecture is
the materialization of
concepts

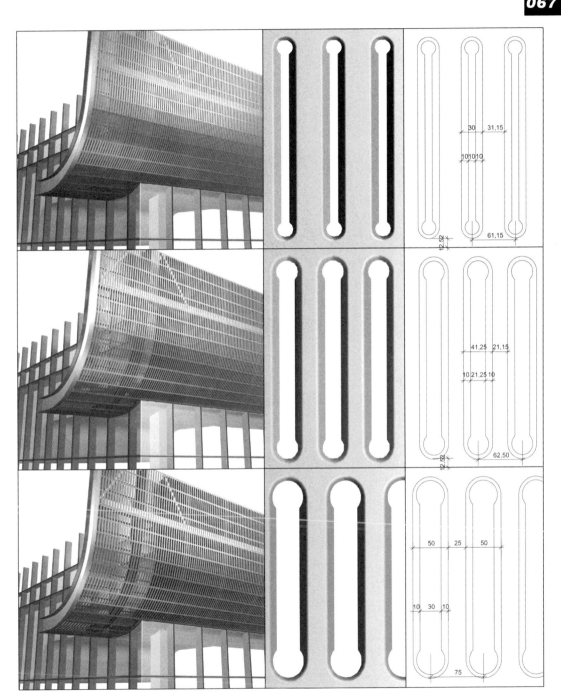

Exterior metal skin perforation studies

The metal exterior skin gives way to a perforated wood surface inside.

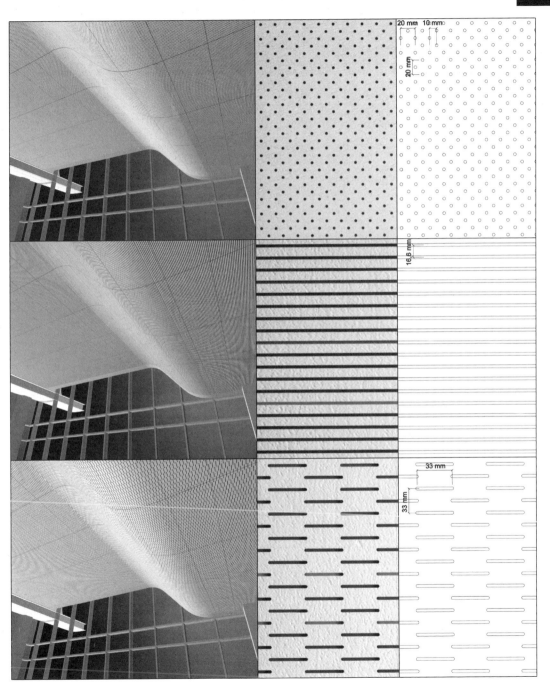

Interior wood skin perforation studies

Can generic contexts
generate
concepts ?

SERVICE DE L'INFORMATION GEOGRAPHIQUE

Etude Zenith
Orthophotoplan
prise de vues du 21 juin 2001
Réf. 2003_5317

DATE D'EDITION	demandeur	ECHELLE
15/07/2003	S.I.C.	1/5000

Strasbourg, Concert Hall, 2003

Megaspan

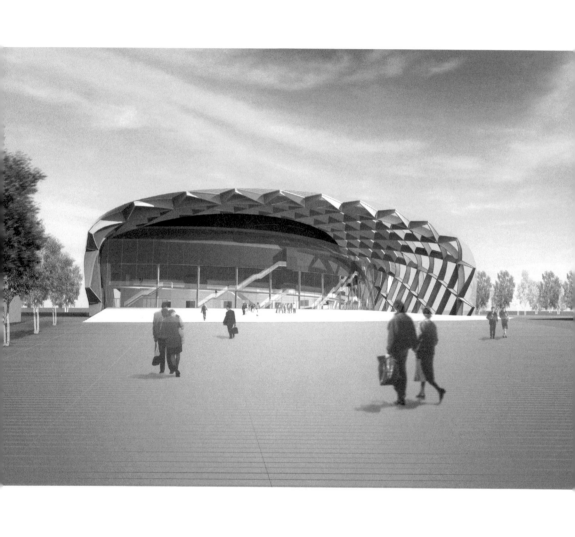

"Zenith" halls are multiprogrammatic arenas aimed at accommodating large crowds for rock concerts, political meetings, and occasional sports events such as skating and basketball. Capacity varies from 3,500 to 8,000. Since the mid-1980s, various city and regional governments throughout France have held competitions for such halls, and more than a dozen have been built. (Examples include the Rouen Concert Hall, described in *Event-Cities 2,* and the Limoges Concert Hall, in this volume.)

Our competition entry for a Zenith hall in Strasbourg aims not only to fulfill the strict programmatic requirements of the hall but also to provide a flagship building for a new cultural and technological district on the outskirts of Strasbourg, along a busy highway leading to the city center.

Our concept inserts a semicircular concert hall into the square defined by a curved envelope above. The simplicity of the geometric strategy allows a generous space to unfold above the entrance and foyer areas of the project. The curved diagonal grid structure spans over 100 meters and covers the hall, foyer, and support spaces.

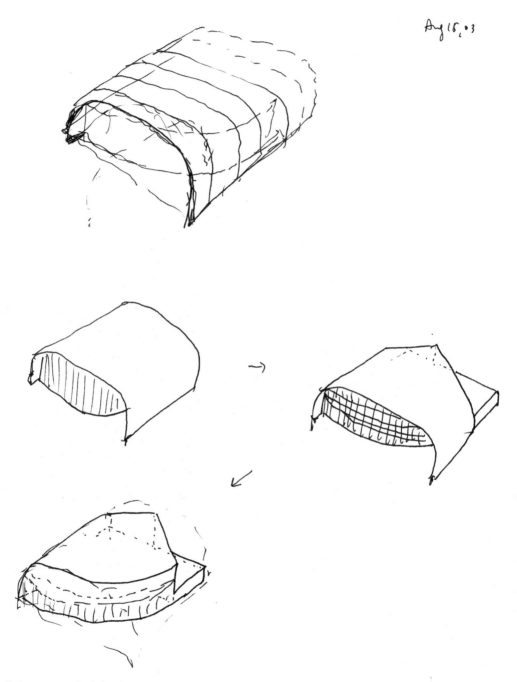

Aug 15, 03

Preliminary conceptual sketches

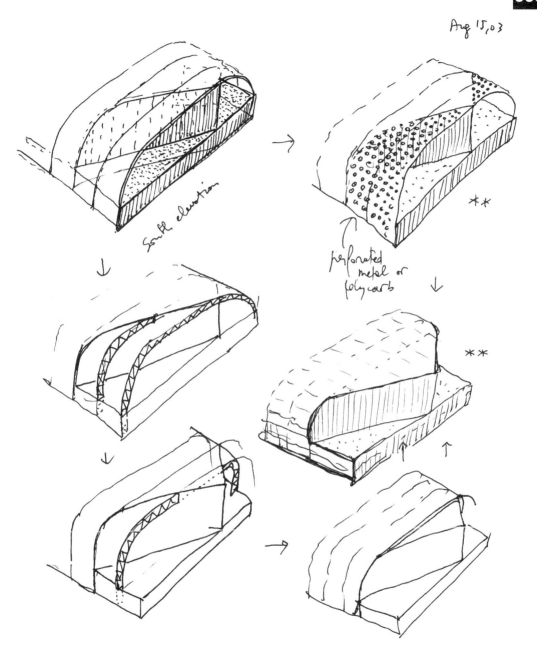

Aug 15, 03

South elevation

perforated
metal or
polycarb

**

**

South elevation studies

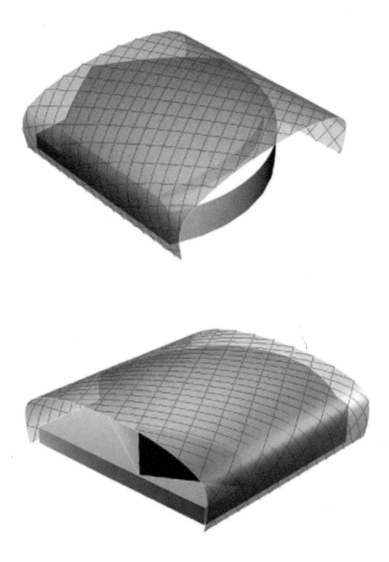

Envelope and massing studies: A semi-circular concert hall is inserted into the square
defined by a curved envelope above.

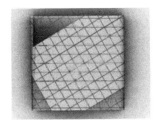

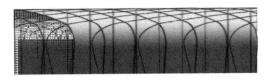

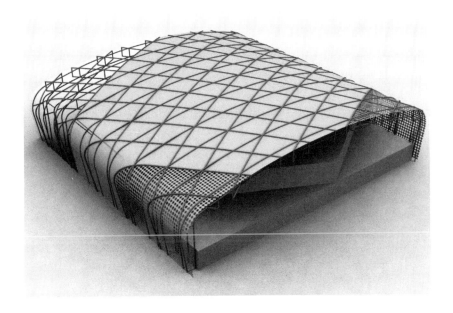

Cladding studies

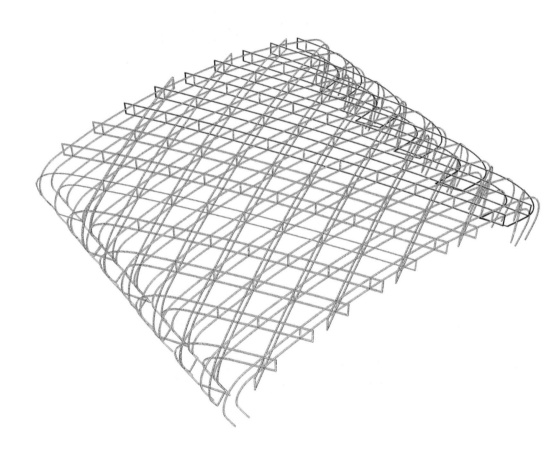

Structural diagram: three-way supported system

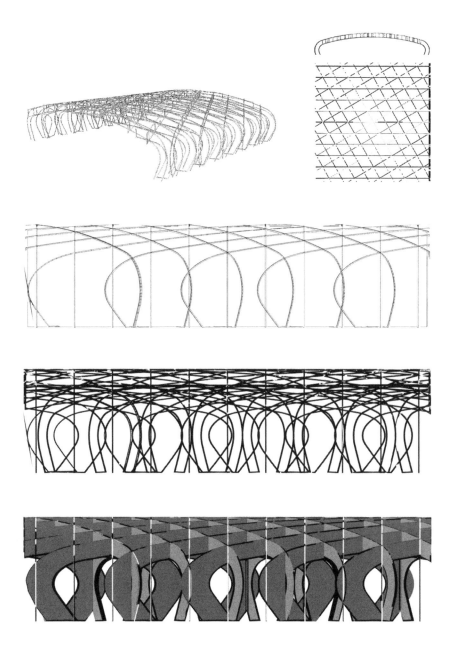

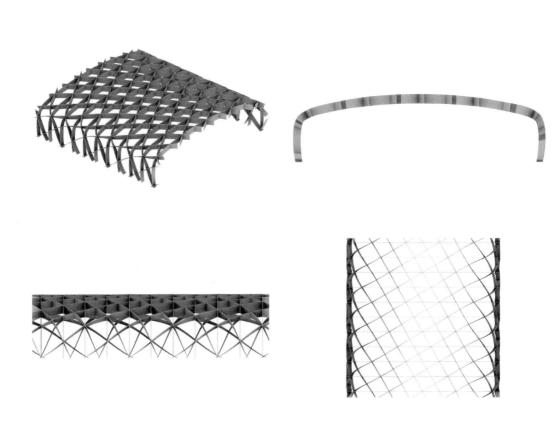

Structural diagrams

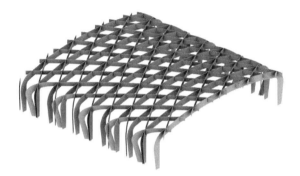

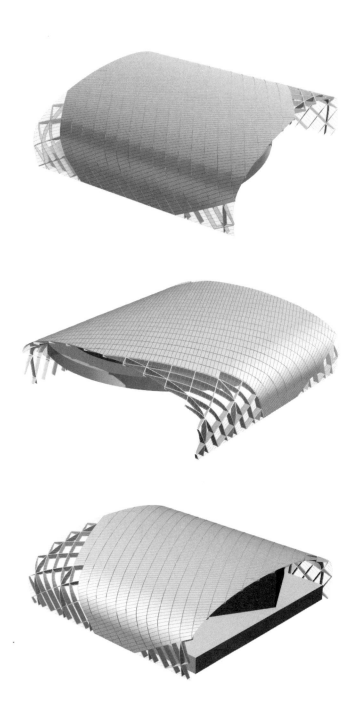

Envelope studies

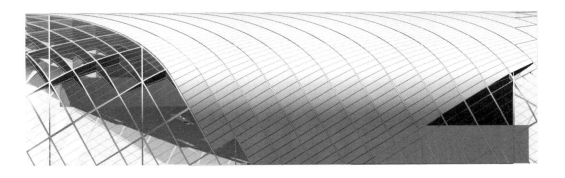

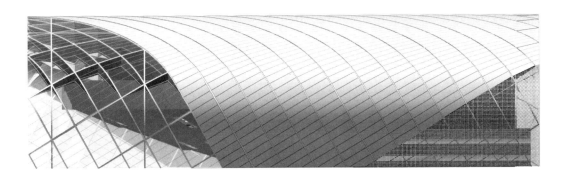

TSTC West Texas
Sweetwater Library

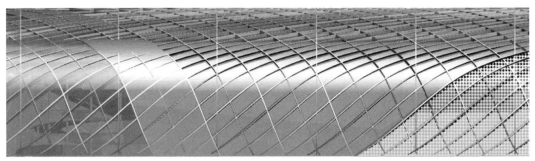

Polycarbonate   Metal cladding   Perforated metal

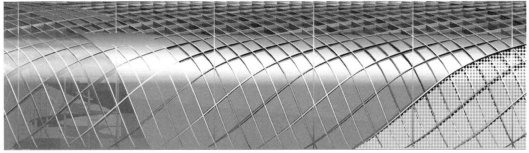

Polycarbonate   Metal cladding   Perforated metal

Facade studies exploring perforation patterns

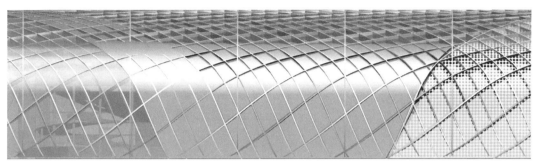

Polycarbonate   Metal cladding   Perforated metal

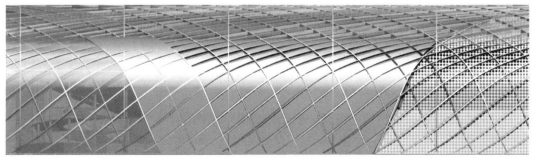

Polycarbonate   Metal cladding   Perforated metal

Night view

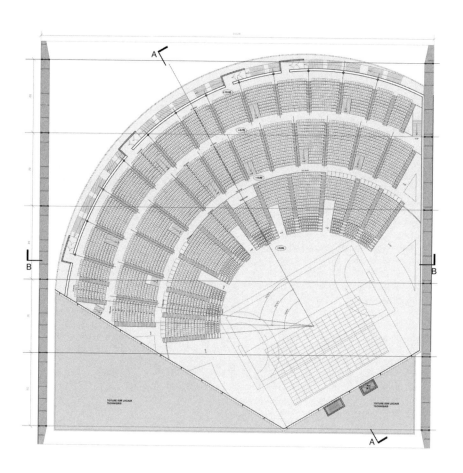

Circle into square
Level +13.40 m

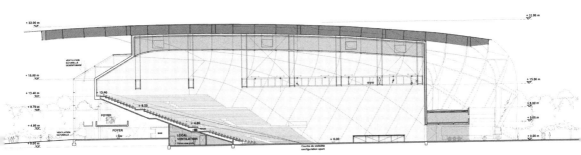

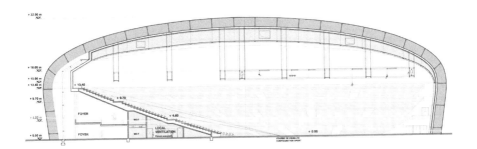

Longitudinal and transverse sections

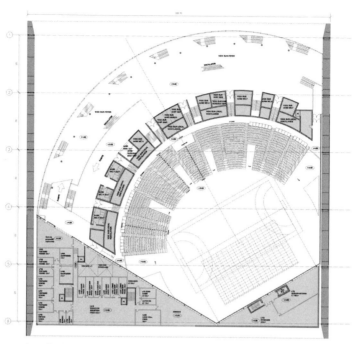

Level +4.80 m

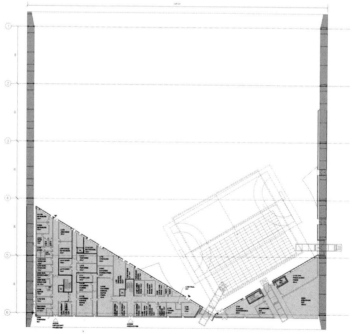

Level 0 m (backstage)

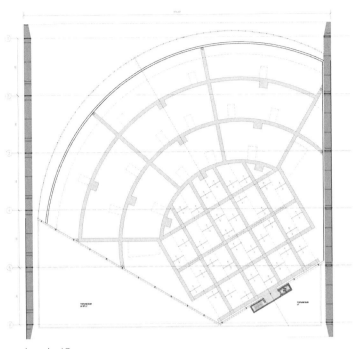

Level +15 m

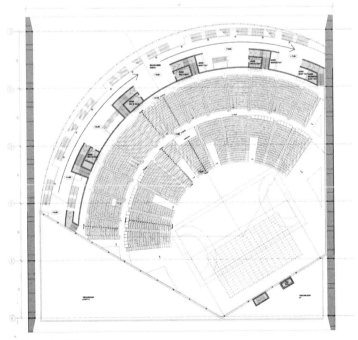

Level +9.70 m

A free-standing object unencumbered by its setting

B.
Reciprocity and Conflict

Among the flawed assumptions that underlay the contextualist movement of the 1980s and 1990s were, first, that a building's relationship to its environment should be conceived primarily in visual terms, and second, that the affiliation should be one of similarity. On the contrary, architecture is connected to its context in multiple ways, and indifference, reciprocity, and conflict are all valid relationships between a building and its environment. If the projects in Part A provided examples of buildings indifferent to their contexts, those in this section exemplify positions between reciprocity and conflict. A strategy of reciprocity, for instance, might mean that a building takes material cues from its environment without mimicking it. Alternatively, materials can be used to make a building stand out from its context, to enunciate an unnatural, alien presence. The projects suggest that architecture of necessity takes a position vis-à-vis its environment, even if it is not always one of complacent agreement.

Pittsburgh, Carnegie Science Center, 2000

Phagocyte

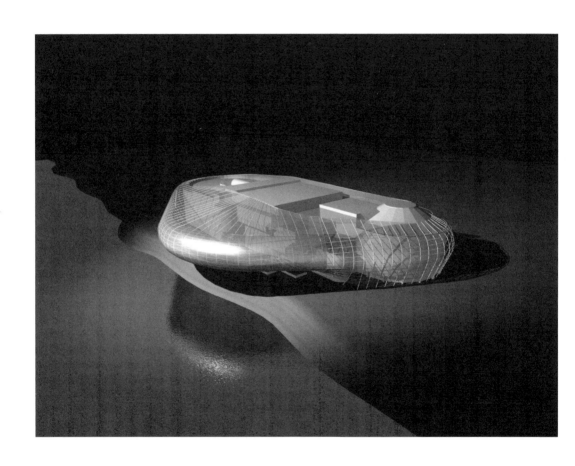

A New Type of Science Center

Today, scientific knowledge is said to double every six months, but this knowledge is largely additive and cumulative, rarely replacing or canceling earlier forms. In the same way, the building proposed in this competition entry does not "cancel" the existing science center structure built a decade earlier, but rather encompasses it, enlarging, extending, and transforming its contours. The project acts as a phagocyte—a cell that engulfs and consumes another body. In the proposal, the existing floors are retained while the old facade is partly removed to allow for a 70,000-square-foot extension to house exhibition galleries. The resulting new outer enclosure simultaneously provides weather protection and support for electronically generated information.

Three goals inform our project:
1. To provide a novel spatial experience while turning the site constraints into opportunities. By enclosing the existing building with a new metal envelope, interstitial spaces are generated where old meets new. The existing building's "outside" is simultaneously the new building's "inside," and the new outer skin is at once the "real" envelope and a support for virtual-reality projections. In defining this new architectural space, the outer surface can be opaque, translucent, or transparent, depending on architectural and programmatic needs. It is simultaneously surface and depth.

2. To define a new type of science center where education and experimentation, technology, and innovation are integrated—a sort of giant laboratory that is accessible to the broadest possible public. To achieve this goal, the project supplies a simple and clear configuration, composed of large floor plates that enable several paths to be taken, allowing for the greatest diversity of information and sensation.

3. To transform the concept into a distinctive landmark in the city panorama, located at the confluence of the Allegheny, Monongahela, and Ohio Rivers: a rounded, polished stainless-steel envelope that is as smooth as a river stone and shines so that it is visible from all around. Strongly differentiated from the adjacent Pittsburgh Steelers' stadium, it looks like nothing else in the city.

Envelope and Vectors

In order to provide visitors with a range of spatial sensations as they move through the building, the existing ramps are maintained and escalators added, along with a circular stair at the junction between the existing and new floor plates. The proposal turns the existing main ramps into a virtual, holographic gallery and adds a pair of glass elevators to the expanded entrance hall. A spectacular new entrance hall, nearly as tall as the building, welcomes individual visitors and large groups. The lobbies and spaces for educational activities on the ground and first floors provide views over the river. These spaces lead to the main education areas of the Science Center, and to the exhibition galleries above via new escalators. The exhibition and educational-program spaces are designed to accommodate nearly one million visitors each year.

Openings at selected intervals in the curved skin allow views toward the river. To the east, a large indoor "eco-sphere" and café offer views of the city as well as constituting a unique, immense space in which a large scientific artifact could be suspended for exhibition.

Science Center Site

Miller
Building

Science Center
Existing Building

Site of the new
football stadium

Existing sports
stadium

Allegheny
River

Ohio River

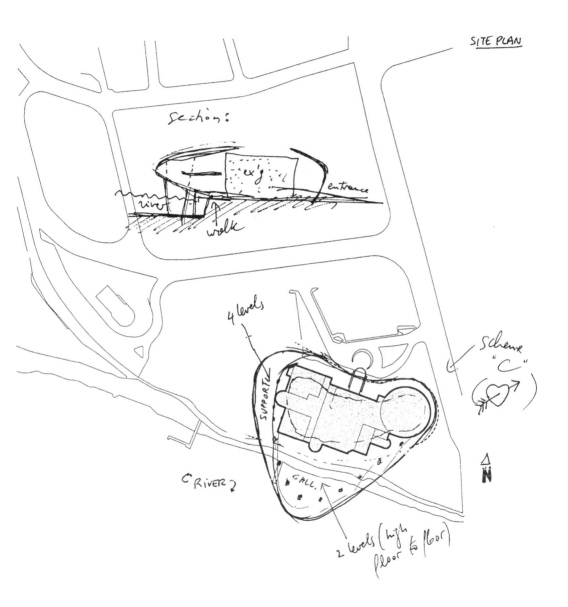

SITE PLAN

Section:

ex'g

entrance

river

walk

4 levels

SUPPORTE

Scheme "C"

C RIVER ?

GALL.

2 levels (high floor to floor)

N

Preliminary conceptual sketches

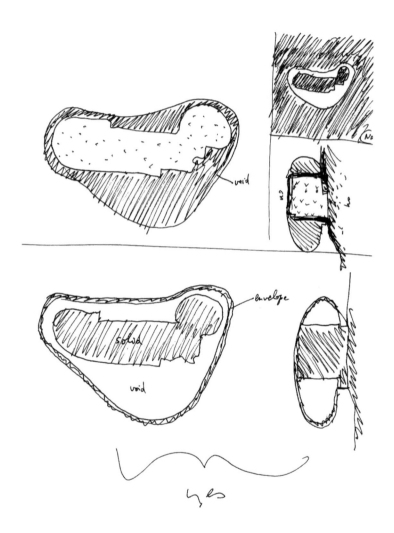

The exterior of the existing structure becomes the interior of the new building.

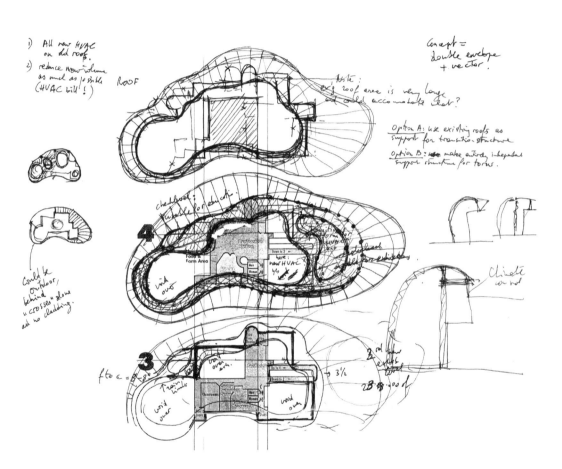

1) All new HVAC on old roof.
2) reduce new volume as much as possible (HVAC bill!)

ROOF

Concept = double envelope + vector.

Aisle: roof area is very large could accommodate that?

Option A: use existing roofs as support for transition structure

Option B: make entirely independent support structure for torus.

Could be outdoor, behind "CROSSES" alone ad no cladding.

Climate on roof

The new polished metal envelope aspires to be as smooth as a river stone.

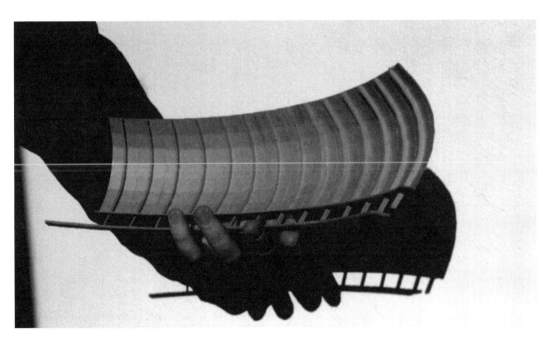

Study models of envelope

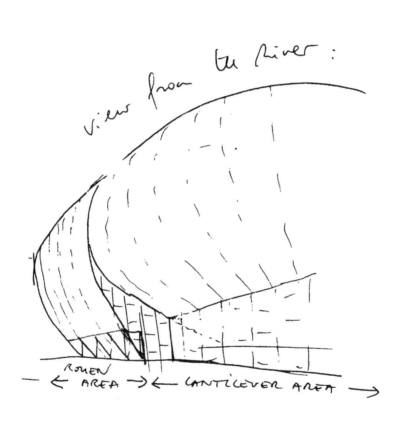

view from the river:

ROUEN AREA → ← CANTILEVER AREA →

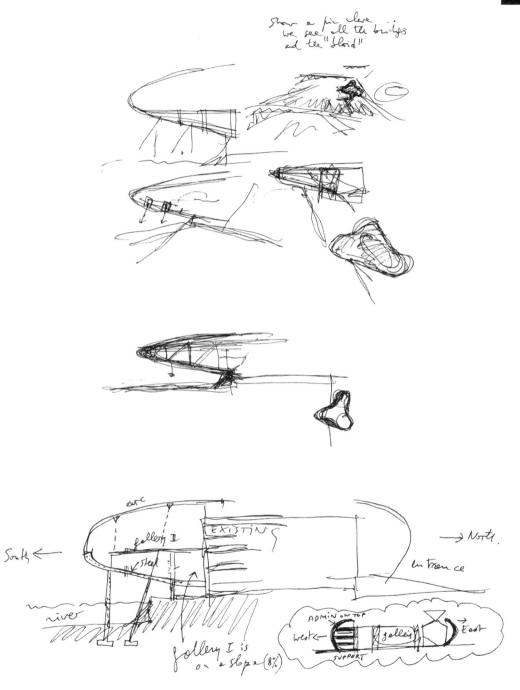

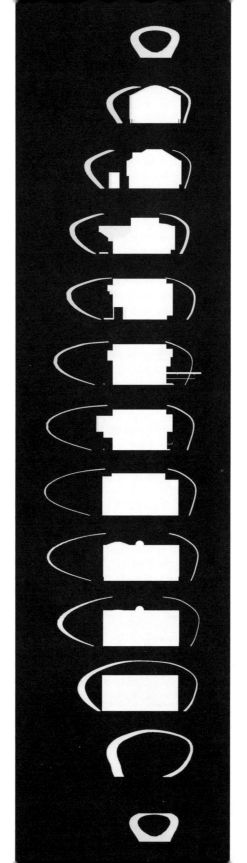

Sectional sequence

Structural Envelope and Economy of Means

Our hypothesis from the outset was to "have our cake and eat it," namely, to create an entirely new building while keeping intact the ten-year-old structural, mechanical, and servicing elements of the older center.

The new envelope wraps around the existing building, completely obscuring the old structure in places, and revealing it through glazing or open ribs in others.

An extremely simple and economical facade system is proposed: self-supporting arcs span between the ground and a light perimeter beam at the top of the existing building. These arcs take advantage of the external envelope's curved form, significantly increasing their efficiency. As all the weight of the new envelope is transferred to the ground, no additional stresses are applied to the existing building along the periphery. A simple weather strip accompanies the perimeter beam and separates inside from outside.

A light, metal "sandwich" skin is stretched over the ribs. Made of steel, aluminum, or titanium, depending on budgetary parameters and market availability, it is composed of one outer layer of metal sheeting, an insulation layer, and an inner layer of light sheet metal. Single or double glazing can be inserted into the skin. At places where the existing building need not be widened (for example, next to the auditorium, to the northeast), the new envelope is reduced to the metal arc frame alone; in these areas, the envelope almost looks like an X-ray image of the old building.

For financial reasons, the proposal opts not to cover the existing roofs, but rather to adjust the curved geometry of the new envelope to render the existing roofs invisible from the surrounding hills.

Proposed Envelope:

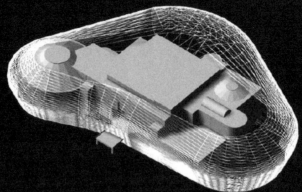

Alternative Envelopes:

Within the general concept, alternative envelopes are possible, extending the building to the west, north, or south.

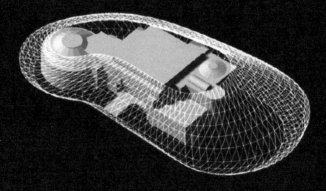

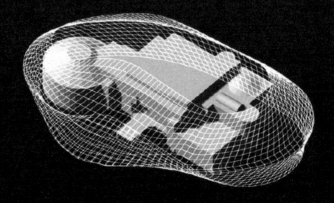

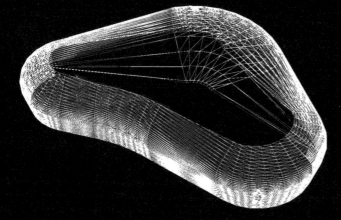

new envelope

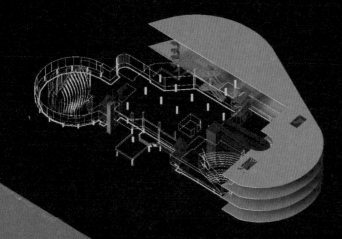

new floorplates with circulation

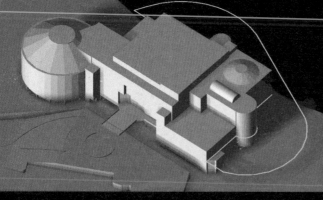

existing building

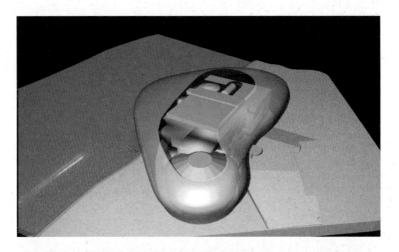

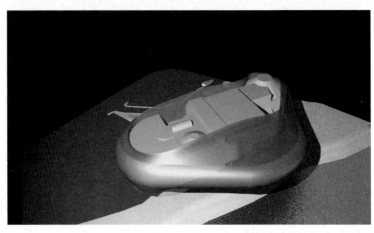

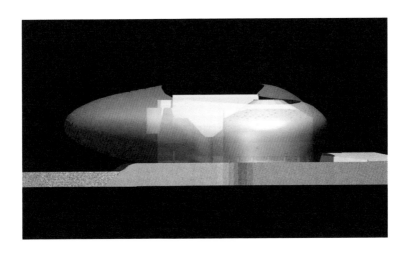

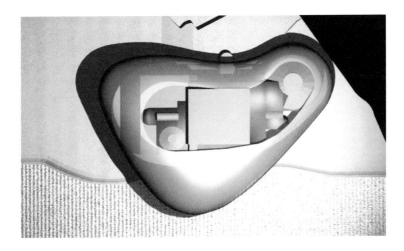

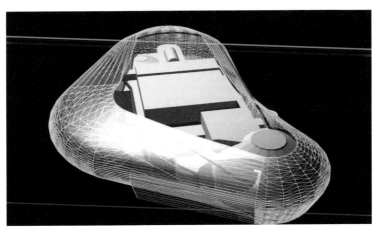

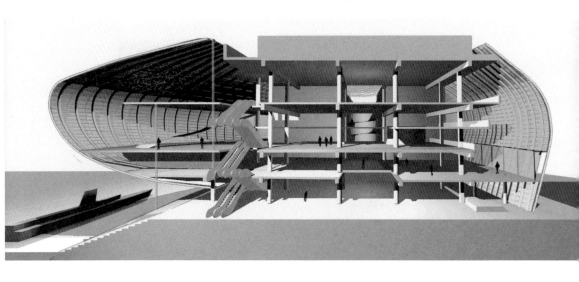

The existing floor plates are retained yet expanded; the old facade is removed but enlarged through a new curvilinear envelope; escalators and panoramic glass elevators are added.

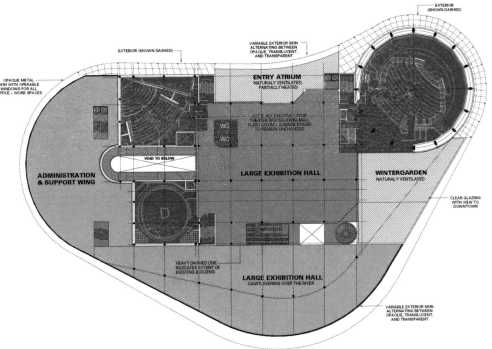

EXTERIOR (SHOWN DASHED)

VARIABLE EXTERIOR SKIN ALTERNATING BETWEEN OPAQUE, TRANSLUCENT, AND TRANSPARENT

EXTERIOR (SHOWN DASHED)

OPAQUE METAL SKIN WITH OPERABLE WINDOWS FOR ALL OFFICE + WORK SPACES

ENTRY ATRIUM
NATURALLY VENTILATED, PARTIALLY HEATED

NOTE: ALL EXISTING LARGE THEATER SPACES (OMNI-MAX, PLANTARIUM + SCIENCE STAGE) TO REMAIN UNCHANGED

WC
WC

VOID TO BELOW

ADMINISTRATION & SUPPORT WING

LARGE EXHIBITION HALL

WINTERGARDEN
NATURALLY VENTILATED

CLEAR GLAZING WITH VIEW TO DOWNTOWN

HEAVY DASHED LINE INDICATES EXTENT OF EXISTING BUILDING

LARGE EXHIBITION HALL
CANTILEVERING OVER THE RIVER

VARIABLE EXTERIOR SKIN ALTERNATING BETWEEN OPAQUE, TRANSLUCENT, AND TRANSPARENT

Ground level

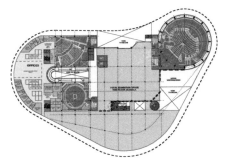

Level 2

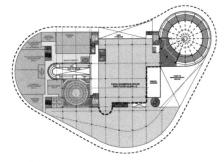

Level 4

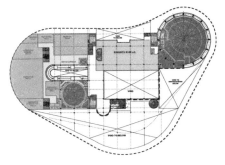

Level 3

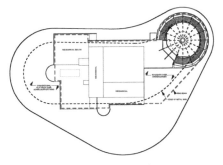

Mechanical penthouse and roof

The new envelope wraps around and expands the existing building.

New entrance hall seen from glass elevator: The juxtaposition of old and new generates an "in-between" space. Context and concept merge in an unexpected reciprocity.

Autonomy =
Concepts that
decontextualize :

Limoges, Concert Hall, 2003–

Concept Recontextualized

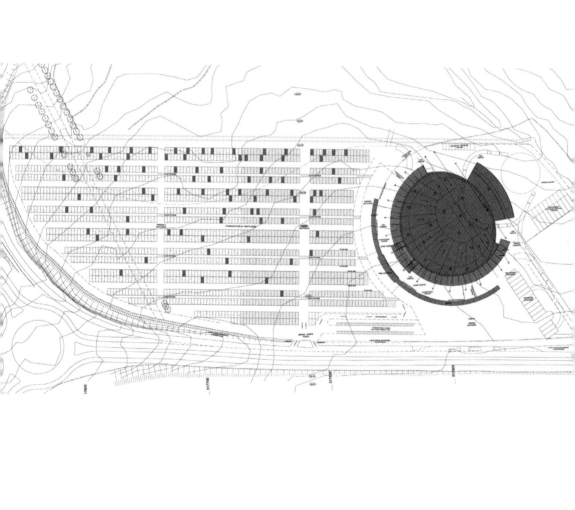

The Zenith Hall for Limoges, in central France, returns to the general envelope concept already explored in our Concert Hall built in Rouen (see *Event-Cities 2*), but transforms it through a new material strategy. If, as has been suggested, architecture is the material-ization of a concept, what if the concept remains the same, but the material changes? We decided to explore the implications of such a transformation.[1]

In Rouen, the outer envelope was made of steel and the inner envelope of exposed con-crete. In Limoges, the outer envelope is made of wood arcs and translucent rigid poly-carbonate sheets and the inner envelope of wood.

The use of wood was suggested by the location of the hall, in a clearing within a large forest, surrounded by trees that are more than 200 years old. The region also has an active lumber industry. In addition, the soft translucency of the polycarbonate allows light to filter in and out of the building. Here, we sought a sort of material reciprocity between concept and context.

The configuration of the double envelope with circulation in between—a scheme advan-tageous for both acoustical and thermal reasons—was modified to respond to several sit-ing issues: whereas Rouen's spiral aimed at channeling sideways the lateral movement of crowds entering the building, Limoges's detached and fragmented envelope opens in two directions, toward both the forest and the road. Between the two envelopes are the movement vectors: two ramps, one extending downward, toward the lower tiers of the auditorium, and the other upward, toward the upper tiers. Additionally, two straight "flying" staircases extend directly toward the top row of seats.

Much of the material treatment is determined by energy conservation and sustainability considerations. The five-centimeter-thick semi-rigid polycarbonate sheeting, with its mul-tiple inner layers of cells, provides excellent insulation value. It can be silk-screened for additional solar protection. Natural ventilation is integrated into the concept, so that the climate of the foyer can be kept at a temperate level, with little additional heating required.

Acoustics play a major role in the treatment of the inner envelope, both internally and externally. In the auditorium's face, strong absorption is required for an 8,000-spectator-capacity hall, while in the large, 1,800-square-meter foyer, absorbent and reflective mate-rials are alternated to generate more varied ambiences and acoustic effects.

1. A comparable experiment was carried out in our School of Architecture in Miami, Florida, which shares a general concept with our project in Marne-la-Vallée, France, but is qualified by a very different context.

tabula rasa = concept

vs.

genius loci = context

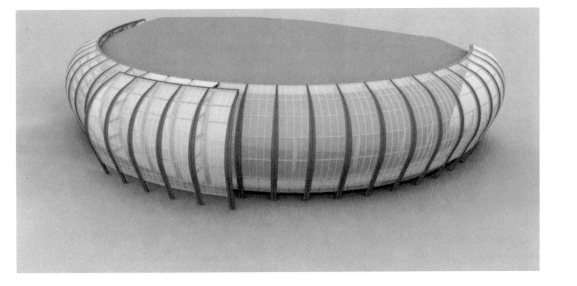

The envelope is offset to create a shielded entrance.

Skin, bracing, and circulation studies

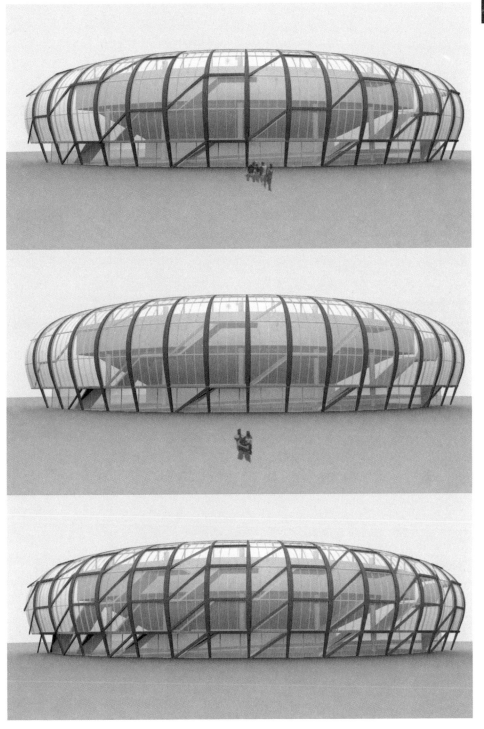

Architects don't choose
Contexts, they choose
concepts .

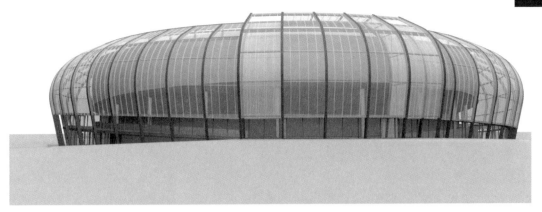

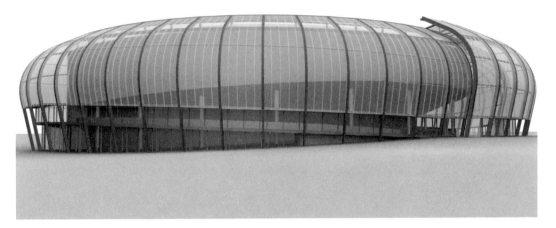

The envelope lifts to follow the incline of the ramp.

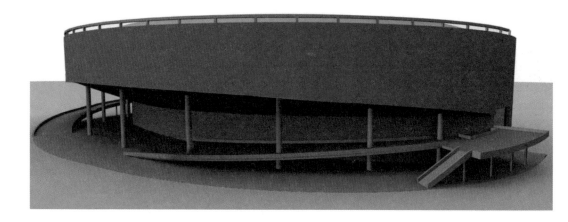

Circulation and auditorium

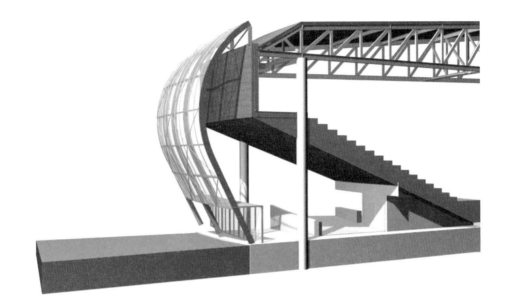

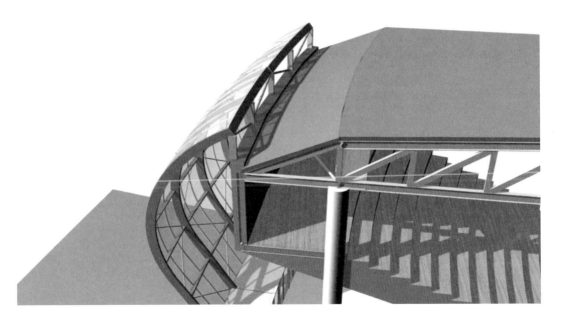

Cutaway views of gridded envelope show structure with circular gutter on the periphery.

Concept vs. context
= or ≠
generic vs. Specific
?

The envelope is composed of translucent polycarbonate panels framed by wood arcs.

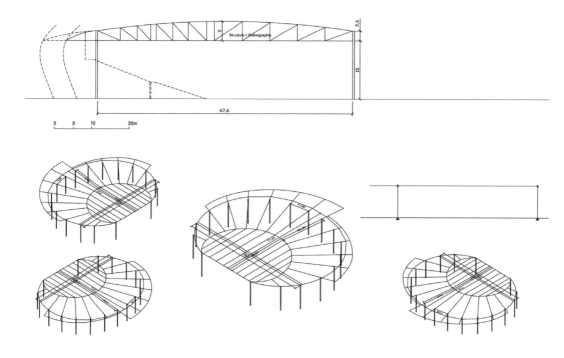

Studies of large-span roof structure

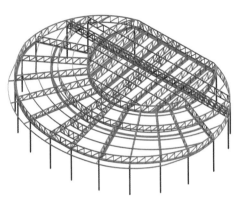

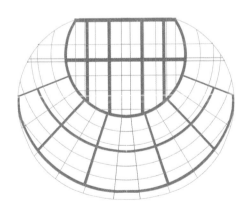

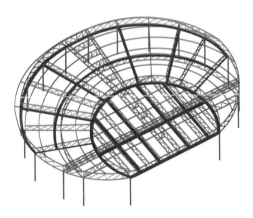

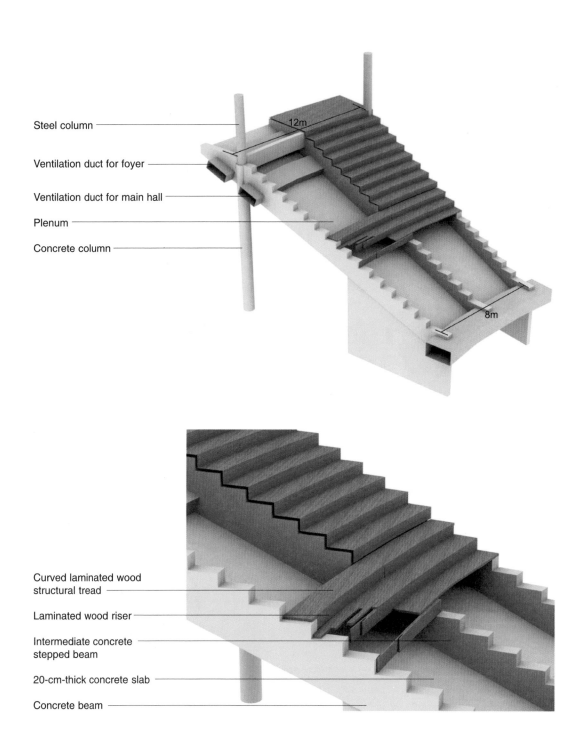

Steel column

Ventilation duct for foyer

Ventilation duct for main hall

Plenum

Concrete column

12m

8m

Curved laminated wood
structural tread

Laminated wood riser

Intermediate concrete
stepped beam

20-cm-thick concrete slab

Concrete beam

Plenum/bleacher study

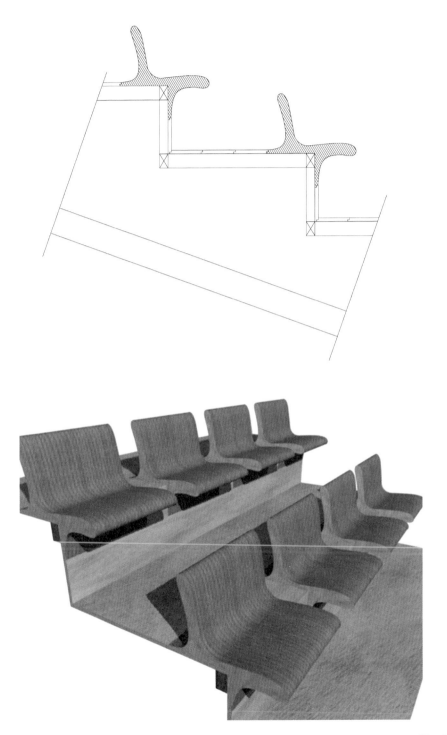

Wood seats

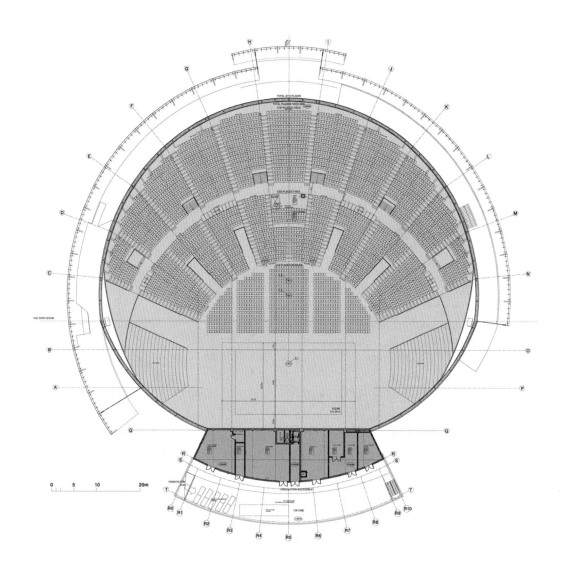

Level +9.50 m: 3,700-seat configuration

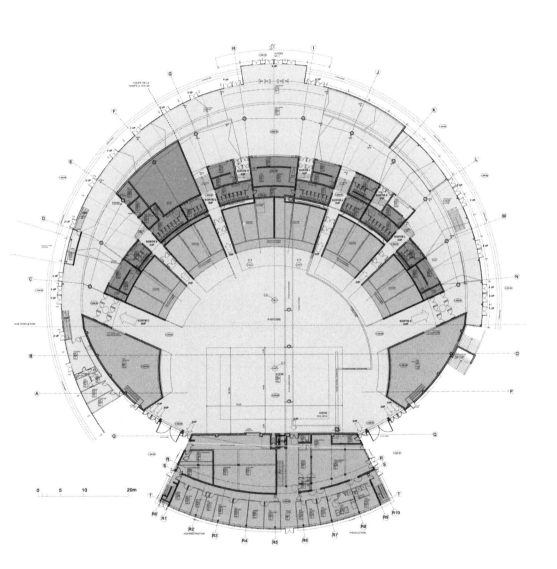

Level 0 m

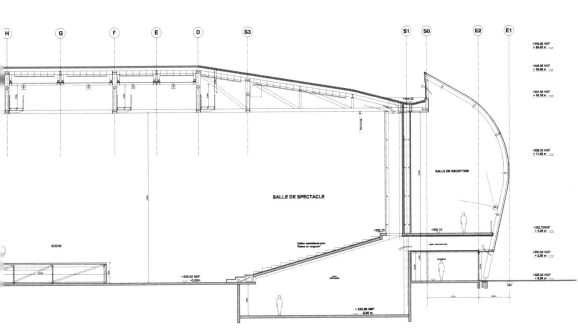

SALLE DE SPECTACLE

SALLE DE RECEPTION

SCENE

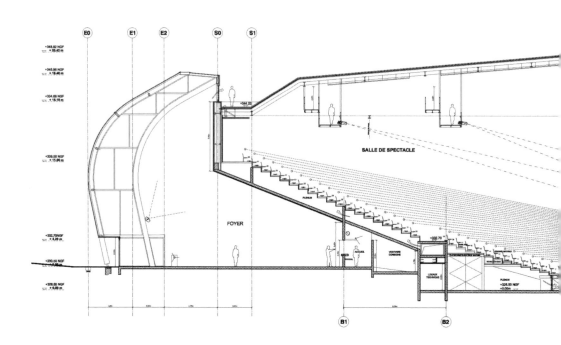

E0   E1   E2   S0   S1

+348,92 NGF
+ 33,42 m

+345,96 NGF
+ 19,46 m

+334,66 NGF
+ 19,16 m

+336,50 NGF
+ 15,00 m

+332,70 NGF
+ 4,20 m

+330,50 NGF
+ 0,00 m

+328,50 NGF
+ 0,00 m

SALLE DE SPECTACLE

FOYER

B1   B2

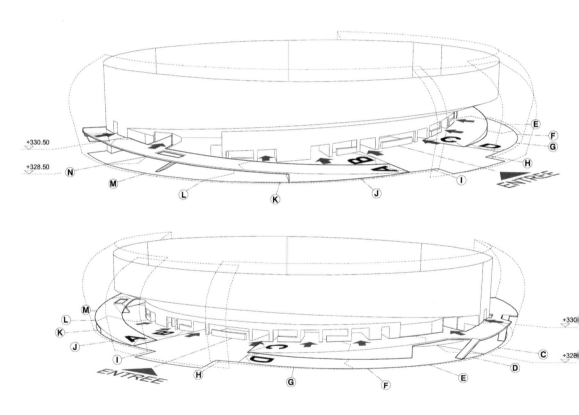

Foyer circulation

Vendée, International Sports Center, 2001

Double Content

Program: a concert hall as a velodrome, a velodrome as a concert hall

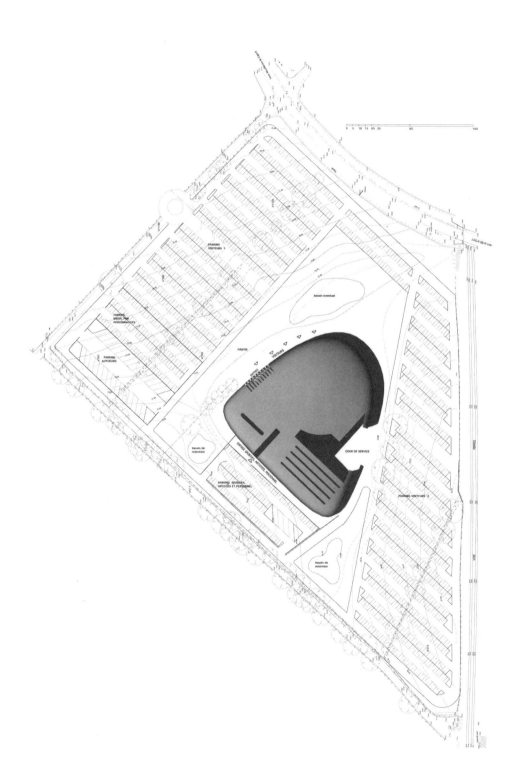

The major challenge of this project, located in a rural area in western France, lies in its content: the building serves as both a velodrome and a concert hall. The double program presents a number of technological and logistical issues: for example, it was stipulated that, once in operation, the reconfiguration of the building from velodrome to concert hall should require a maximum of eight people working no more than eight hours.

Can content lead to concept? Here, what the building does programmatically is as important as what it looks like. However, our proposal calls for a rounded metal envelope, clearly differentiated from the surrounding rural context, that hints at the technological transmission of sports information and music news through the global media.

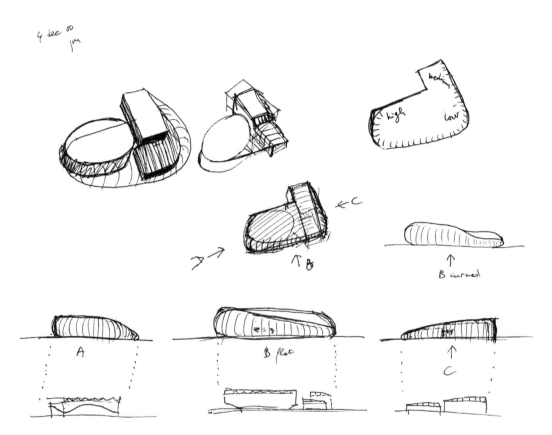

Preliminary sketches

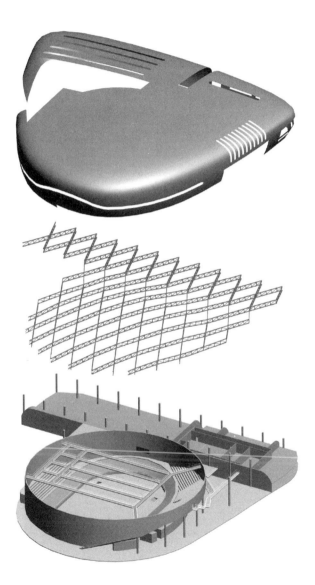

The abstract envelope mediates between context and content.

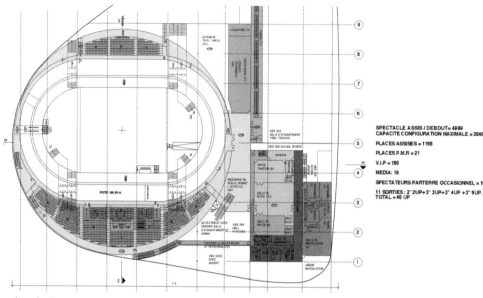

Level +1

SPECTACLE ASSIS / DEBOUT = 4999
CAPACITE CONFIGURATION MAXIMALE = 2848 P.

PLACES ASSISES = 1158

PLACES P.M.R = 21

V.I.P = 150

MEDIA: 19

SPECTATEURS PARTERRE OCCASIONNEL = 150

11 SORTIES : 2" 2UP+3" 3UP+3" 4UP +3" 5UP.
TOTAL = 40 UP

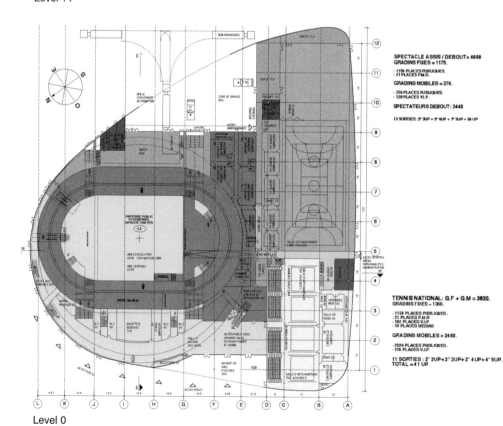

Level 0

SPECTACLE ASSIS / DEBOUT = 4999
GRADINS FIXES = 1175.

- 1154 PLACES PUBLIQUES.
- 21 PLACES P.M.R.

GRADINS MOBILES = 376.

- 256 PLACES PUBLIQUES.
- 120 PLACES V.I.P.

SPECTATEURS DEBOUT = 3448

13 SORTIES: 3" 3UP + 3" 4UP + 7" 5UP = 58 UP

TENNIS NATIONAL : G.F + G.M = 3820.
GRADINS FIXES = 1360.

- 1158 PLACES PUBLIQUES.
- 21 PLACES P.M.R
- 162 PLACES V.I.P
- 19 PLACES MEDIAS

GRADINS MOBILES = 2460.

- 2334 PLACES PUBLIQUES.
- 126 PLACES V.I.P

11 SORTIES : 2" 2UP+3" 3UP+2" 4UP+ 4" 5UP.
TOTAL = 41 UP

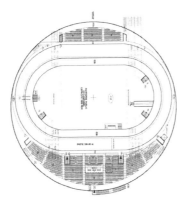

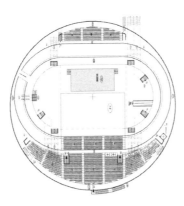

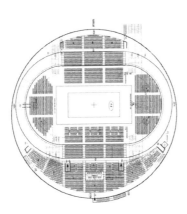

Content as concept: The building must be reconfigurable as either concert hall or velodrome.

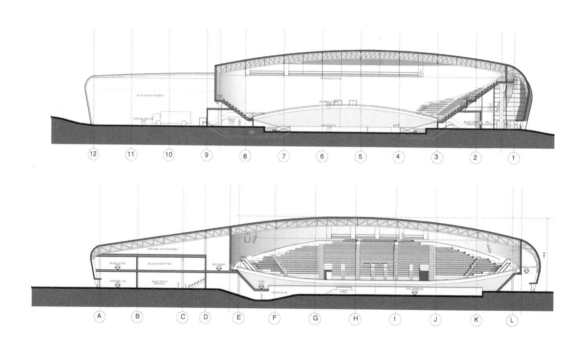

Transverse sections

Double content: entrance views

East and northwest elevations

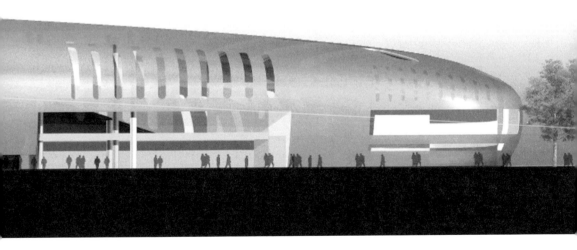

C.
Contextualizing Concept

This section presents two dyads of projects that stem from a common idea, in order to explore how concepts adapt to their environments. To use an example from another field, just as Darwin's finches on Galápagos evolved from one "founder" population into numerous species with each occupying a particular niche, a concept can mutate as it is inserted into different contexts. Sometimes the resulting architectural species may appear similar while functioning quite differently, as in the case of the projects for Rome and Antwerp; in other cases, as at Troy, New York, and São Paulo, they may retain little visual resemblance but still share a basic concept. Adaptation is universal but its techniques are infinite.

Rome, Italian Space Agency, 2000

Fractal Cantilever

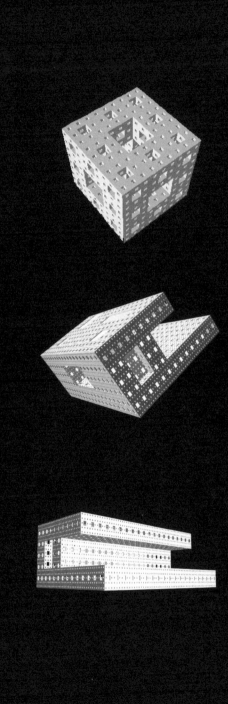

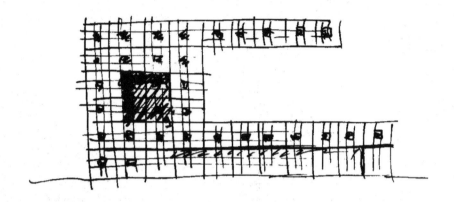

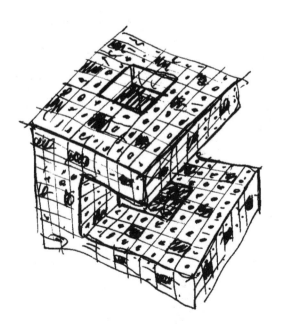

Remembering Menger's sponge (See *Event-Cities 2*, p. 425.)

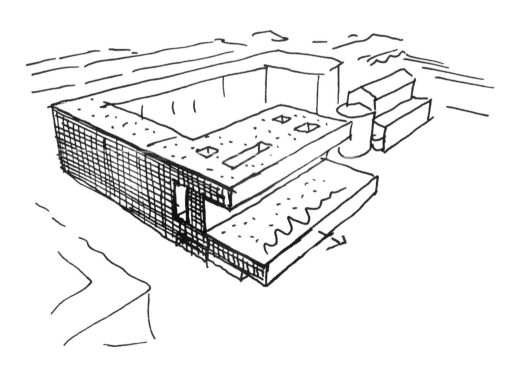

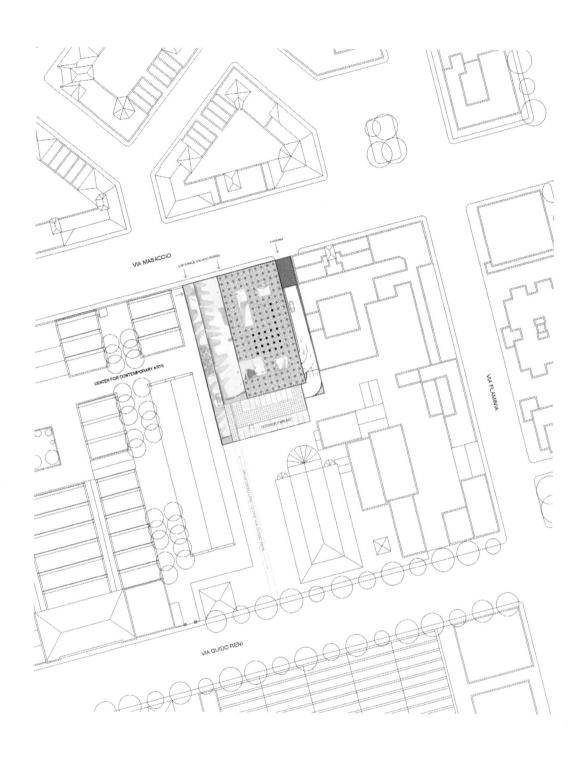

VIA MASACCIO

ENTRANCE (PEDESTRIAN)

PARKING

CENTER FOR CONTEMPORARY ARTS

OUTDOOR PARKING

PROPOSED LINK TO THE VIA GUIDO RENI

VIA FLAMINIA

VIA GUIDO RENI

The Italian Space Agency (ASI) oversees scientific, technological, and industrial developments related to the conception, design, construction, and launching of satellites in orbit. Its new headquarters were to be located in Rome, north of the historic center.

Design Strategy
The approach was to devise an overriding concept that could accommodate site requirements and energy conservation goals, as well as provide required green spaces, functional flexibility, and an image or identity to the project—all in a single move.

Underlying the proposal was the fractal notion of self-similarity. Inspired by the photographs of Earth taken by orbiting satellites, which reveal the fractal nature of landscapes, the project develops a three-dimensional pattern, analogous to Menger's sponge (an idea investigated in the extension for The Museum of Modern Art, described in *Event-Cities 2*).

Concept Enters Context and Content
First, the 25-meter-high existing street wall massing of Via Masaccio was extended, using a perforated concrete panel system that both continued the masonry and fenestration patterns typical of the neighborhood and offered a new contemporary identity.

The flexibility of the "fractal" architectural solution permitted not only the integration of the site with the functional program but also the introduction of several outdoor spaces, from the ground-level patio to the top-floor office patios.

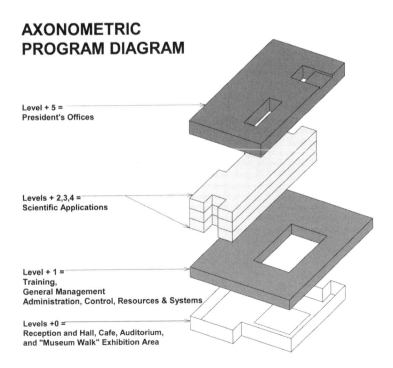

AXONOMETRIC PROGRAM DIAGRAM

Level + 5 =
President's Offices

Levels + 2,3,4 =
Scientific Applications

Level + 1 =
Training,
General Management
Administration, Control, Resources & Systems

Levels +0 =
Reception and Hall, Cafe, Auditorium,
and "Museum Walk" Exhibition Area

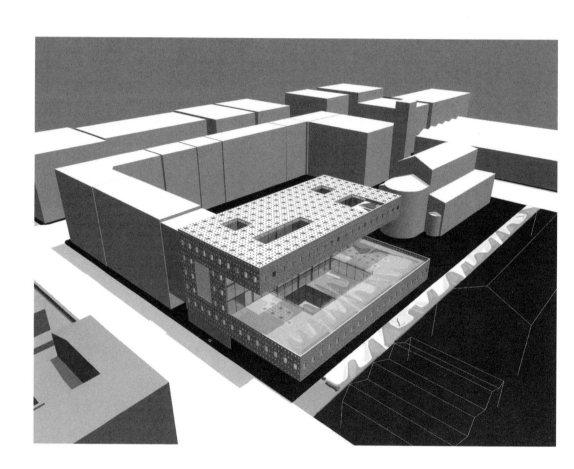

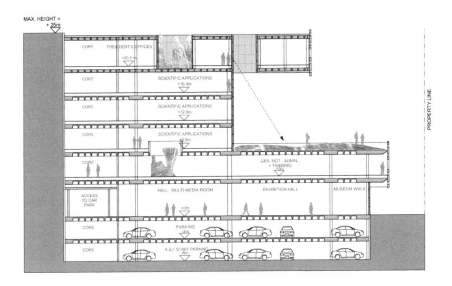

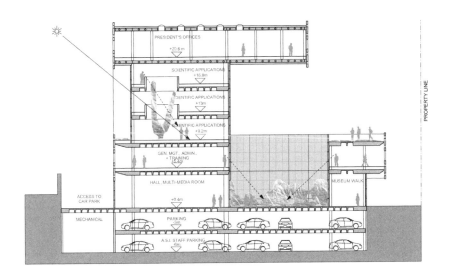

The building's fractal organization allows for the creation of patios at several levels.

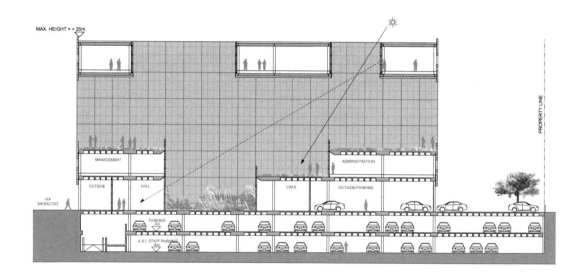

MAX. HEIGHT = + 25m

MANAGEMENT

ADMINISTRATION

OUTSIDE   HALL

CAFE   OUTSIDE/PARKING

VIA
MASACCIO

PARKING
-3m

A.S.I. STAFF PARKING
-6m

PROPERTY LINE

The patios are conceived as "voids" in the cantilever and as surfaces on the lower levels.

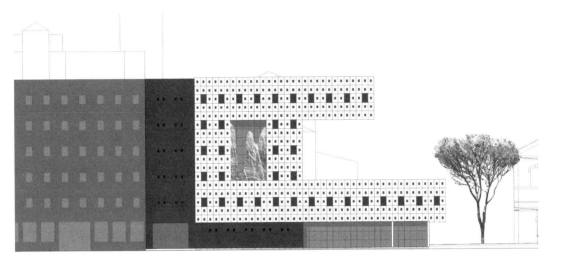

North elevation, from Via Masaccio: A perforated concrete panel system both continues the masonry and fenestration patterns of the neighborhood and offers a new contemporary identity.

West elevation: The thermal mass of the precast facade acts as a barrier to heat and direct sunlight during the day. Windows, including the smaller facade openings, provide both natural light and high- and low-level manual operation, optimizing ventilation.

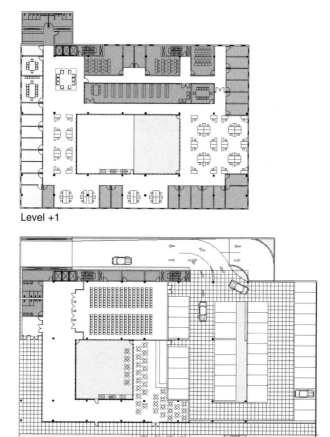

Level +1

Level 0

Levels +1 and 0: The ground floor contains a reception hall, exhibition space, café, and auditorium; the first floor houses management, training, and administration.

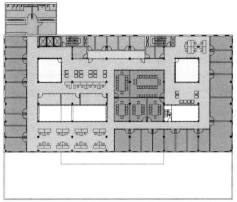

Level + 5

Level + 3/4

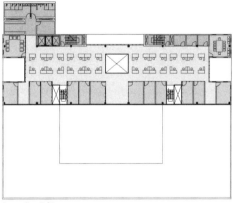

Level + 2

Levels +5, +3/4, and +2: Level 5 holds the president's offices.
Levels 2 to 4 house scientific applications.

Facade Functions

Small facade penetrations above and below the main fenestration provide manually operable high- and low-level openings that optimize the stack-driven ventilation within each floor plate while keeping the work plane draft-free. During mild seasons the occupants can regulate the openings to control the ventilation adjacent to their work area.

Small low-powered "window fans" integrated into the facade and located in penetrations at alternating low and high levels between the windows mechanically boost the ventilation effect when required and allow the building to be ventilated and cooled at night.

Office Distribution Systems

A raised floor scheme that incorporates the systems for electrical power, information technology, and air circulation avoids the need for a lowered ceiling. The underside of the ceiling slab exposes thermal mass within the space, absorbing some of the heat generated during the day and lowering the peak internal temperature gain. The waffle slab is developed on the 900 x 900-mm building module so that partitions, located on the ribs of the slab, can be flexibly reconfigured on the building grid.

Structure

The top floor cantilever structure is a one-story-high Vierendeel truss, extending north-south in plan. The truss cantilevers 10.8 meters, but can be penetrated for access. It is made of steel so that it can be erected without being propped. Lateral stability for the structure is provided by cast-in-place shear walls. These are located on the east, west, and south sides of the building, leaving the glazed facade free of structure.

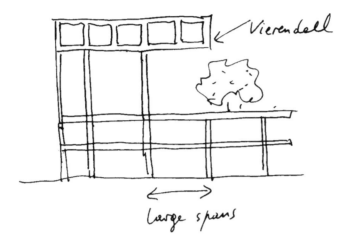

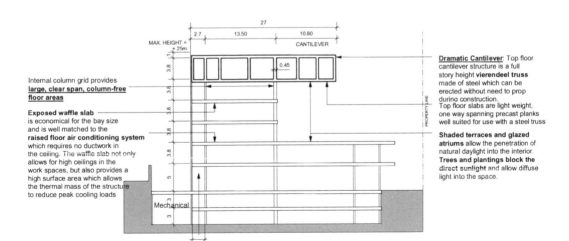

Internal column grid provides **large, clear span, column-free floor areas**

Exposed waffle slab is economical for the bay size and is well matched to the **raised floor air conditioning system** which requires no ductwork in the ceiling. The waffle slab not only allows for high ceilings in the work spaces, but also provides a high surface area which allows the thermal mass of the structure to reduce peak cooling loads

Dramatic Cantilever: Top floor cantilever structure is a full story height **vierendeel truss** made of steel which can be erected without need to prop during construction. Top floor slabs are light weight, one way spanning precast planks well suited for use with a steel truss

Shaded terraces and glazed atriums allow the penetration of natural daylight into the interior. **Trees and plantings block the direct sunlight** and allow diffuse light into the space.

Core: distribution of air, power and data to all floors

Structural concept: The top floor is a full-story-height Vierendeel truss that cantilevers 10.8 meters.

Second-floor garden patio

Antwerp, Museum aan de Stroom, 2000

Fractal Matrix

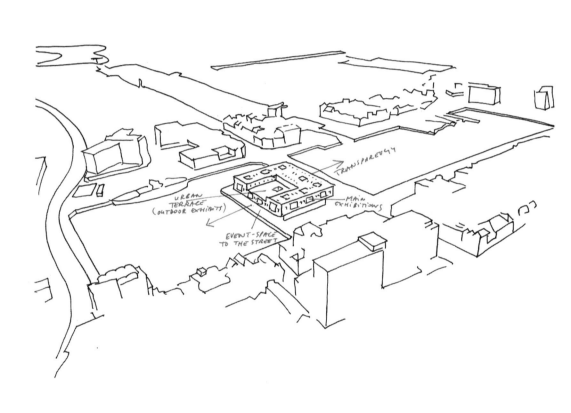

TRANSPARENCY

URBAN
TERRACE
(OUTDOOR EXHIBITS)

MAIN
EXHIBITIONS

EVENT-SPACE
TO THE STREET

The new Museum aan de Stroom (MAS), or Museum on the River, located in a rapidly developing section of Antwerp's working harbor, is designed to house four disparate collections of artifacts currently located in smaller, out-of-date museum buildings. The common denominator of the existing Vleeshuis, Volkskunde, Scheepvaarrt, and Industrial Heritage collections—which range from examples of heavy industrial machinery from the early 20th century to shipbuilder's models,19th-century embroidery, children's toys, and 16th-century landscape paintings—is the history of this Dutch port city.

The creation of the new museum raises the following questions: How can the history of the construction of the metropolis be exhibited? How can the local, metropolitan, and international dimensions of the city's life be integrated in the new museum? How can the historical memory of the city be inserted into and linked with the dynamics of present time in a contemporary manner? How can one give a recognizable overall identity to the museum, one that simultaneously responds to the changing urban environment and to the multiplicity of the collections?

Fractal Scaling

The design for MAS explored a concept that was simultaneously urban, architectural, and curatorial, moving from the largest scale to the smallest, from the city to the room to the pins used to hang art. The variable scales of disparate collections within one museum suggested once again an analogy with fractal theory, whereby apparent complexity can be explained through multiple scales of self-similarity. Our earlier research on museum design revealed the potential relevance of fractal diagrams, in particular Menger's sponge, a volume that can be infinitely hollowed, as square voids are surrounded repeatedly by voids one-third their size (described in The Museum of Modern Art section in *Event-Cities 2*). The implications for architecture, which is made of solids and voids, surfaces and volumes, on multiple scales, are worth exploring. In the context of the city of Antwerp, one can observe the engineering of Antwerp cathedral, which is made up of fractal triangles, as are many other Gothic works of architecture. Similarly, in his classic Flemish landscape painting *The Harvesters*, Pieter Brueghel juxtaposed multiple self-similar forms, creating tensions between similarities by "fractalizing" triangles, circles, and rectangles.

The proposed MAS design uses a simple linear fractal strategy to bring together the scale of the city—its street and dock patterns, as well as the fenestration of its dockside warehouses—with the vastly varying scales of the museum exhibits.

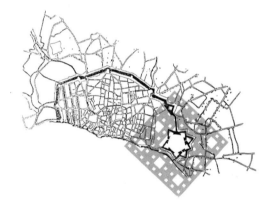

1450 Emergence of the pattern of the urban core
1650 The scale of the military system

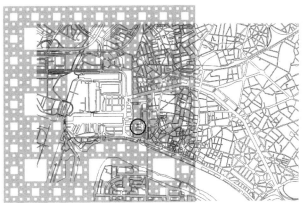

1830 The proliferation of the medieval pattern
2000 The scale of industry

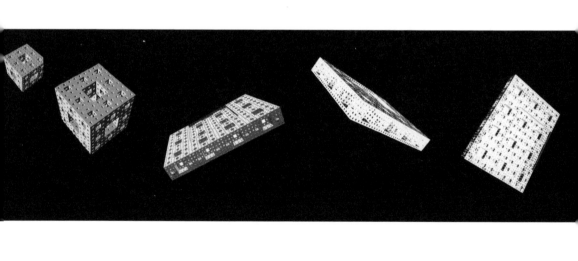

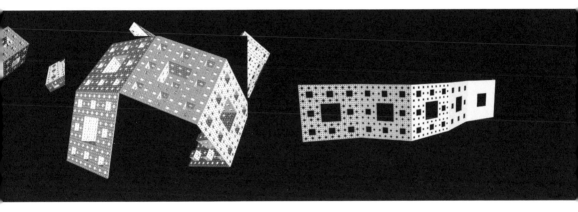

Degrees of transparency in two- and three-dimensional envelopes

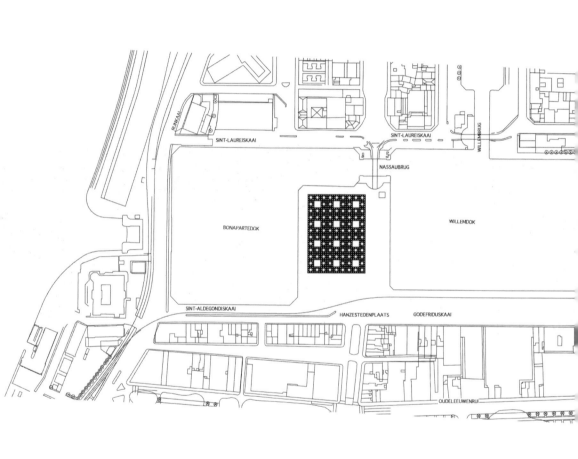

A Loop in Time

The museum building acts as a transfer point connecting the east-west and north-south axes of the city. Accessible from all directions, its covered entrance gallery leads through the reception area to the escalators and up to the galleries for the permanent exhibitions. A grand stairway descends back to the city. A continuous movement loop is created, extending from the city to the exhibitions and back to the city again.

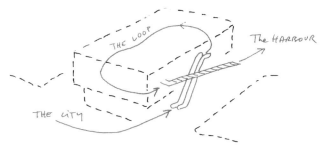

Urban Loggias

Outdoor urban loggias extend the permanent exhibition galleries into the city. They can accommodate both large objects that need little protection from the weather, like industrial artifacts, and large displays, such as fabric signs or screens for projected images. The urban loggias, which open to the river, port, and city, become the articulation between the museum and the urban center.

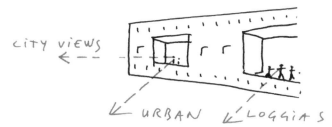

Event-Space, Openness

At times when there is no installation in the ground-level temporary exhibition gallery, this area can be an urban event-space, an extension of the city, fully open from east to west. An urban terrace at the top level provides another space for gatherings.

Public Spaces

The entrance lobby, café, and bookstore give direct access to the temporary exhibition gallery. Escalators lead to the permanent exhibitions on the middle level. An educational strip spans the entire length of the permanent exhibition spaces and provides various interactive displays. Conference halls, a documentation center, and classrooms for educational activities and programs are located on the upper level and open onto a grand terrace with framed views of the city.

Non-Public Spaces

All non-public spaces are located in the southeast part of the building, so that loading docks and depot, and spaces for workroom, logistics, and administration are contiguous and can be accessed separately from the public areas.

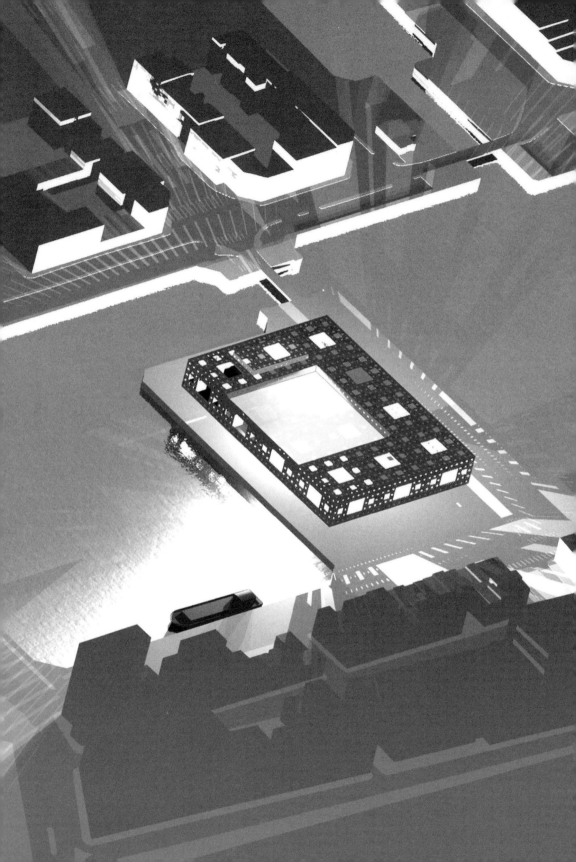

The Galleries Concept: The Time Matrix

The specific qualities of the four collections require that different scenarios be accommodated. Therefore, a concept has been devised that permits several possible readings, depending on the visitor's route: namely, a matrix with temporal and thematic axes.

This concept opens the potential for numerous paths and "stories" of the city. One can, for example, conceive of histories of the city based on themes (urbanization, contemporary relevance, multiple interpretations, city on the river), questions (where, from what, who, how), size (from small to large), or on the collections' respective identities. A north-south thread, for instance, affords visitors a chronological reading of the city, as they move through artifacts interwoven from the four collections. One can even blend together several readings and histories.

Regardless of the selected curatorial sequence, all routes provide panoramic views of the surrounding cityscape, thus creating a constant oscillation between history and the present.

This proposal features four large gallery spaces, each 900–1,300 square meters in size, 17.5–25 meters wide, and 52 meters long. To avoid monotony, each space is given a different atmosphere by varying the width, materials, and light conditions. For example, the gallery for a historical collection might have dark wood floors and paneling with northern light, while the gallery holding the Industrial Heritage collection might feature a concrete floor with filtered southern light.

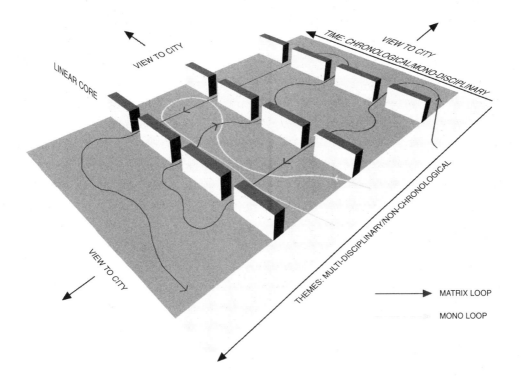

LINEAR CORE

VIEW TO CITY

VIEW TO CITY

TIME: CHRONOLOGICAL/MONO-DISCIPLINARY

VIEW TO CITY

THEMES: MULTI-DISCIPLINARY/NON-CHRONOLOGICAL

MATRIX LOOP

MONO LOOP

The galleries: a matrix with temporal and thematic axes

Concept —not form—
is what distinguishes
architecture from mere building

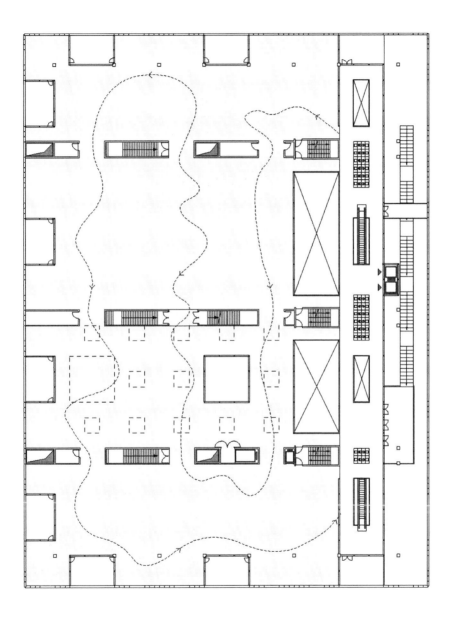

First floor: Several possible routes or "narratives" are possible.

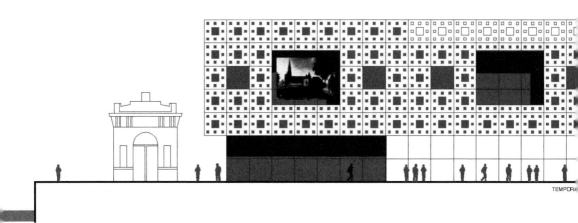

TEMPOR

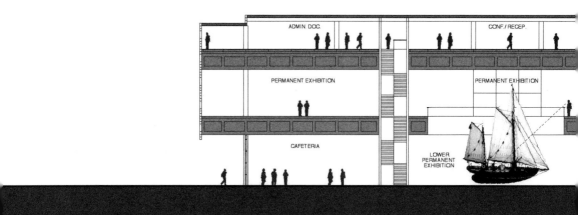

Longitudinal elevation and section

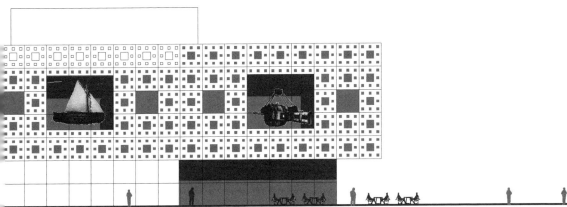

Ϙ EVENT-SPACE)

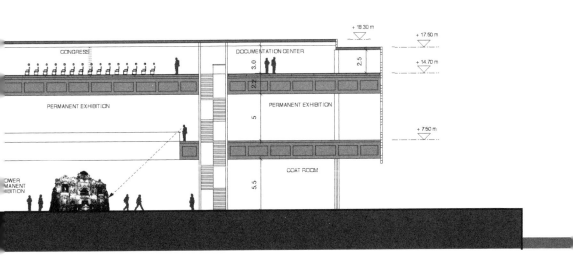

São Paulo, Museum of Contemporary Art, 2001

A Vertical Museum Sketchbook

"The Museum is about art, but also about the city"

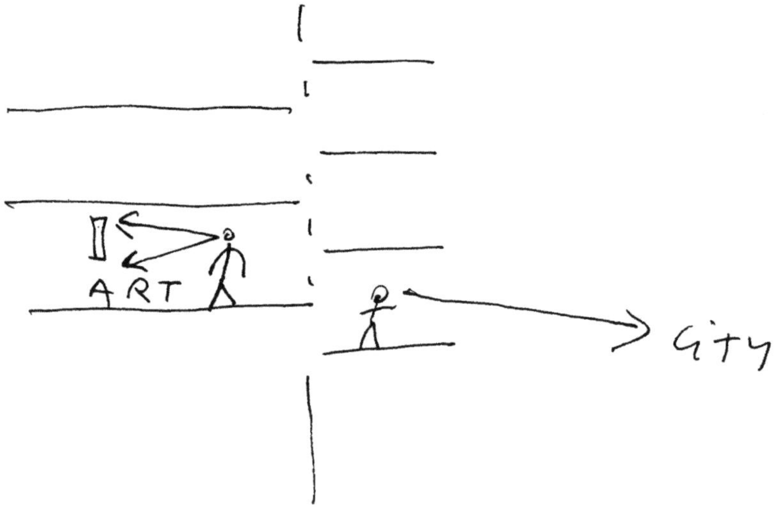

ART

city

Art and the City

Buildings can be introverted or extroverted. Stressing the privacy of aesthetic experience, most museums tend to be the former, as in the case of Frank Lloyd Wright's Guggenheim Museum in New York, an assertive but inward-oriented building that does not allow visitors to view the city around it. Located in a dynamically growing section of São Paulo, the new home for the Museu de Arte Contemporânea (MAC) provides an opportunity to develop a different type of museum, in which the city is an integral part of the museum experience, and in which the perception of art and the city intertwine in an unprecedented way.

The innovative nature of the new building is expressed by a simple formulation: the museum must not be just a container; it must also provide a context for the art of its time, setting it into a relationship with both the history of art and the dynamic of the surrounding city. Much as the city has been an informing stimulus for 20th-century art, so might public, urban experience define the 21st-century museum.

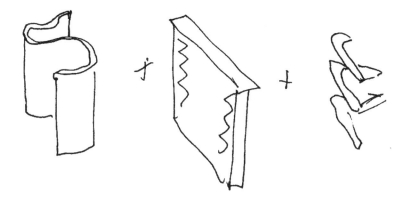

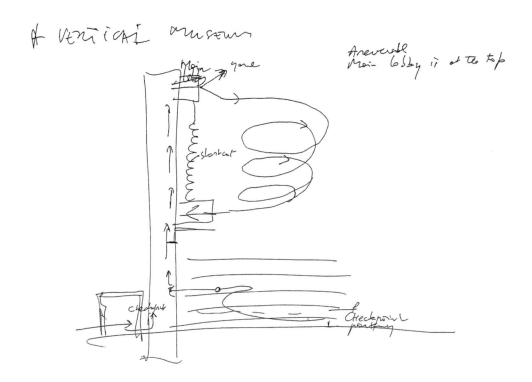

A vertical museum: five levels of car park on the ground, three levels of galleries in the air

A Vertical Museum Manifesto

The following terms describe the proposal for the new museum:

1. It is vertical.

2. Movement within it is visible from outside through a panoramic gallery ramp and glass envelope.

3. Its aim is to make art and the city interact.

To achieve this, the architecture of the museum consists of three elements:

1. Large, open floor plates within a free-flowing envelope

2. A linear vertical core containing all fire stairs, elevators, plumbing, and mechanical systems

3. A city street in the air, composed of curvilinear ramps with city views, linking the gallery floors through movement. Cantilevering beyond the glass, the edge of the ramp acts as a sun shade in the hot Brazilian climate.

Site Constraints

Based on a footprint of approximately 1,600 square meters per floor, the building necessarily consists of ten levels above ground and one below. The museum itself, not including the automobile parking levels, occupies 12,500 square meters, distributed over six levels and a roof garden. Parking occupies the first four levels above ground, since geological conditions do not permit deeper excavations.

Mediating between art, education, scholarship, and entertainment, the new MAC suggests five programmatic families:

1. Exhibition galleries

2. Lobby, restaurant, shop, and retail services

3. Support (administrative, curatorial, conservation, etc.)

4. Auditorium and meeting rooms for the public

5. Parking

Identifying these five programmatic families led to an important part of the museum concept.

Project

A publicly accessible covered lobby on the ground floor contains an information center, bookstore, and ticket booth. The main lobby, however, is situated at the top of the building; the visitor ascends by elevator and then walks down along the external ramp to and through the galleries below. A restaurant and sculpture garden are located on the roof.

Circulation throughout the galleries occurs via the ramps as well as by means of elevators or "short-cut" stairs between floors. Importantly, the ramps will serve as an "in-between" space, physically mediating between the collections and the city, and providing locations for exhibiting new art forms with public content and public modes of address.

The structure supporting the floor plates may be either a large span (12–15 meters) on all floors, or Vierendeel trusses every other upper floor, allowing two gallery floors to be column-free.

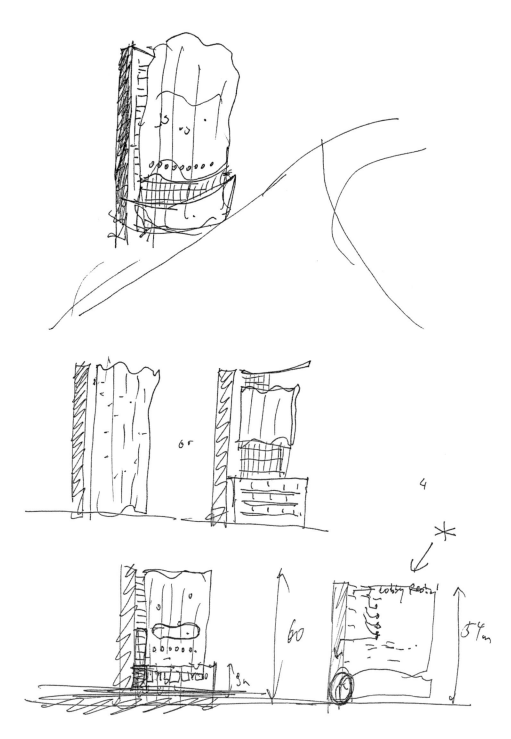

First sketches before visiting the site

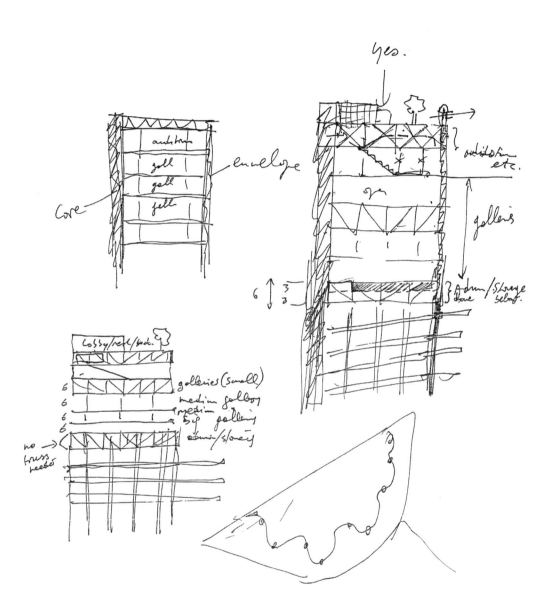

Testing structural configurations

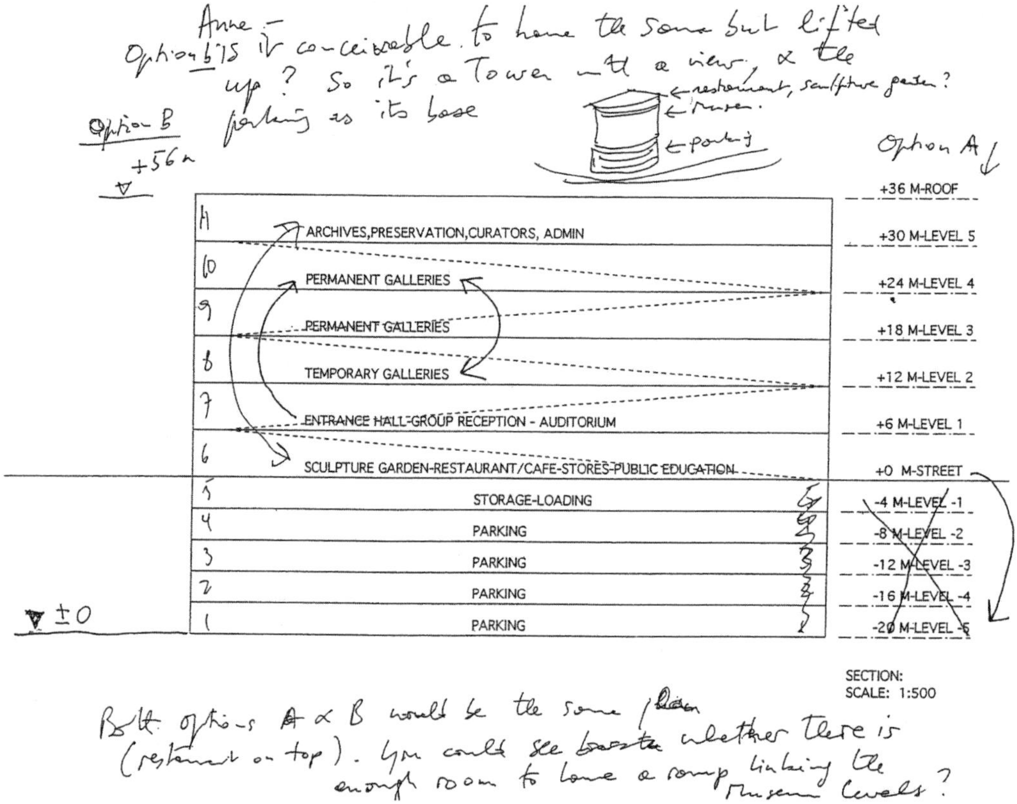

Anne —

Option B: Is it conceivable to have the same but lifted up? So it's a Tower with a view, & the parking as its base

Option B
+56 m
▽

← restaurant, sculpture garden?
← museum.
← parking

Option A ↓

		+36 M-ROOF
11	ARCHIVES, PRESERVATION, CURATORS, ADMIN	+30 M-LEVEL 5
10	PERMANENT GALLERIES	+24 M-LEVEL 4
9	PERMANENT GALLERIES	+18 M-LEVEL 3
8	TEMPORARY GALLERIES	+12 M-LEVEL 2
7	ENTRANCE HALL-GROUP RECEPTION - AUDITORIUM	+6 M-LEVEL 1
6	SCULPTURE GARDEN-RESTAURANT/CAFE-STORES-PUBLIC EDUCATION	+0 M-STREET
5	STORAGE-LOADING	-4 M-LEVEL -1
4	PARKING	-8 M-LEVEL -2
3	PARKING	-12 M-LEVEL -3
2	PARKING	-16 M-LEVEL -4
1	PARKING	-20 M-LEVEL -5

▽ ±0

SECTION:
SCALE: 1:500

Both options A & B would be the same plan (restaurant on top). You could see whether there is enough room to have a ramp linking the museum levels?

Programmatic interchangeability

Museum in the air

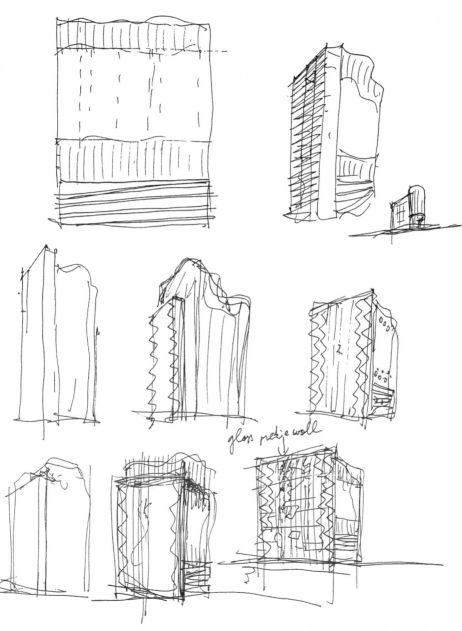

glass media wall

A linear core and a curvilinear envelope

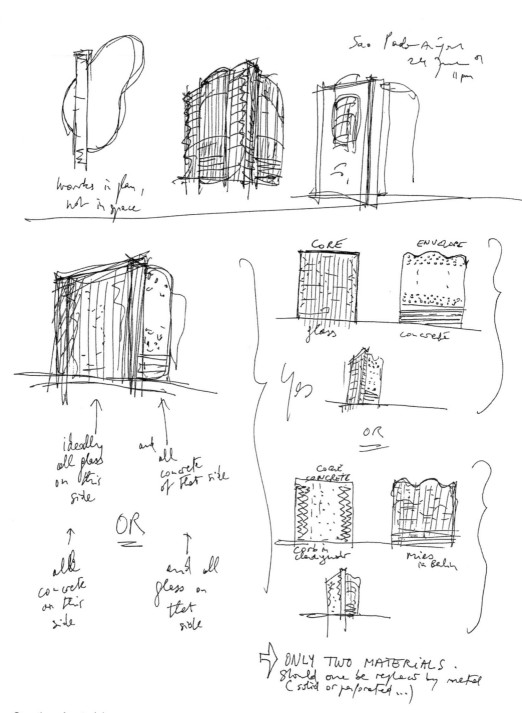

Sao Paulo Airport
24 June 07
11 pm

Workes in plan,
not in space

CORE

glass

ENVELOPE

concrete

Yes

OR

ideally
all glass
on this
side

and all
concrete
of that side

OR

all
concrete
on this
side

and all
glass on
that
side

CORE
CONCRETE

Corb in
Chandigarh

mies
in Berlin

ONLY TWO MATERIALS.
Should one be replaced by metal
(solid or perforated ...)

Question of materials

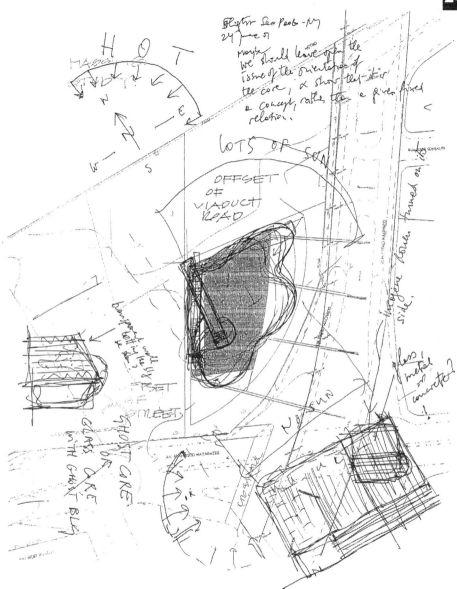

Visiting São Paulo and the Site

The new museum sits on a reclaimed industrial site that has been turned into a new business center, sandwiched between railway lines and a main avenue, and flanked by an elevated highway. It acts as a pivot for this part of the city.

The question is whether the building core should be parallel to the site boundary line established by recent history, or perpendicular to the river, along the axis laid by nature. The decision is made to follow nature, as Oscar Niemeyer did in the nearby Memorial da America Latina.

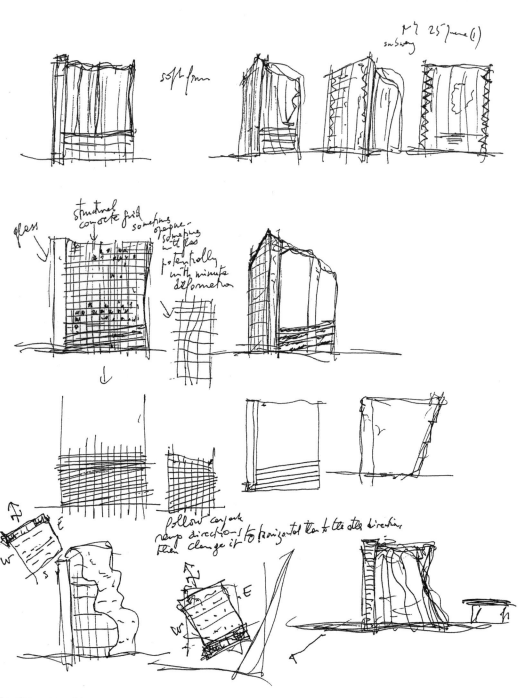

Envelope geometries

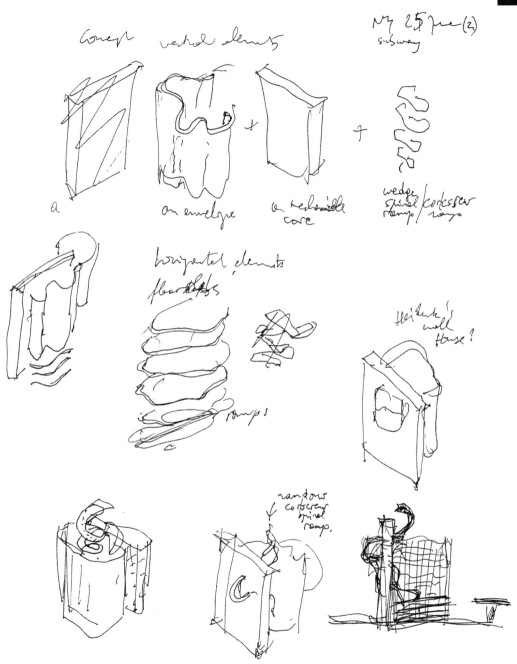

Concept   vertical elements

NY 25 June (2)
subway

a

an envelope

a mechanical core

wedge
spiral / corkscrew
ramp / ramps

horizontal elements

floor slabs

ramps

c

Heiduk's wall House?

random corkscrew spiral ramp.

Introducing movement vectors

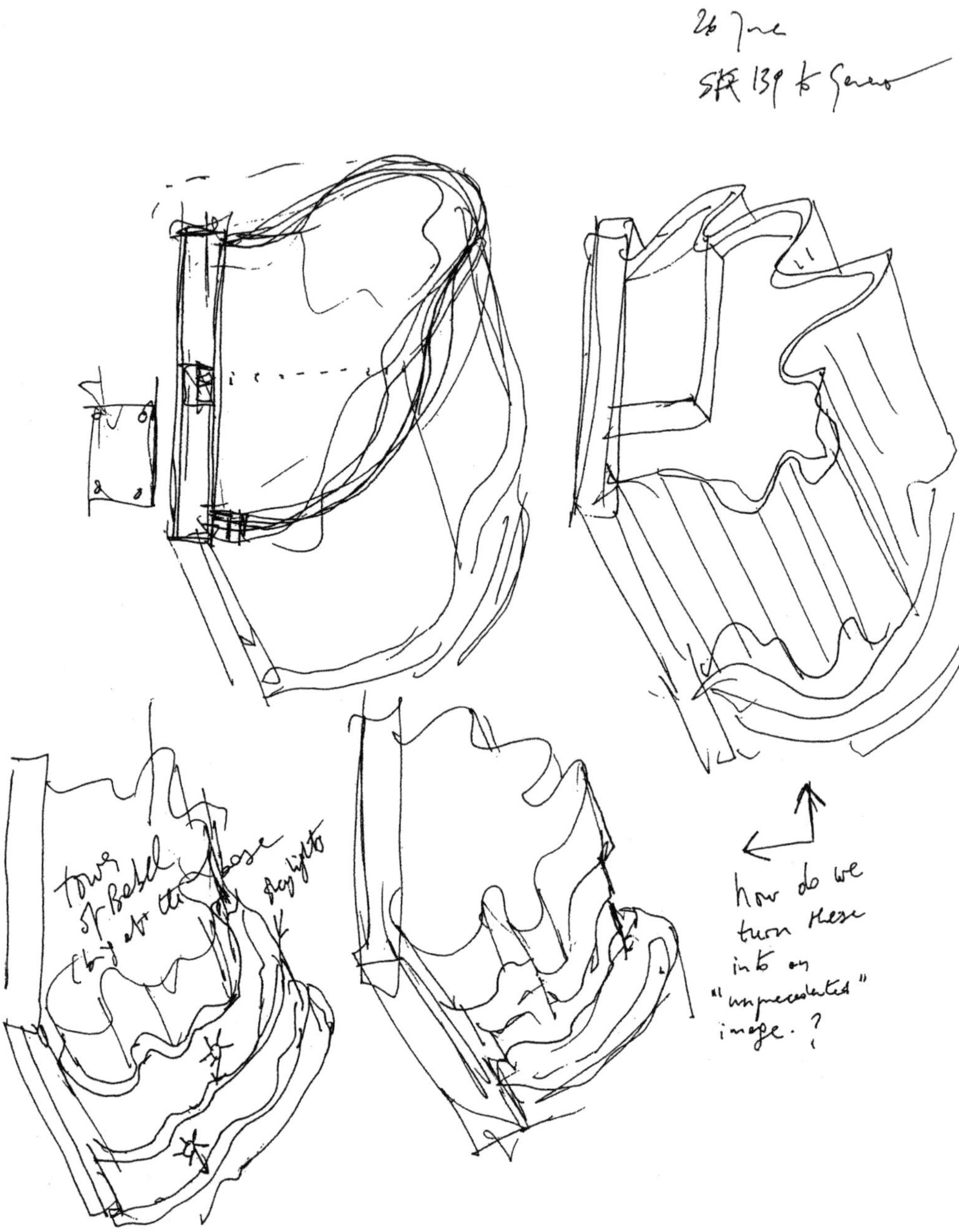

tower
of Babel (blog at the apse)
(Bing at the apse) skylights

how do we turn these into an "unprecedented" image. ?

Question of image

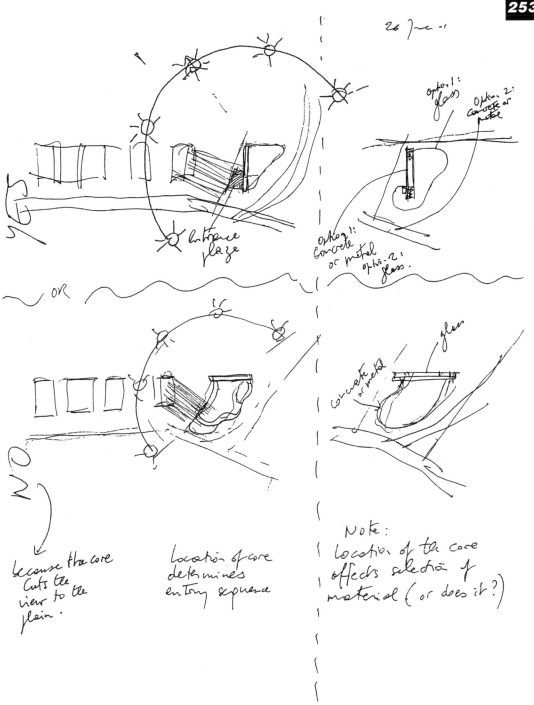

26 June -1

option 1: glass

option 2: concrete or metal

option 1: concrete or metal

option 2: glass.

entrance plaza

OR

NO

glass

concrete or metal

because the core cuts the view to the plain.

Location of core determines entry sequence

Note:
Location of the core affects selection of material (or does it?)

Finalizing the building's orientation

Concepts qualify
or disqualify
contexts ...

- - - - - - - -

contexts qualify
or disqualify
concepts ...

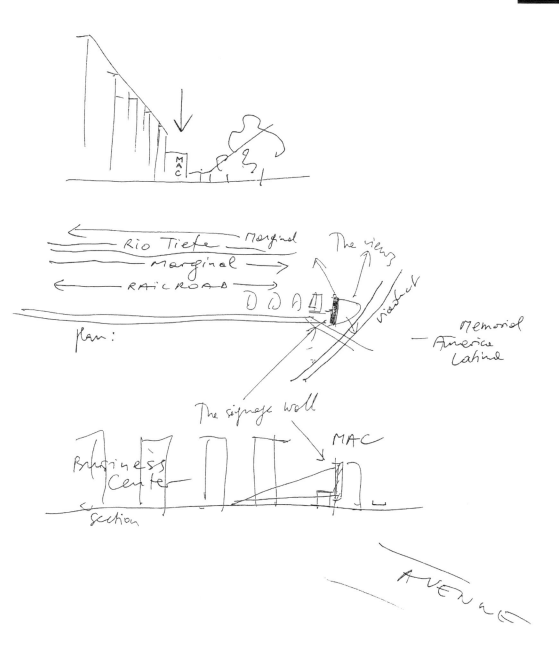

Rio Tiete — Marginal

Marginal →

← RAILROAD →

plan:

The views

viaduct

Memorial
— America
Latina

The signage wall

MAC

Business
Center

Section

AVENUE

Site plan issues: responding to site constraints

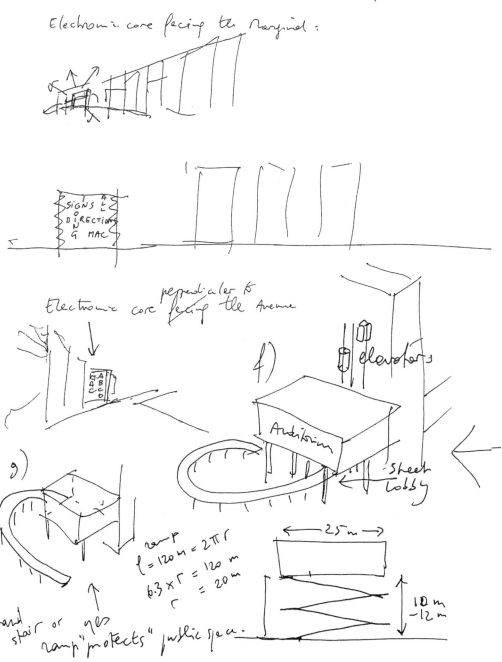

26 June 2

Electronic core facing the marginal:

SIGNS
O
DIRECTION
&
MAC

A
L
L
R
P

Electronic core perpendicular to facing the Avenue

f)

elevators

Auditorium

Street Lobby

g)

ramp
$\ell = 120 m = 2\pi r$
$6.3 \times r = 120 m$
$r = 20 m$

⟵ 25 m ⟶

10 m
-12 m

grand stair or yes ramp "protects" public space.

Public space, urban space

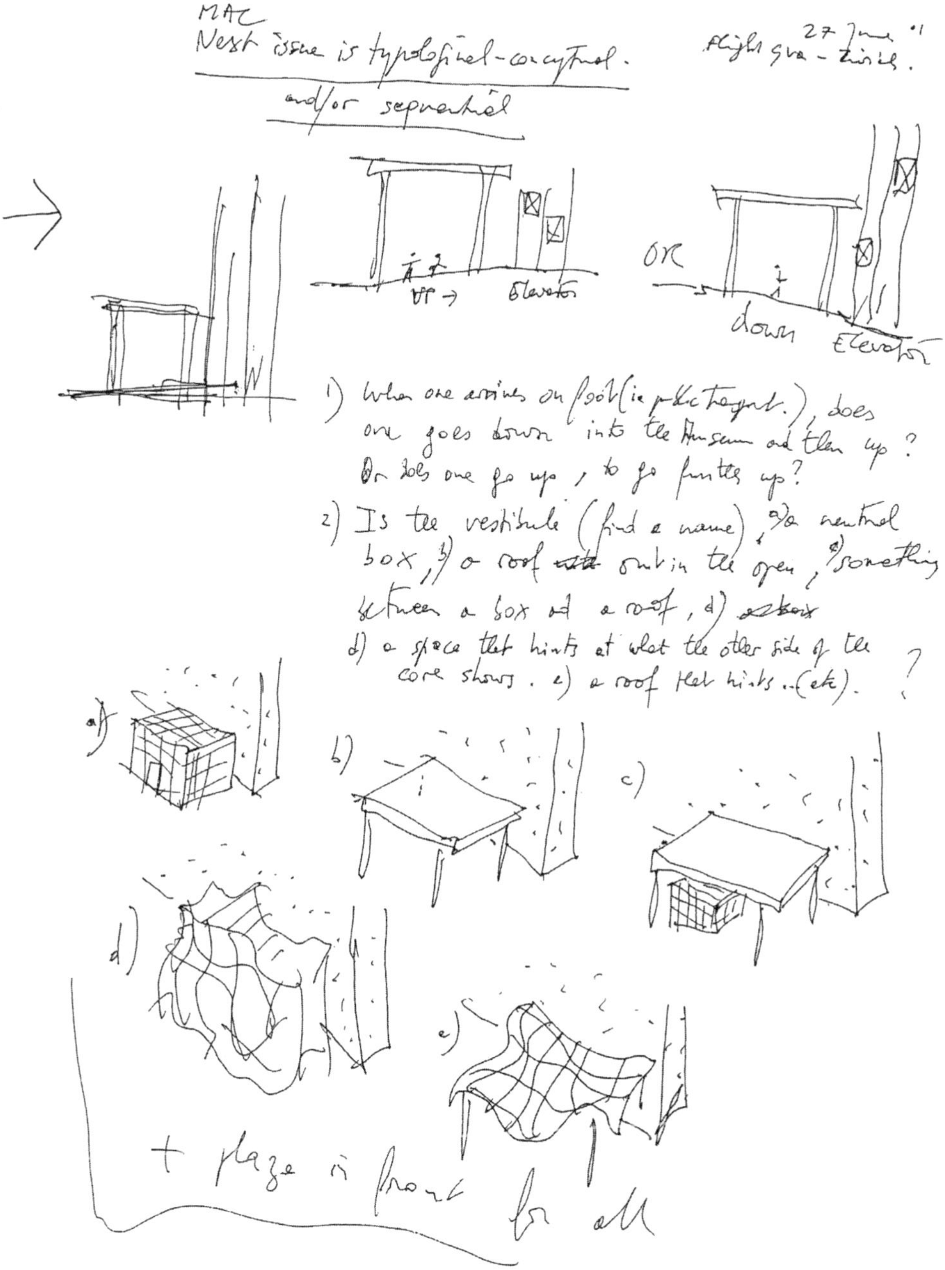

MAC
Next issue is typological-conceptual.
and/or sequential

flight sur - zürich. 27 June '11

or

down Elevator

1) When one arrives on foot (ie public transport), does one goes down into the Museum and then up? Or does one go up, to go further up?

2) Is the vestibule (find a name) a) a neutral box, b) a roof out in the open, c) something between a box and a roof, d) a box

d) a space that hints at what the other side of the core shows. e) a roof that hints ..(etc). ?

a)

b)

c)

d)

e)

+ plaza in front for all

The street-level entrance lobby is intended as a symbolic gift from the museum to the city and its inhabitants: a grand, covered public space that accommodates temporary public art installations and includes an information area, souvenir and book kiosk, and ticket booth. Access to this ground-floor lobby is free, but visitors pay to reach the "sky lobby" entrance to the museum. The street-level lobby also leads directly to the auditorium above, encouraging public forums and events while permitting the museum collections to be isolated after-hours.

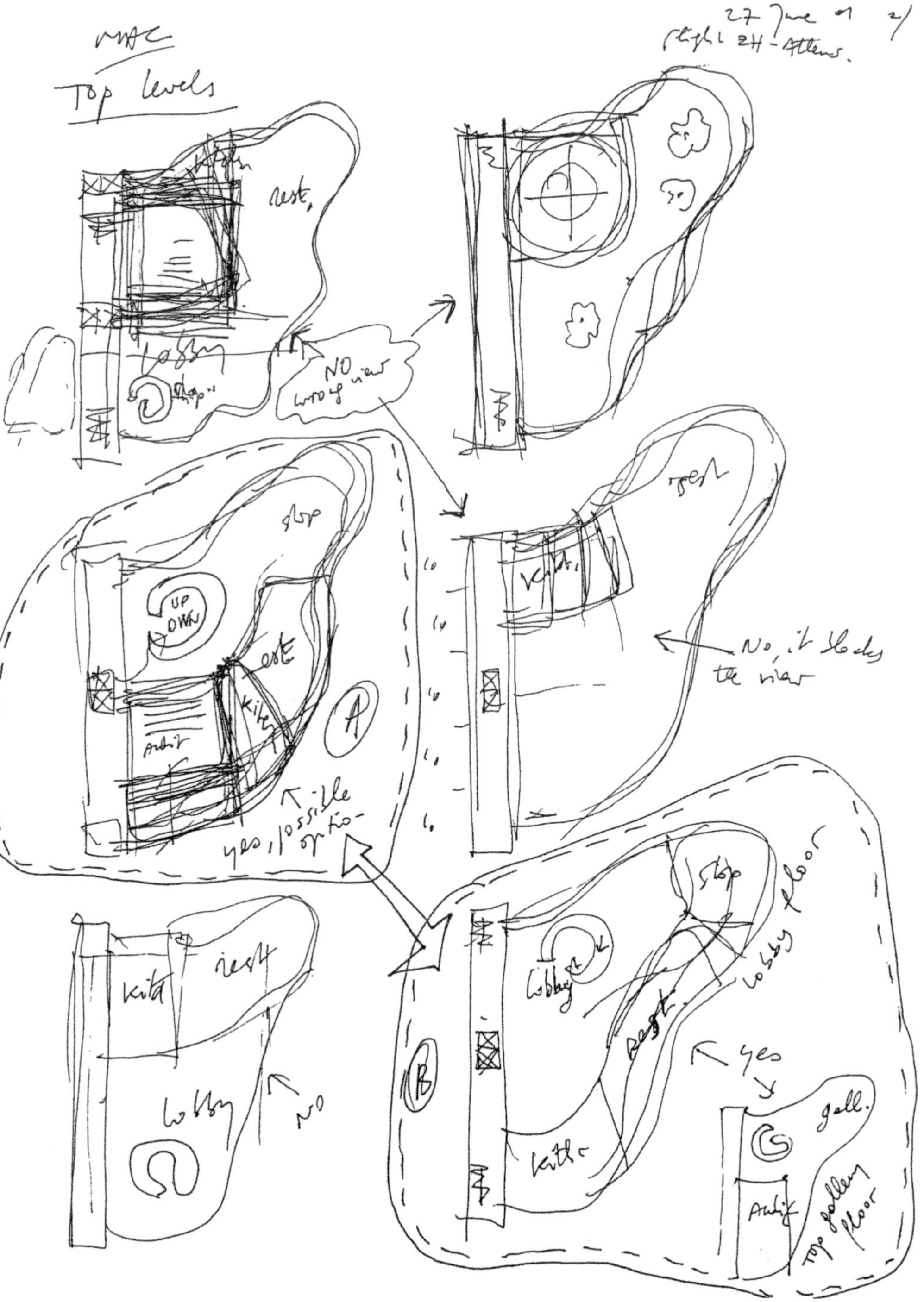

NYAC
Top levels

rest.

stop

NO
wrong view

27 June '01
flight ZH - Athens.

rest

No, it blocks
the view

stop

UP
OWN

rest

kitch

Audit

A

yes, possible
option

kitch   rest

lobby   no

stop   lobby floor

lobby   rest

B   yes

kitch

Audit

gall.

C

Top gallery floor

Finalizing the Concept

In finalizing the double envelope, vertical core, floor plates, and upper-level ramps, the question is: should the ramps be expressed directly in the elevations, or hidden behind a continuous skin?

It is decided to express the ramps in the museum galleries, creating a unique urban context for the display of art. Additional layout alternatives for the sky lobby are also explored.

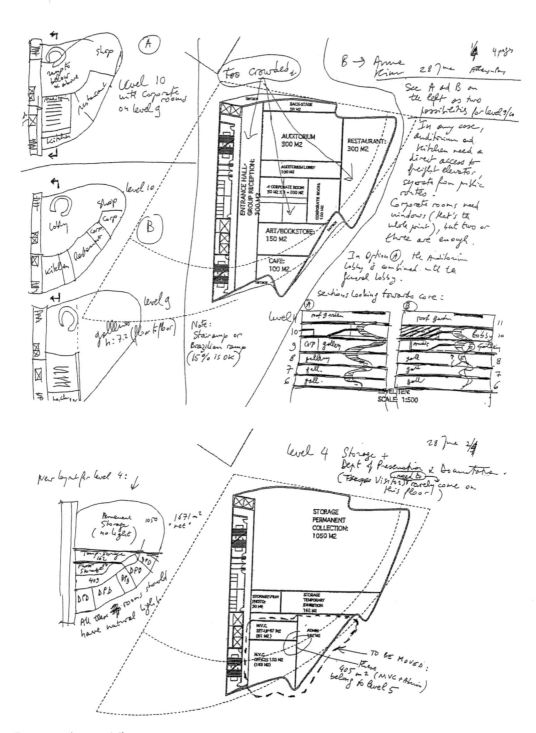

Programmatic permutations

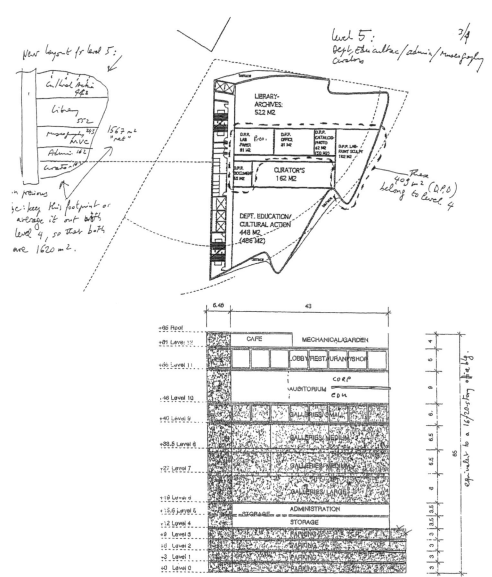

Testing Alternative Layouts

Various locations for the museum activities are tested, with a goal of maximum effect paired with maximum flexibility.

Experiments are conducted using various volumetric treatments and material options, including glass, metal, and concrete. All are possible, but a glass envelope with tinted concrete ramps inside is selected.

Last, the auditorium is located in relation to the street rather than to the sky, encouraging public accessibility. The auditorium acts as a protective cover for the street entrance; its stair-ramp defines the public plaza and provides an easy exit to the street.

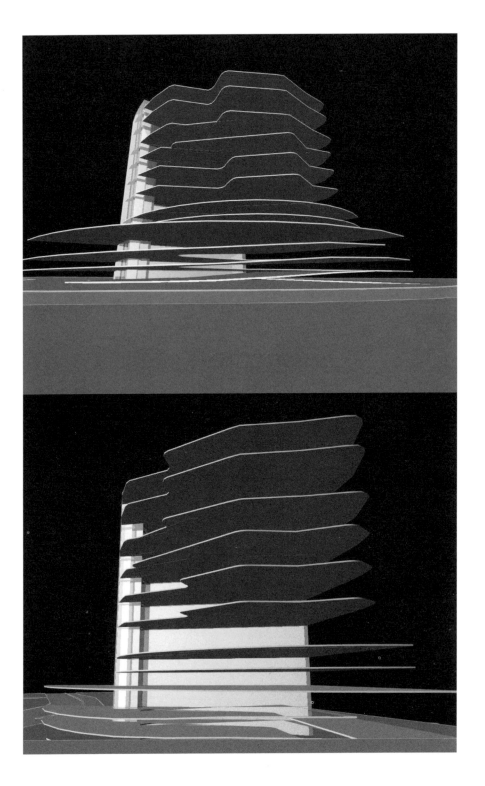

1.2 X 2.4 GLASS STACKED
SOUTH VIEW

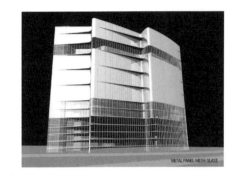

METAL PANEL-MESH-GLASS

1.2 X 2.4 GLAZING - STACKED
NORTH VIEW

1.2 X 2.4 METAL PANEL-GLASS-MESH
NORTH VIEW

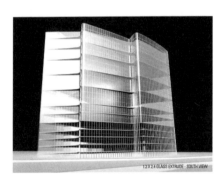

1.2 X 2.4 GLASS EXTRUDE - SOUTH VIEW

CONCRETE MESH-TAPERED VOLUME
WITH TERRACES

1.2 X 2.4 GLASS EXTRUDED
NORTH VIEW

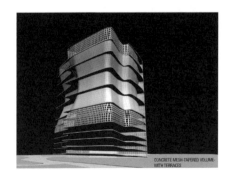

CONCRETE MESH-TAPERED VOLUME
WITH TERRACES

Testing possible configurations

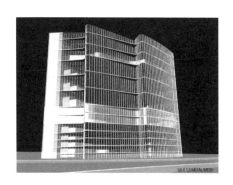

0.6 X 1.2 METAL MESH

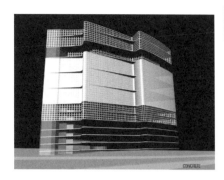

CONCRETE

1.2 X 2.4 METAL MESH -EXTRUDED- NORTH VIEW

CONCRETE

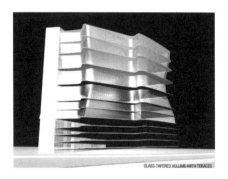

GLASS-TAPERED VOLUME-WITH TERRACES

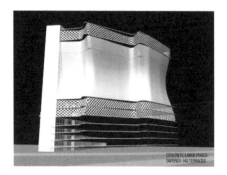

CONCRETE-LARGE PIXELS-
TAPERED -NO TERRACES

CONCRETE-SMALL PIXELS
TAPERED VOLUME-TERRACES

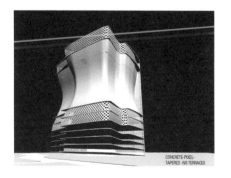

CONCRETE-PIXEL-
TAPERED -NO TERRACES

(Valentin to work on them)

Elevations

Concept: The building has only two elevations,
i.e. the service core and the curvy wall

Options for the curved wall:

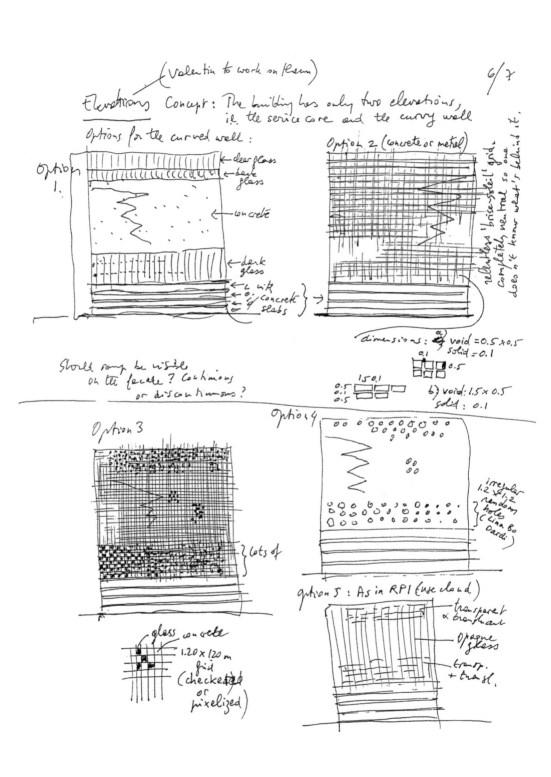

Option 1.

← clear glass
← dark glass
← concrete
← dark glass

← w/ or concrete slabs }

Option 2 (concrete or metal)

relentless "brise-soleil" grid.
Completely neutral so one
doesn't know what's behind it.

dimensions: a) void = 0.5 × 0.5
solid = 0.1

0.1 0.5

1.5 0.1
0.5
0.1
0.5

b) void: 1.5 × 0.5
solid: 0.1

Should ramp be visible
on the façade? Continuous
or discontinuous?

Option 3

} lots of

glass concrete
1.20 × 120 m
grid
(checkered
or
pixelized)

Option 4

irregular
1.2 × 1.2
random
holes
(Lina Bo
Bardi)

Option 5: As in RPI (use cloud)

transparent & translucent
opaque glass
transp. + transl.

The Outer Envelope

Glass is selected for the outer envelope, with a solid material providing an inner envelope that surrounds the galleries and protects artworks from external light. The ramps between these two envelopes are made of tinted concrete, as are the major movement vectors (stairs and elevators). The contrast between the warm, red tones of the tinted concrete and the shimmering whitish or pale green hues of the glass will be a major "sign" for the project. The glass will be transparent, translucent, opaque, and printed. Its modalities will evoke the quality of light befitting a museum.

Transparent on the south side, the glass gradually becomes nearly opaque on the sunnier north side, through the use of screen printing. Spandrel glass (inexpensive opaque glass with insulation behind it) is used wherever appropriate for art or energy conservation.

Energy conservation issues are of primary concern today and the building is designed accordingly: the naturally ventilated area of the ramps acts as a buffer zone, minimizing energy costs in the galleries.

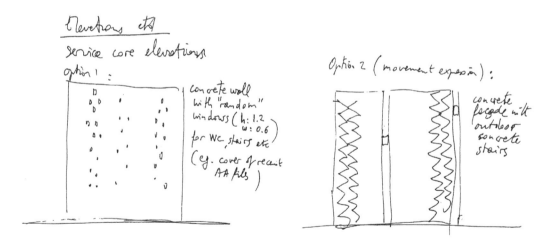

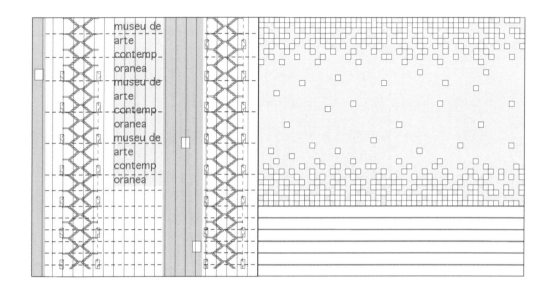

museu de
arte
contemp
oranea
museu de
arte
contemp
oranea
museu de
arte
contemp
oranea

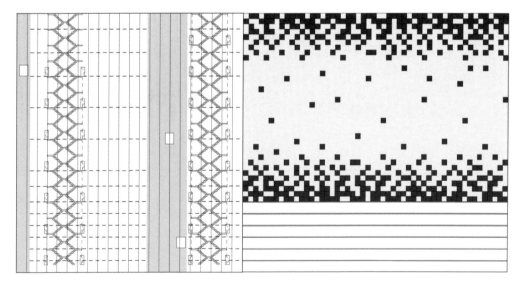

Glazed linear core, concrete curved envelope

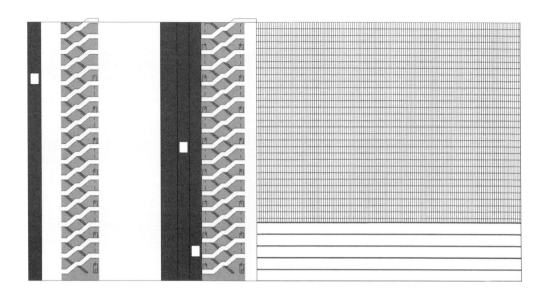

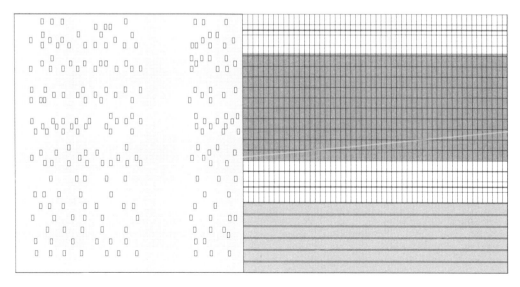

Concrete linear core, glazed curved envelope

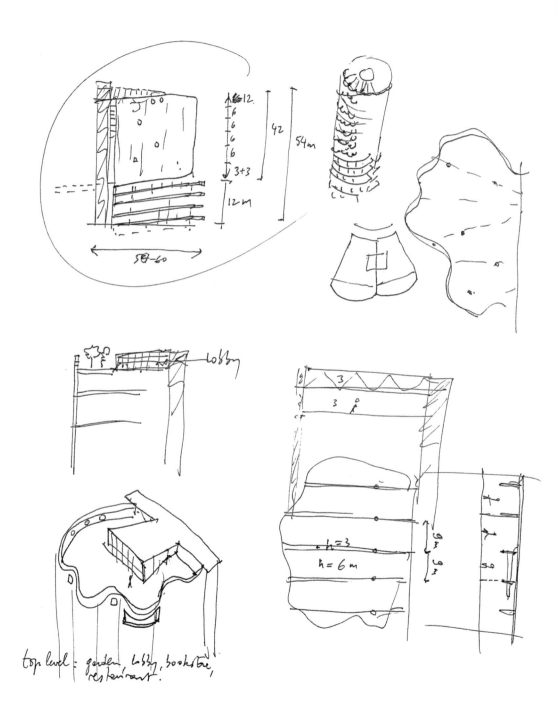

12.
6
6
6
6
3+3
42
54m
12m
50-60

lobby

h=3
h=6m
9m
9m
3
3

top level = garden, lobby, bookstore, restaurant.

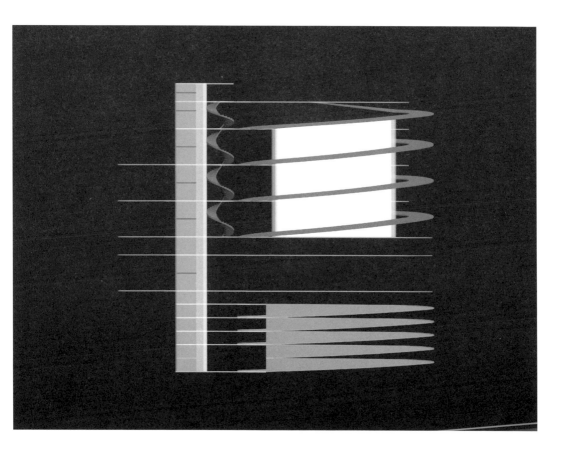

A vertical core and ramps connect the floors.

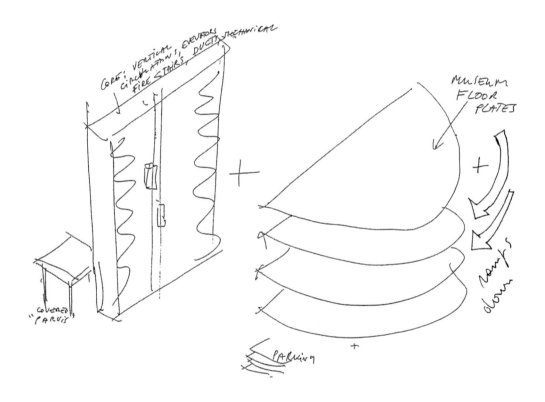

Planned functional dissociation: The core is highly specialized, the floor plates are flexible, and the ramps support the envelope.

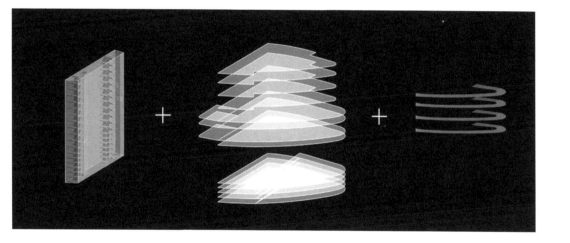

The three elements of the museum: a vertical core, open floor plates,
and ramps forming a city street in the air

MAC July 1

Double envelope

Paris – NY AF008

solid wall (structure)

ramp with sculpture

glass wall

ramps in one direction with printed glass

floors not shown

ramps in the other direction

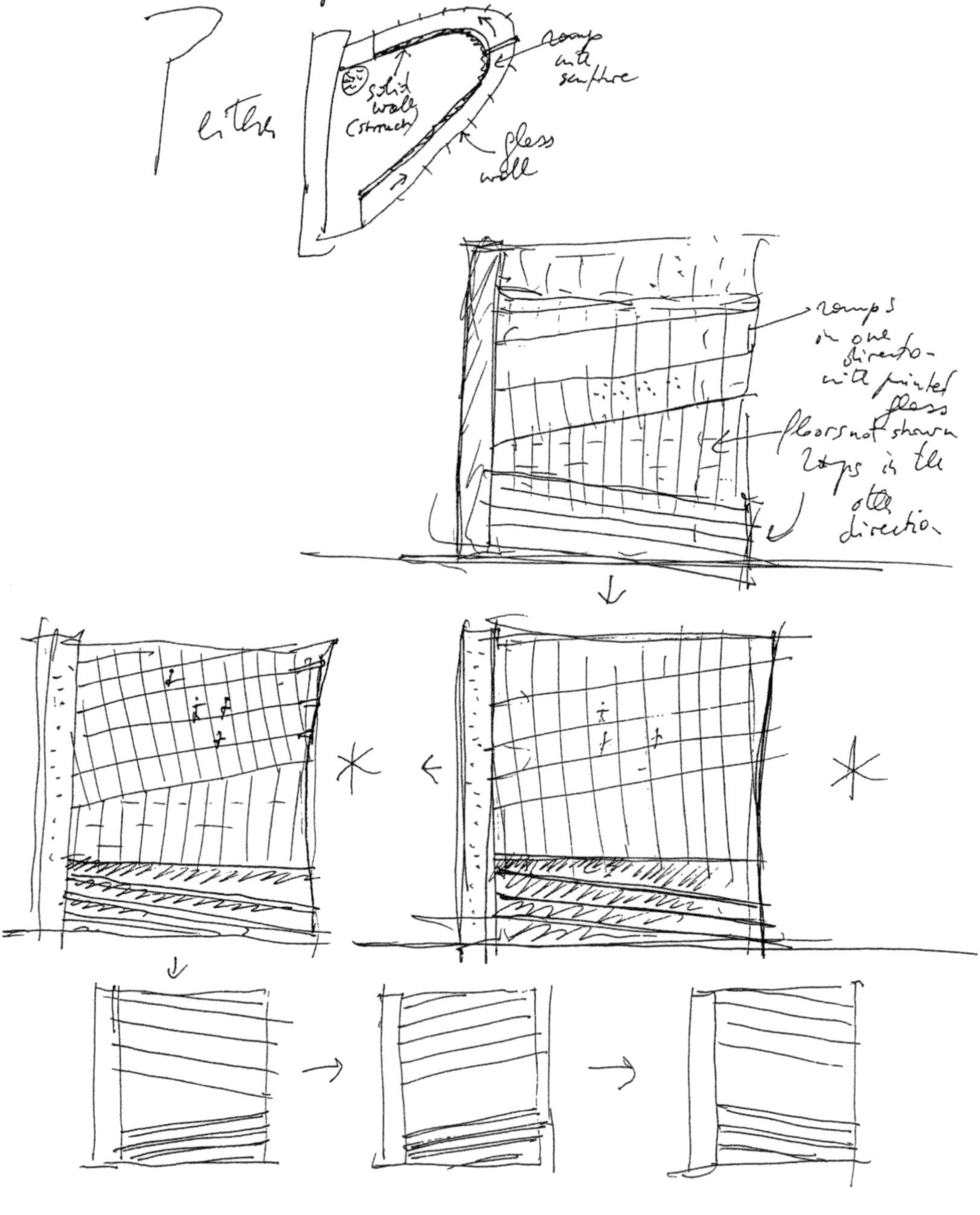

A & B are both ok

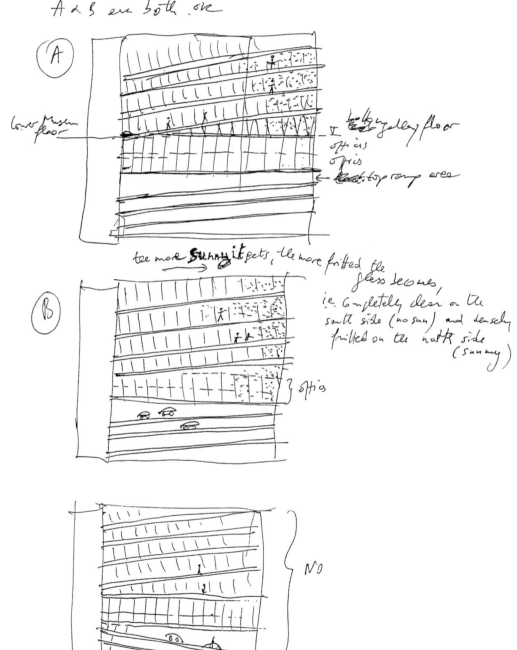

A

lower museum
floor

gallery floor
offices
offices
rooftop ramp area

the more sunny it gets, the more fritted the
glass becomes,
i.e. completely clear on the
south side (no sun) and densely
fritted on the north side
(sunny)

B

offices

} NO

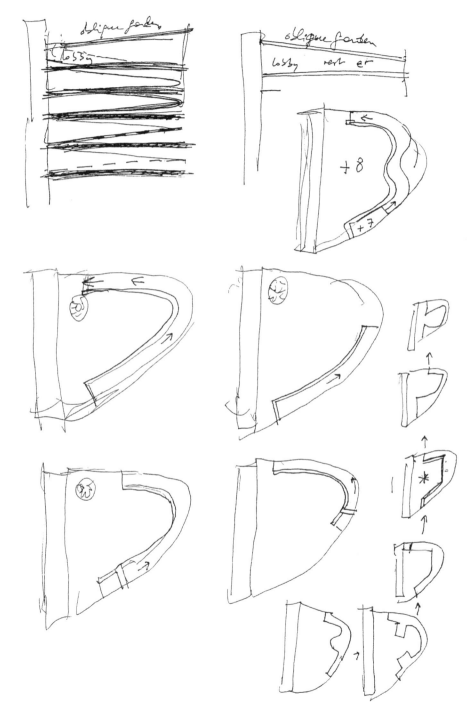

A RAMP GOES FROM GALLERIES TO GALLERIES

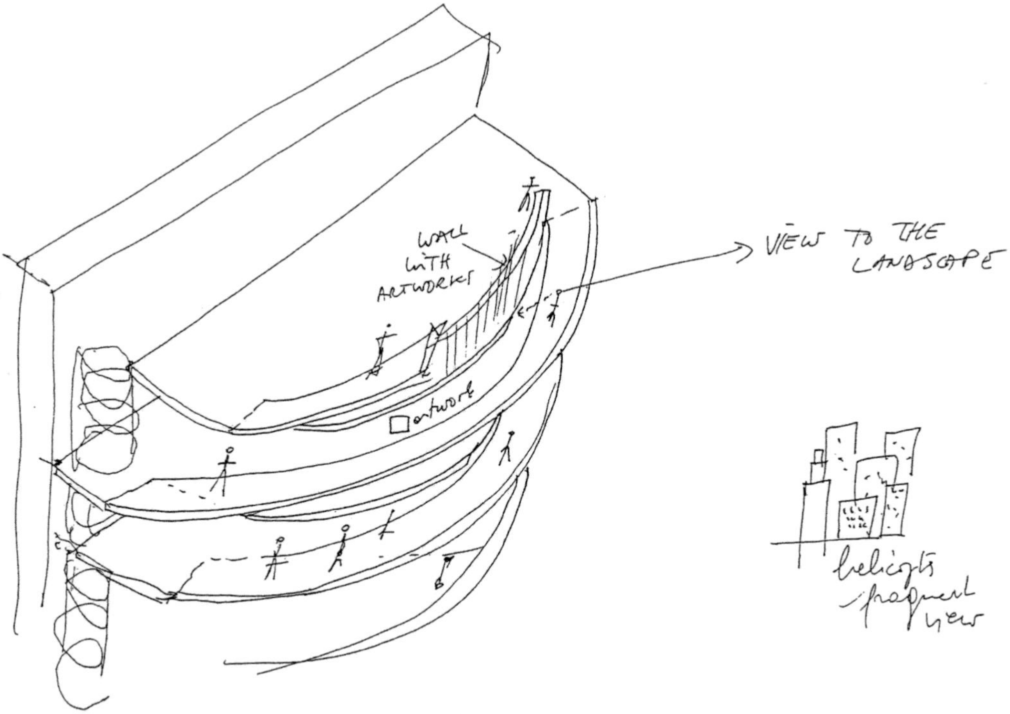

WALL
WITH
ARTWORKS

☐ artwork

VIEW TO THE
LANDSCAPE

helights
fragment
view

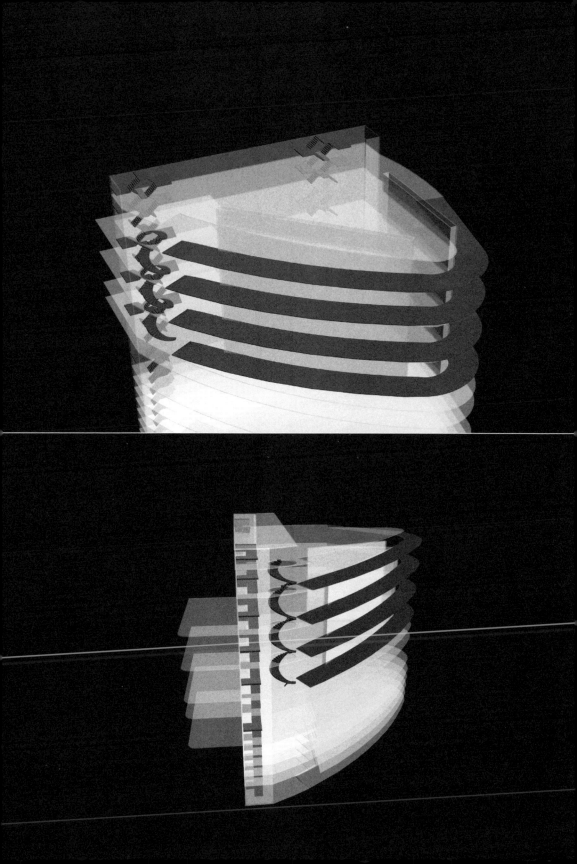

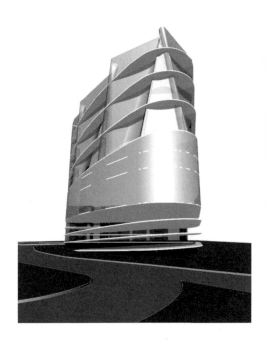
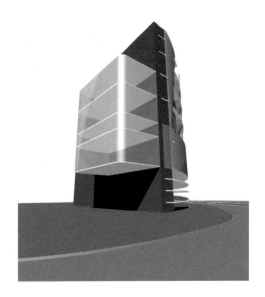

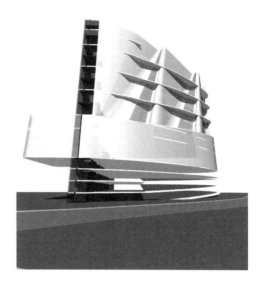

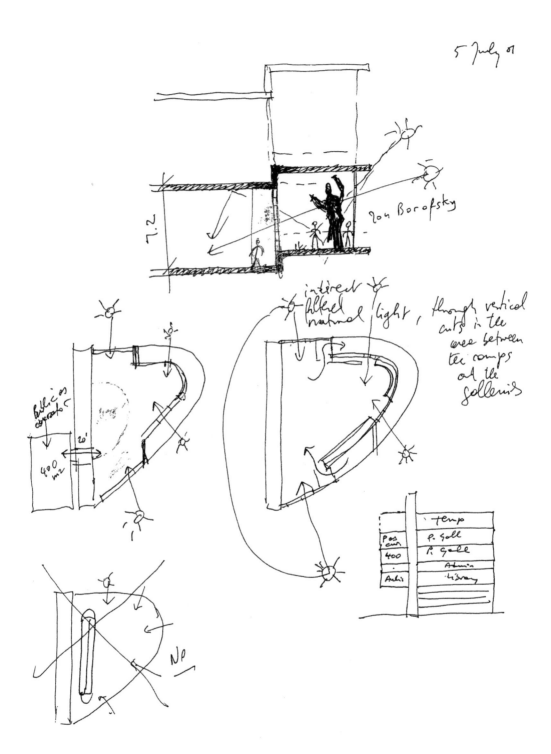

5 July 01

Jon Borofsky

indirect filtered natural light, through vertical cuts in the area between the ramps and the galleries

The Galleries

The museum's collection and exhibition programs straddle two centuries, creating numerous challenges. The size, scale, and viewing context of the artworks range from intimate pieces to large-scale installations; from relatively private viewing situations to open, public contexts; and from contemporary works that require expansive space and light to emerging art forms that occupy little space, produce their own light, or demand public forms of address. Our scheme recognizes these needs within the historical collection as well as in recent works involving video, interactive art, and electronic installations.

The ramps provide a new and paradigmatic exhibition context for art forms that are not easily contained within conventional galleries or that require public or social means of address. Based on the observation that no museum to date has accounted for the role of the public in the arts or for the museum's relations to its expanding numbers of visitors, the proposal calls for a building that is at once art space and social space. The ramps provide contexts for public exhibitions as well as gathering or lounging environments, accommodating video and electronic art in addition to sculptures. The immediate backdrop, visible through the glass envelope, is the city: the ramps offer a visual link between the museum and São Paulo while providing a dramatically illuminated urban presence in the night sky.

The wide 1,600-square-meter floor plates of the exhibition galleries allow flexibility in partitioning, permitting intimate viewing contexts as well as extensive environments similar to the open spaces of industrial lofts. Consciously avoided is the longitudinality, or "linear march through time," common to most museum spaces. This enables curators to establish different relations among periods, movements, and artistic media.

Drawing on the idea that pure space and diffused light are the optimum conditions for viewing art, the galleries are characterized by simplicity and sobriety. White-painted walls and natural-colored materials, such as glass, wood, concrete, and metal, are used throughout. Dark wood floors are suggested for the permanent collections, with perhaps poured concrete for the contemporary and temporary exhibition galleries, attending to the need for nonabrasive surfaces for floor-mounted sculptures and installations.

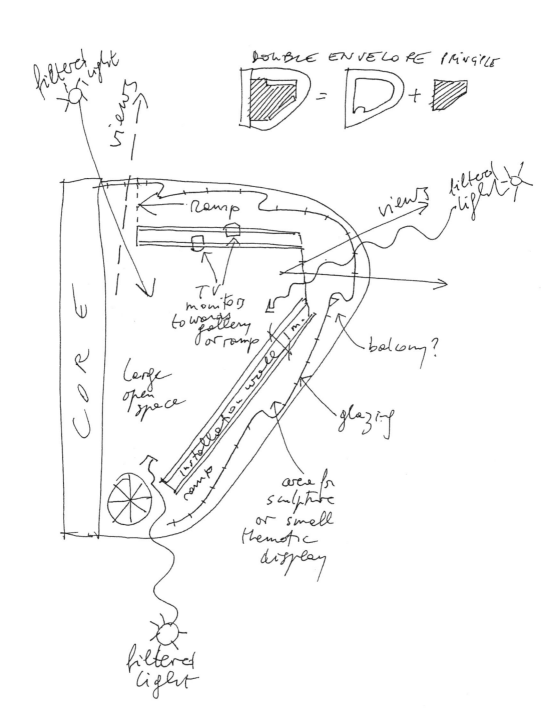

DOUBLE ENVELOPE PRINCIPLE

filtered light

views 5

filtered light

Ramp

views

CORE

TV monitor towards gallery or ramp

Large open space

installation wall

ramp

balcony?

glazing

area for sculpture or small thematic display

filtered light

Gallery floor plates

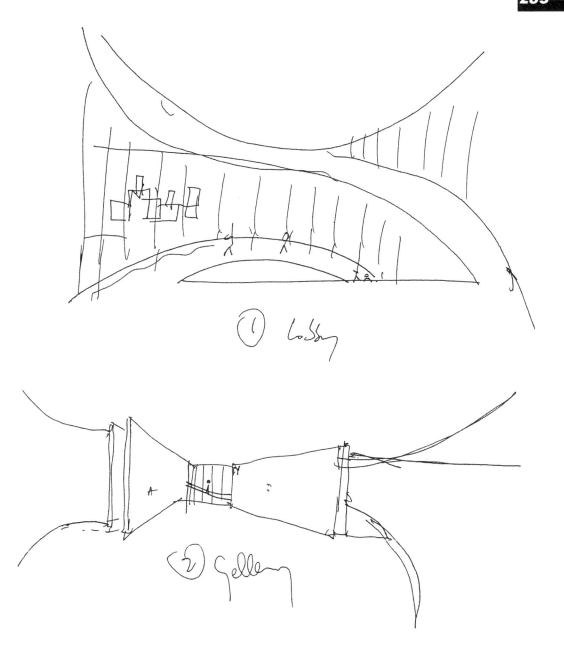

① Lobby

② Gallery

Selecting views

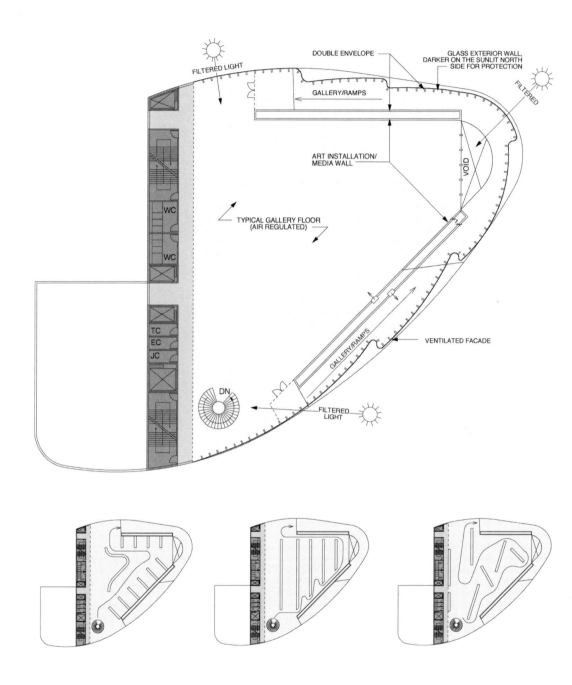

DOUBLE ENVELOPE

GLASS EXTERIOR WALL,
DARKER ON THE SUNLIT NORTH
SIDE FOR PROTECTION

FILTERED LIGHT

FILTERED

GALLERY/RAMPS

ART INSTALLATION/
MEDIA WALL

VOID

WC

WC

TYPICAL GALLERY FLOOR
(AIR REGULATED)

TC
EC
JC

GALLERY/RAMPS

VENTILATED FACADE

DN

FILTERED
LIGHT

Typical gallery plan and options

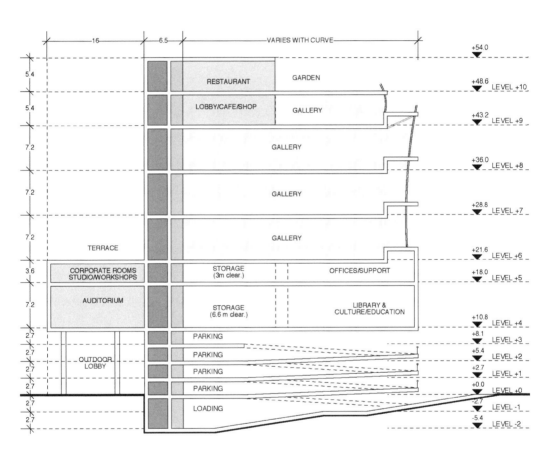

Base section

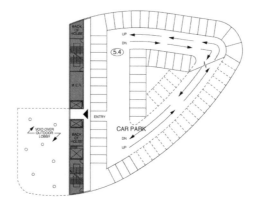

Level +2

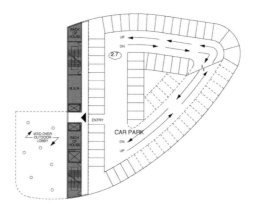

Level +1

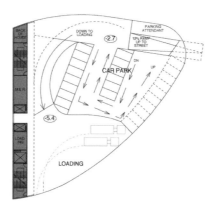

Level -1

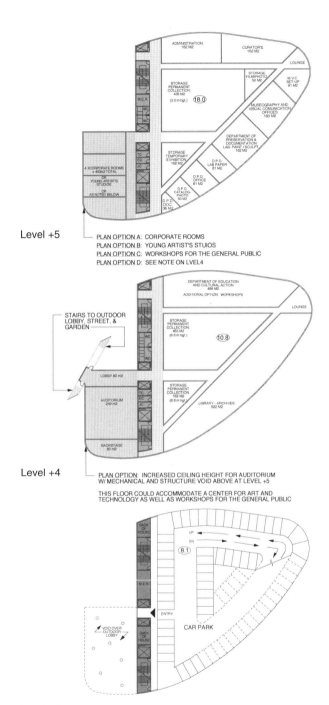

Level +5

PLAN OPTION A: CORPORATE ROOMS
PLAN OPTION B: YOUNG ARTIST'S STUIOS
PLAN OPTION C: WORKSHOPS FOR THE GENERAL PUBLIC
PLAN OPTION D: SEE NOTE ON LVEL4

Level +4

PLAN OPTION: INCREASED CEILING HEIGHT FOR AUDITORIUM
W/ MECHANICAL AND STRUCTURE VOID ABOVE AT LEVEL +5

THIS FLOOR COULD ACCOMMODATE A CENTER FOR ART AND
TECHNOLOGY AS WELL AS WORKSHOPS FOR THE GENERAL PUBLIC

Level +3

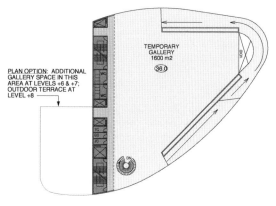

Level +8

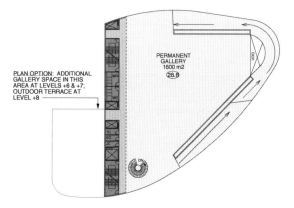

Level +7

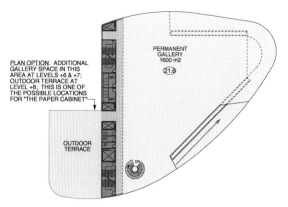

Level +6

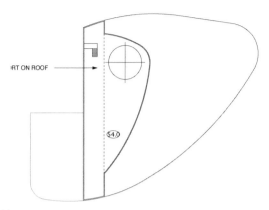

'RT ON ROOF →

54.0

Level +11

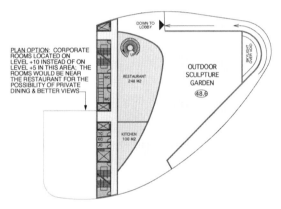

DOWN TO
LOBBY

PLAN OPTION: CORPORATE
ROOMS LOCATED ON
LEVEL +10 INSTEAD OF ON
LEVEL +5 IN THIS AREA; THE
ROOMS WOULD BE NEAR
THE RESTAURANT FOR THE
POSSIBILITY OF PRIVATE
DINING & BETTER VIEWS

WC

WC

RESTAURANT
248 M2

OUTDOOR
SCULPTURE
GARDEN

48.6

SKYLIGHT OVER VOID

TC
EC
JC

KITCHEN
100 M2

Level +10

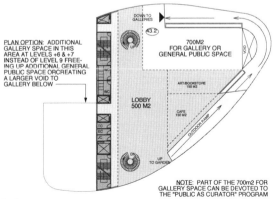

DOWN TO
GALLERIES

43.2

700M2
FOR GALLERY OR
GENERAL PUBLIC SPACE

PLAN OPTION: ADDITIONAL
GALLERY SPACE IN THIS
AREA AT LEVELS +6 & +7
INSTEAD OF LEVEL 9 FREE-
ING UP ADDITIONAL GENERAL
PUBLIC SPACE ORCREATING
A LARGER VOID TO
GALLERY BELOW

WC

LOBBY
500 M2

ART/BOOKSTORE
150 M2

CAFE
150 M2

OUTDOOR RAMP

TC
EC
JC

DN

UP
TO GARDEN

NOTE: PART OF THE 700m2 FOR
GALLERY SPACE CAN BE DEVOTED TO
THE "PUBLIC AS CURATOR" PROGRAM

Level +9

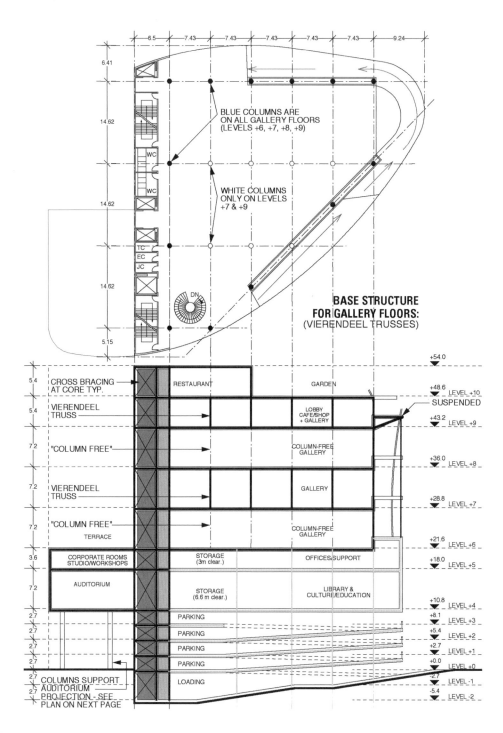

BASE STRUCTURE
FOR GALLERY FLOORS:
(VIERENDEEL TRUSSES)

BLUE COLUMNS ARE
ON ALL GALLERY FLOORS
(LEVELS +6, +7, +8, +9)

WHITE COLUMNS
ONLY ON LEVELS
+7 & +9

Structural diagrams

BASE MECHANICAL SYSTEMS DIAGRAM

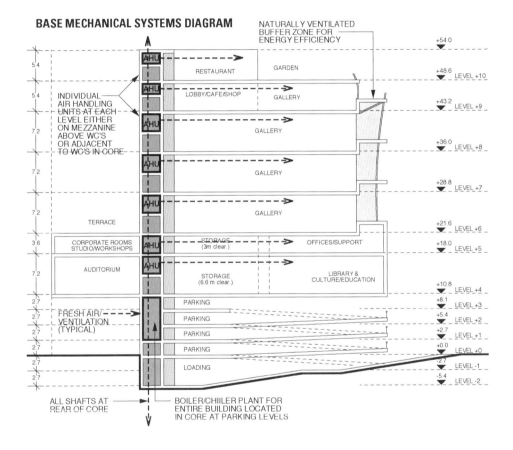

NATURALLY VENTILATED
BUFFER ZONE FOR
ENERGY EFFICIENCY

INDIVIDUAL
AIR HANDLING
UNITS AT EACH
LEVEL EITHER
ON MEZZANINE
ABOVE WC'S
OR ADJACENT
TO WC'S IN CORE

FRESH AIR/
VENTILATION
(TYPICAL)

ALL SHAFTS AT
REAR OF CORE

BOILER/CHIILER PLANT FOR
ENTIRE BUILDING LOCATED
IN CORE AT PARKING LEVELS

RESTAURANT · GARDEN
LOBBY/CAFE/SHOP · GALLERY
GALLERY
GALLERY
GALLERY
TERRACE
CORPORATE ROOMS STUDIO/WORKSHOPS · STORAGE (3m clear.) · OFFICES/SUPPORT
AUDITORIUM · STORAGE (6.6 m clear.) · LIBRARY & CULTURE/EDUCATION
PARKING
PARKING
PARKING
PARKING
LOADING

+54.0
+48.6 LEVEL +10
+43.2 LEVEL +9
+36.0 LEVEL +8
+28.8 LEVEL +7
+21.6 LEVEL +6
+18.0 LEVEL +5
+10.8 LEVEL +4
+8.1 LEVEL +3
+5.4 LEVEL +2
+2.7 LEVEL +1
+0.0 LEVEL +0
-2.7 LEVEL -1
-5.4 LEVEL -2

5.4
5.4
7.2
7.2
7.2
3.6
7.2
2.7
2.7
2.7
2.7
2.7
2.7

Air-treatment principles

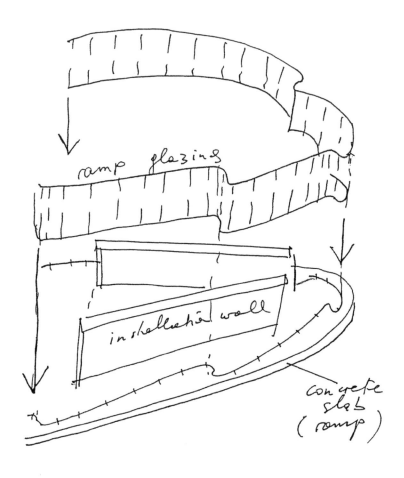

ramp glazing

installation wall

concrete
slab
(ramp)

double envelope principle:
ramp area acts as a protective
buffer zone. With appropriate
ventilation, it will minimize
energy consumption in the galleries.

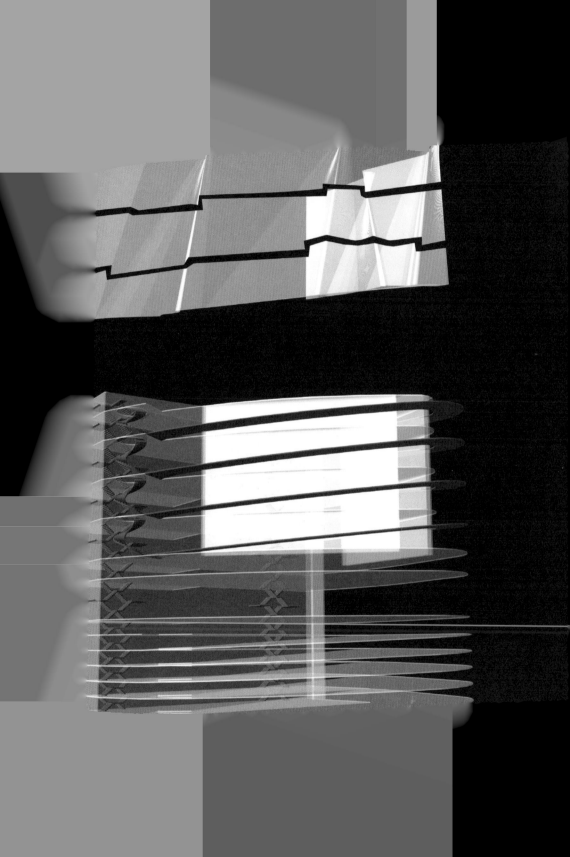

Landing on MAC

The ramps serve as an in-between space, physically mediating between the collections and the city.

Sky lobby interior

Gallery interior

*Troy, Electronic Media and
Performing Arts Center, 2001*

Double Envelope

The new Electronic Media and Performing Arts Center, located in the historical master plan of a respected academic institution in upstate New York, aims to establish a new, contemporary dialogue with the city and region as a whole. The object is to move the 19th-century Rensselaer campus into the 21st century, by extending it to its western corner. Intended for the city as much as for artists, researchers, and students, the multi-programmatic facility must be easily accessible from both town (below) and campus (above). To this end, the site's steep slope presents a major challenge.

The building seeks to bring together 21st-century electronic media technology with contemporary and traditional performing arts. It includes a 1,200-seat theater, a 400-seat recital hall, three black-box experimental theaters, audio-video production facilities, a radio station, multimedia galleries, music practice rooms, dance studios, and spaces for other related activities.

A site strategy is combined with a programmatic one. The design calls for inserting the building partly into the slope—a glowing transparent and translucent glass cube, distinct from, yet complementary to the brick and concrete architecture of the campus. Upon entering the building, the visitor encounters a uniquely three-dimensional experience, simultaneously seeing above and below, left and right.

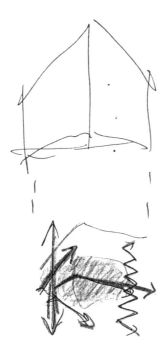

Double Envelope with movement in-between

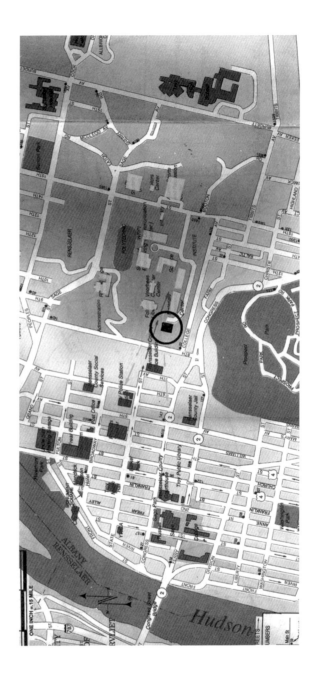

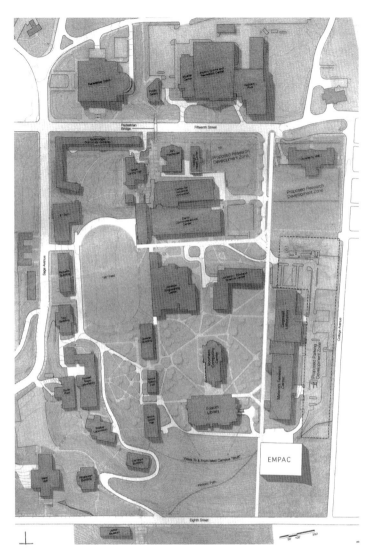

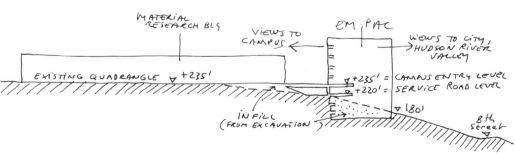

The historical campus master plan

The concept for the building consists of two envelopes with circulation in between. This simple notion allows maximum spatial flexibility inside the innermost envelope, and permits the main circulation routes to be revealed on the glazed outer envelope. The movement of visitors between the two envelopes is a spectacle of its own. At night, the building becomes a shadow theater of real people and virtual images.

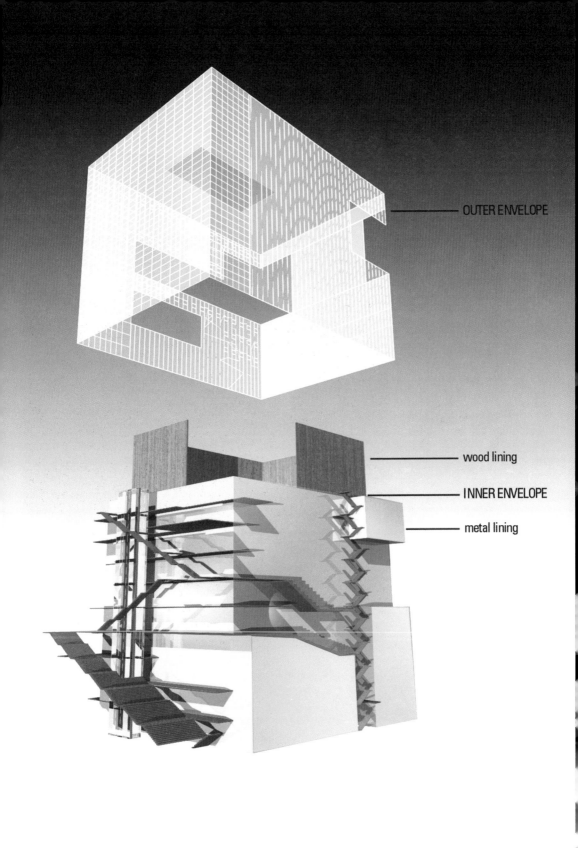

OUTER ENVELOPE

wood lining

INNER ENVELOPE

metal lining

A program's intricate interactions

Double Envelope Strategy

The glass of the outer envelope takes many forms: single or double glazing, transparent or translucent, printed or fitted, textured or reflective, opaque or clear, crystalline or industrial. The inner envelope is clad mainly in wood. For the interiors of the inner envelope, particularly of the theater and recital hall, adjustable sound-absorptive wood surfaces are integrated in the architectural details.

The concept of the double envelope is carried further inside the building, with acoustical barriers following the same principle of the box inside a box. Hence, the inner envelope has thickness and mass for sound insulation. Its interior lining provides absorption and reflection for sound control.

Interacting Identities

Each major programmatic entity (theater, black box, Audio Video Communications, recital hall, music practice rooms) is organized on its own clearly identifiable level. Six main levels and four alternating mezzanine levels allow a simple reading. All of the individual lobbies interact with the main circulation and social space of the building. The design's double objectives are identity and interaction: Densely packed multiple programs lead to a new 21st-century culture of crossovers. A montage of attractions is contained within a single glass volume, with the vertical lobby collecting and linking all activities.

The vertical stacking of public functions is made possible by the location of the building on a steep slope. By providing egress at grade on four different levels, the context has been turned into a major asset.

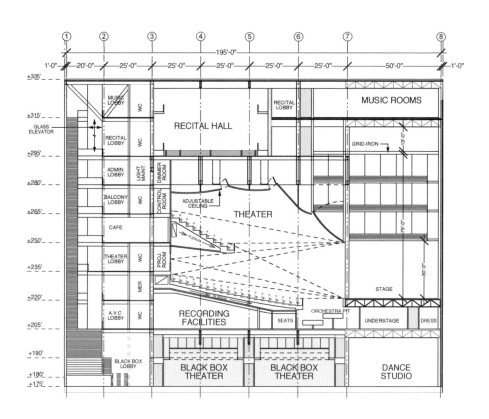

Longitudinal section (perpendicular to the slope)

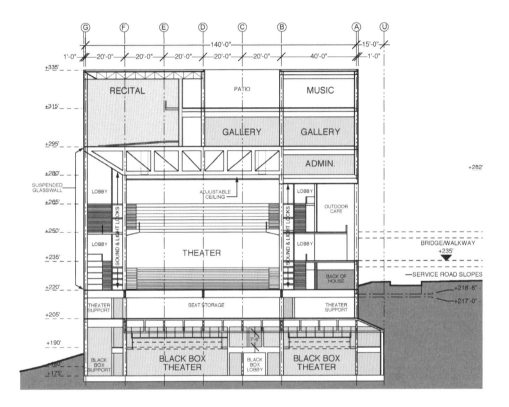

Transverse section (along the slope)

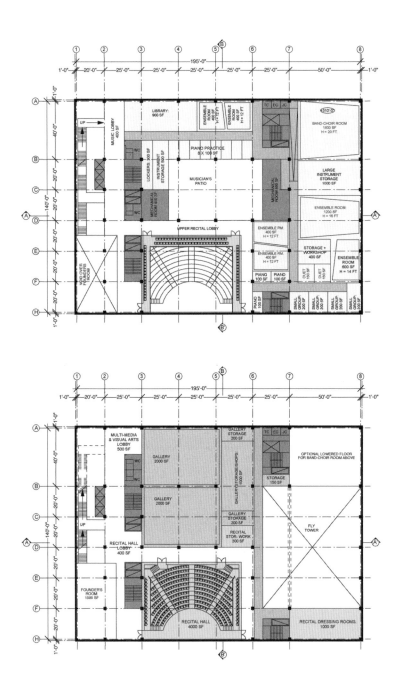

From top to bottom:
Level 6: Upper recital and music spaces
Level 5: Founders room, recital hall, and Multimedia and Visual Arts gallery

From top to bottom: Sky lounge, recital hall, and sky lobbies

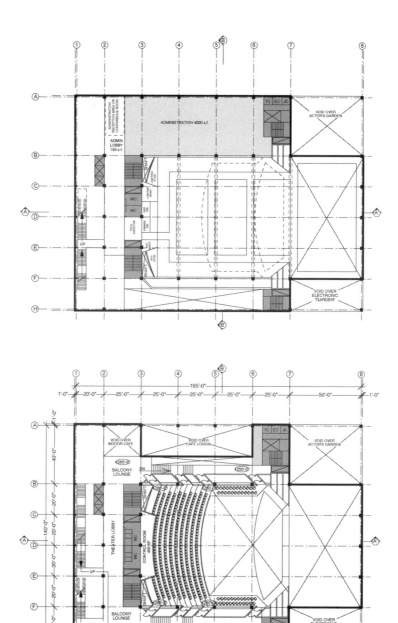

Level 4 Mezzanine: Administration
Level 4: Balcony

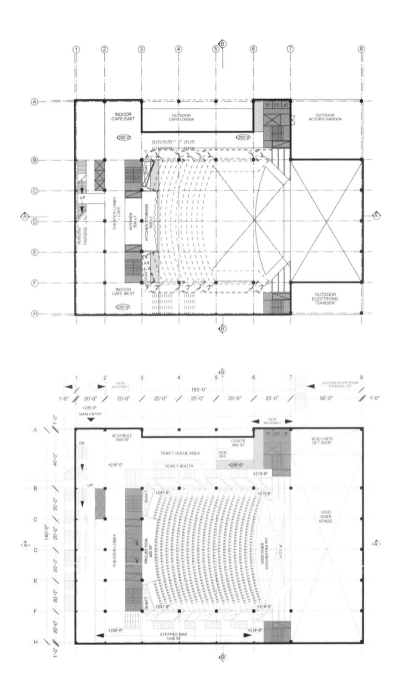

Level 3 Mezzanine: Café
Level 3: Main entrance and theater: Visitors enter the building at mid-level and have the sensation of being suspended in mid-air. Moving past the vestibule, they find elevators, stairs, ticket booth, coatroom, and the main theater lobby, which features views towards the valley.

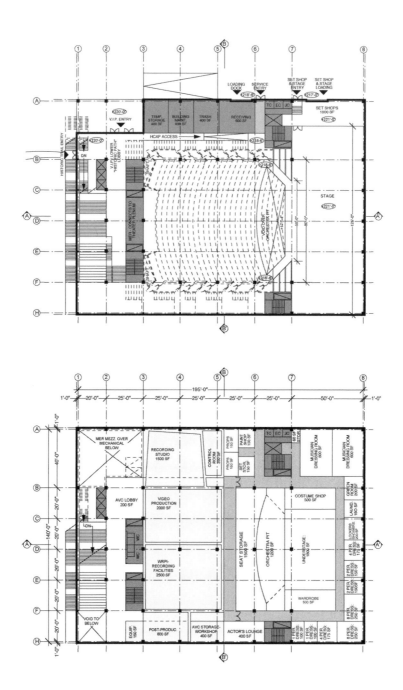

Level 2 Mezzanine: Stage and loading
Level 2: Audio Video Communications and understage

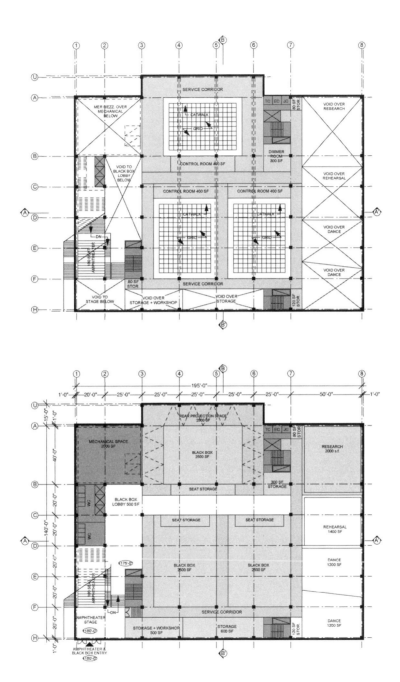

Level 1 Mezzanine: Upper black box
Level 1: Black box, dance, and rehearsal spaces

Concepts clarify concisely;
Concise concepts antagonize

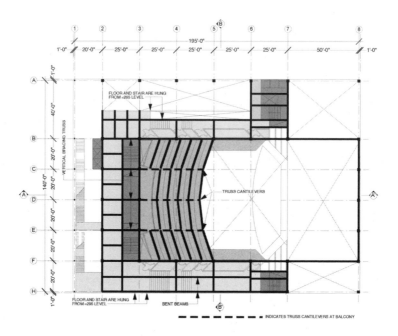

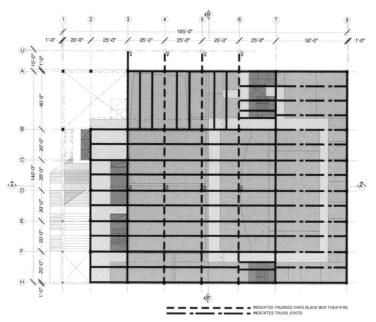

Structural diagrams: level 4 and 2 framing plans

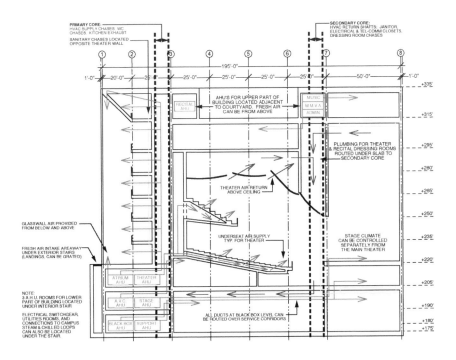

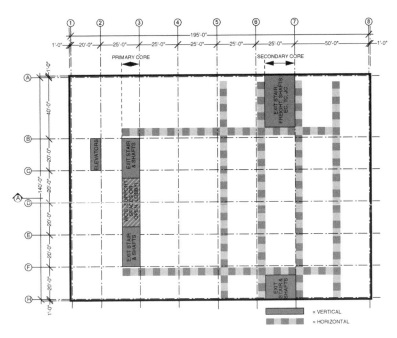

MEP and service diagrams

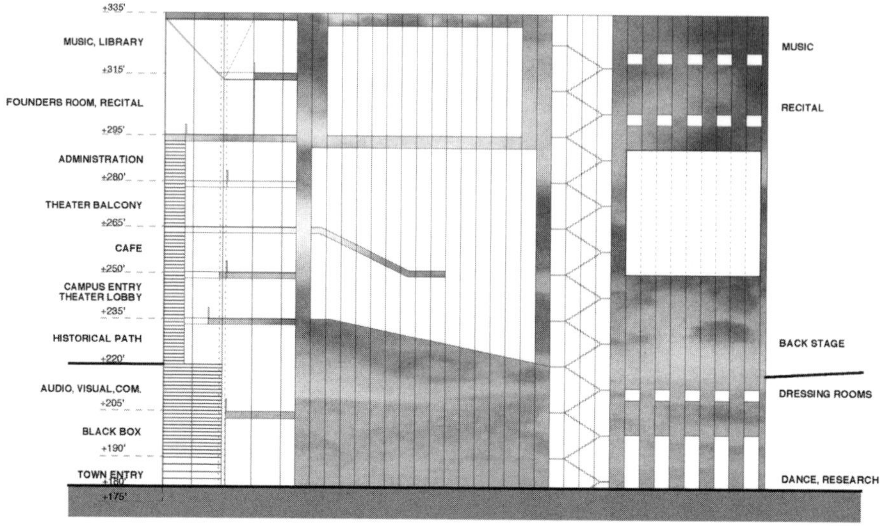
+335'
MUSIC, LIBRARY
+315'
FOUNDERS ROOM, RECITAL
+295'
ADMINISTRATION
+280'
THEATER BALCONY
+265'
CAFE
+250'
CAMPUS ENTRY
THEATER LOBBY
+235'
HISTORICAL PATH
+220'
AUDIO, VISUAL,COM.
+205'
BLACK BOX
+190'
TOWN ENTRY
+180'
+175'
MUSIC
RECITAL
BACK STAGE
DRESSING ROOMS
DANCE, RESEARCH

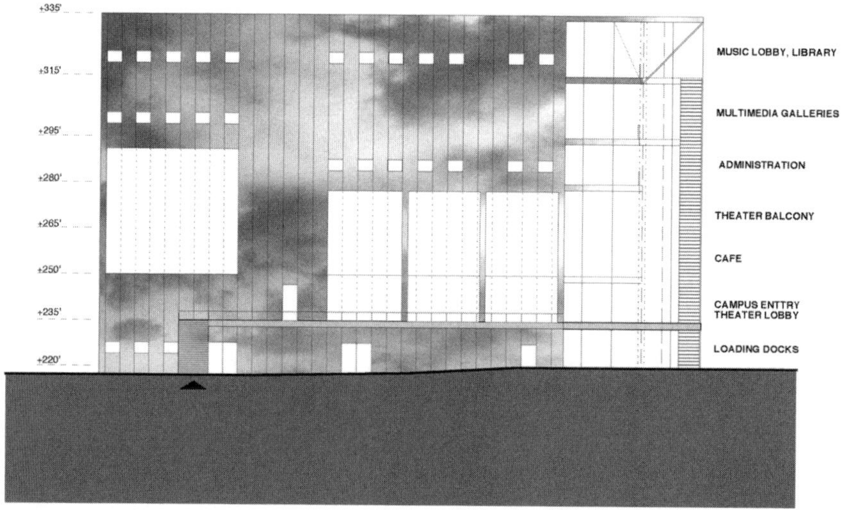
+335'
+315'
+295'
+280'
+265'
+250'
+235'
+220'
MUSIC LOBBY, LIBRARY
MULTIMEDIA GALLERIES
ADMINISTRATION
THEATER BALCONY
CAFE
CAMPUS ENTTRY
THEATER LOBBY
LOADING DOCKS

West and east elevations: The concept of the glass envelope is "crystal clear." Using a combination of conventional and advanced building techniques, such as curtain wall, spandrel glass, and point-fixed clear glass, allows the cost and code-related energy requirements to be met.

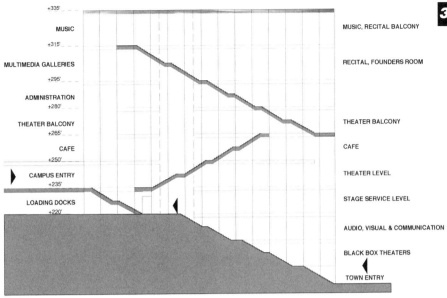

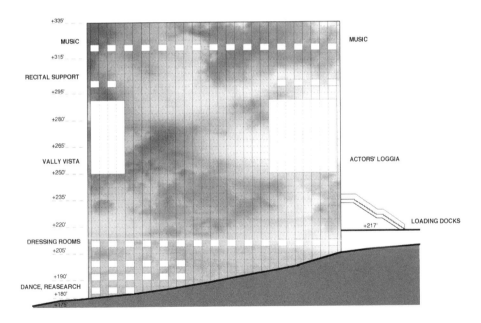

North and south elevations: While the north facade features point-fixed single glazing, or possibly a double-glazed curtain wall, the south elevation most likely consists of photovoltaic panels that capture solar energy. The energy gained from the south facade exactly fulfills the energy needs of the atrium behind the north facade: a zero-sum strategy. The photovoltaic cells can take the form of either panels or a film applied to the glazing surface (in this case, low-cost spandrel glass cladding the masonry wall of the fly tower).

D.
Conceptualizing Context

It is ironic that while architects are often the most vocal champions of the city, many of their greatest works lie in distinctly un-urban environs—in the closest earthly manifestations of the proverbial tabula rasa favored by many 20th-century modernists. Indeed, according to conventional wisdom, maintaining the purity and coherence of an architectural work is easier the fewer external constraints there are to negotiate. In the city, a rat's nest of zoning laws, infrastructure, vociferous neighbors, historical layers, and local (and sometimes national) politics render the likelihood of realizing a lucid concept near impossible. The only solution is to incorporate the constraints into the concept. That strategy was adopted for our projects in Athens, New York, and Cincinnati. One of these sites is a culturally and historically loaded national capital, one is an international cultural capital, and the last is a crowded university campus for which a building had to be literally squeezed into the space left between existing structures. In each instance we sought to turn the complexities of the context into an architectural concept.

New York, Museum for African Art
Version 1, 2000–02

Wood Curves, Glass Box

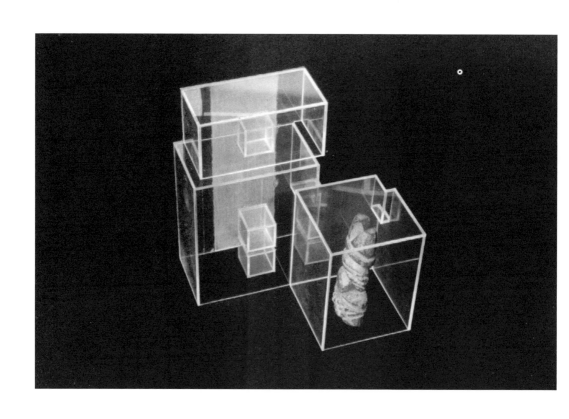

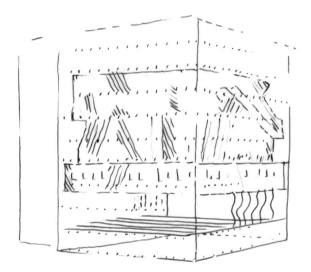

An institution known for its creative scholarship and lively exhibition programs, the Museum for African Art (MAA) plans to move from its current limited facilities to a new, freestanding building located on upper Fifth Avenue, on the southern edge of Harlem. The proposed design for the new building juxtaposes MAA's historic aim of exhibition with an increased focus on audience and accessibility. It combines traditional wood with a contemporary glass structure, and provides an emblem of access and participation for its visitors.

Contexts

Zoning constraints in the site area required a street-wall facade, aligned with existing residential buildings along Fifth Avenue, and with a typical setback on the higher floors, precluding a design as expressive as at the Guggenheim Museum or the Metropolitan Museum of Art. The rigid constraints, however, could be turned to an advantage: The glass cube would conform to the strict zoning envelope on the outside, bringing light and views where necessary, while inside, a free-flowing wood enclosure would house the exhibition galleries, public spaces, and offices.

The building is intended to be both a resource and a stimulus. It includes flexible, dramatically lit galleries characterized by an invisible integration of advanced technology, areas for education and research, multipurpose social spaces, and comfortable working environments for the staff. The entrance, retail area, and café in the ground-floor lobby offer the dynamism of an African bazaar, while a rooftop sculpture garden overlooks Central Park. Importantly, the museum is designed to suggest the creative multiplicity of African cultures while avoiding literal references.

Soaring glass walls on the perimeter of the structure afford views toward Central Park. In this manner, MAA will become the only museum on Fifth Avenue that exposes the park landscape to visitors and staff circulating through the building, as escalators, elevators, and stairs are all located on the periphery of the building.

Locating the fixed elements of circulation and servicing on the periphery of the floor plate allows maximum flexibility in the interior spaces. The structural system also permits three floors entirely without columns—the lobby, large gallery for temporary exhibitions, and event-space situated under the roof garden.

Zoning Constraints:

Special Park Improvement District, district C-4.6
100% lot coverage allowed, no rear yard requirements
FAR of 10.0 for community facility use +
FAR of 3.4 for commercial use

+210' max.

special park improvement district height
limit = 210'-0" (max. # of stories = 19)

+150' max.
+125' min.

special park improvement district
mandates a streetwall of 125' min./
150' max. on wide streets; setback
10' above 150'

special park improvement district
mandatory streetwall requirement
(125' min./150' max.) continues for
first 50'-0" on a narrow street

The 125' min./150' max. streetwall
may continue for an additional 20'
beyond which the underlying
district regulations take effect (C-4.6)

District C-4.6 maximum streetwall = 85'-0"
Above 85' on a narrow street, a min. setback of
20'-0" is required, and a sky plane exposure
ratio of 2.7:1 must be observed

district C-4.6 regulations
option to continue streetwall
mandatory streetwall

+210' max.
+150' max.
+125' min.

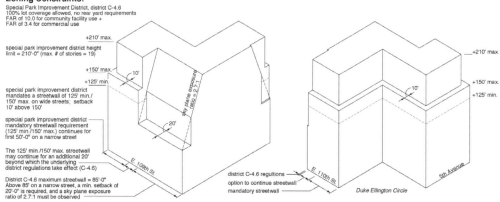

Zoning Strategy:

Because of the streetwall requirement on Duke Ellington Circle
and part of 110th Street, and because of Edison's interest in
having a tall building with views, it makes sense for the bulk
to be located on thenorthern part of the site.

Large functional footprints can be achieved on all
office floors even after the 10' setback.

+210' max.

+150' max.

The maximum streetwall height of 150'
is used for the Edison building so that
it appears as a seperate mass from the
museum building. This also maximizes
the number of floors with larger footprints.

The Edison (academy + headquarters) program does not fill
out the maximum zoning envelope. With the bulk shifted to the
north of the site, the south mass can become quite variegated
within the zoning envelope allowing for outdoor playgrounds.

(zoning envelope indicated in red)

The program of the Museum is smaller
than what the maximum zoning envelope
will allow. Since the 5th Avenue streetwall
is mandatory and must go to a min. of +125'
the massing is ultimately a box to 125'.

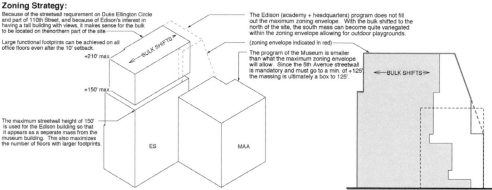

Zoning and massing

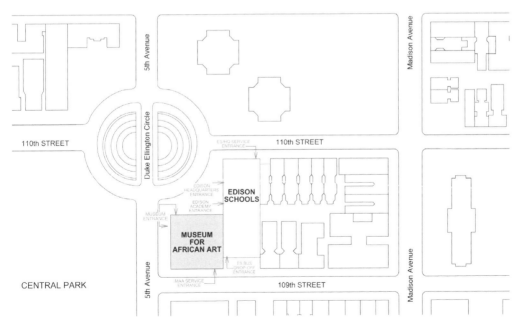

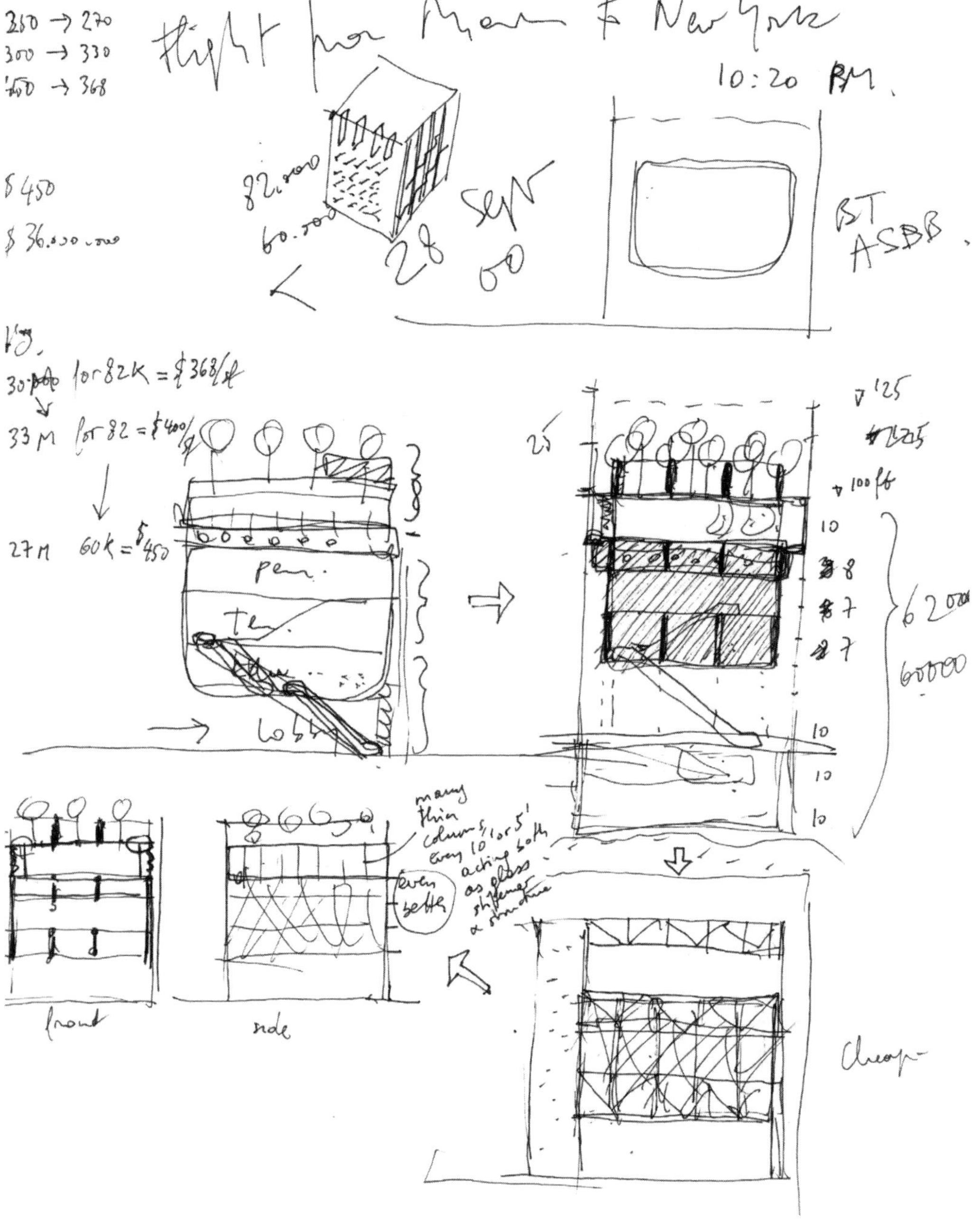

flight from Miami to New York 10:20 PM.

250 → 270
300 → 330
450 → 368

$ 450
$ 36.000.000

28 SEP 00

BT ASBB.

82.000
60.000

30.000 for 82K = $368/ft
33 M for 82 = $400/ft
27 M 60K = $450

pen.
Ten.
LOB

25

125
$225
100 ft
10
8
$7
$7
10
10
10

62000
60000

many thin columns 1 or 5' every 10' acting both as glass stiffener & structure
even better

front   side

Cheap

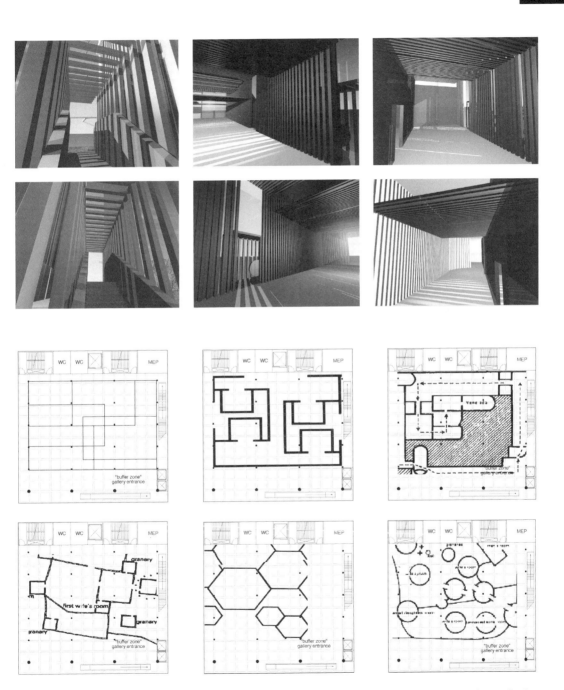

Flexible galleries accommodate multiple types of organization.

1.

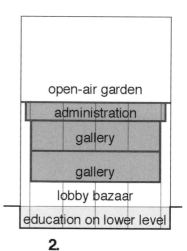

2.

open-air garden

gallery

gallery

lobby bazaar

education on lower level

1.

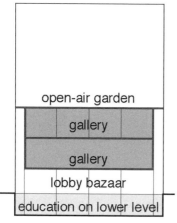

open-air garden

administration

gallery

gallery

lobby bazaar

education on lower level

2.

Change and Flexibility
An important consideration in planning the museum is programmatic change and flexibility. The basis of the project is the glass enclosure, with the wood sanctum standing as the penetrable core of the museum experience. This principle provides a concept and identity for the museum that remains equally strong regardless of the size or scale determined by budgetary constraints.

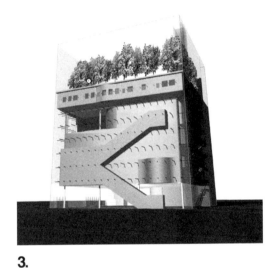

3.

5. Museum as currently proposed.

open-air garden
administration
gallery
gallery
education
lobby bazaar

3.

open-air garden
event space
administration
gallery
gallery
education
lobby bazaar

5.

In the proposed system, the glass can abide by zoning regulations for the area surrounding the park, while the wood interior might be two, three, or four stories high, without changing the general concept of the project.

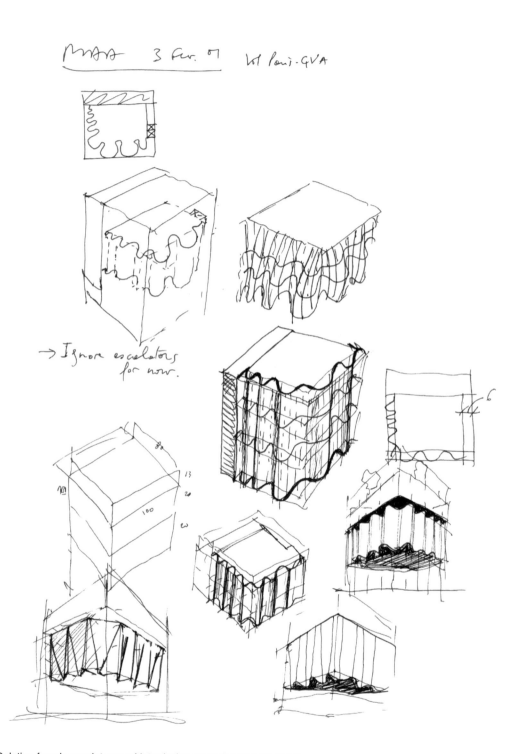

Deleting facade escalators and introducing an undulating envelope

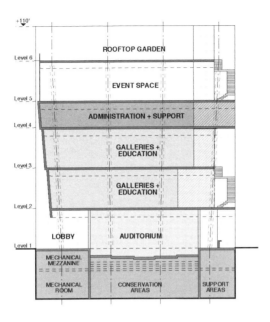

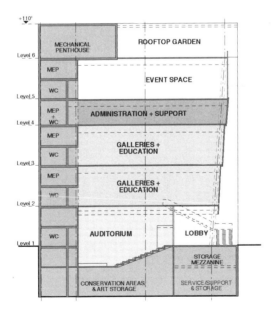

Program sections looking east and south

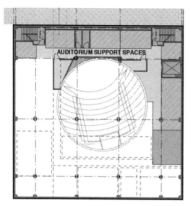

Cellar mezzanine

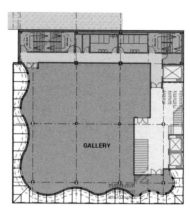

Level 2

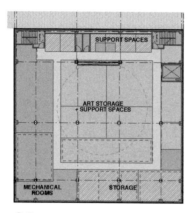

Cellar

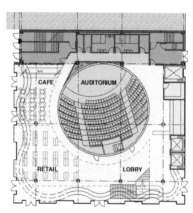

Ground level

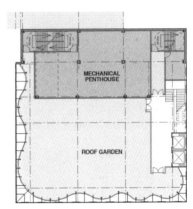

Level 4

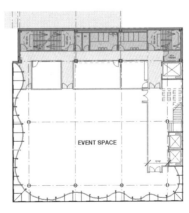

Penthouse / roof

Level 3

Level 5

Sectional perspective looking west, toward the park

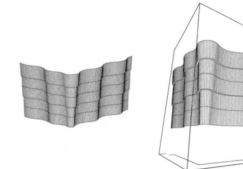

Wood curves inside a glass box

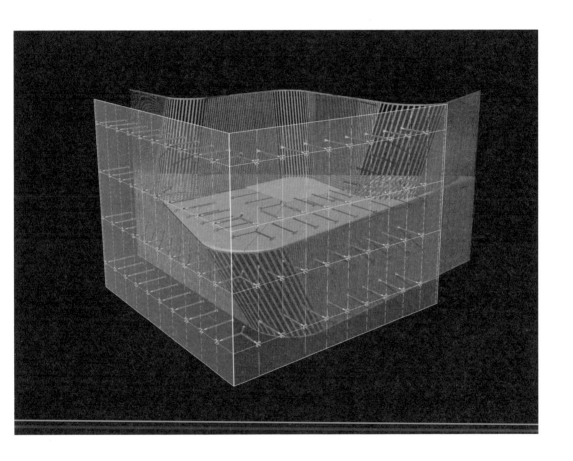

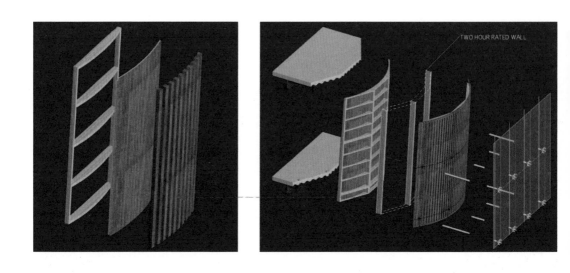

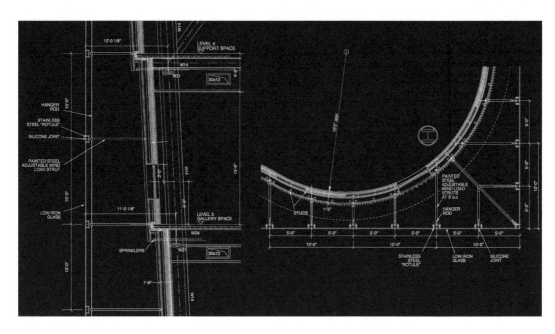

Details of wood and glass envelopes

Structural Principle:

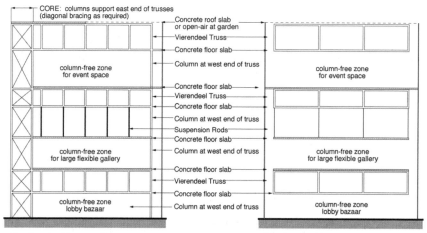

Section looking south   Section looking east

Structure

The structure for the Museum has been developed to create large, open-plan spaces at the ground, third, and sixth levels, using full-floor-height Vierendeel steel trusses. Three levels of trusses are introduced—between the second and third levels, the fifth and sixth levels, and the seventh and eighth levels. Typically each truss level supports the two floor slabs directly above and below it, with the exception of the middle truss, from which the fourth level is also hung.

Four trusses, spaced approximately 30 feet apart and spanning 80 feet from east to west, are provided on each level, with steel beams, spaced 10 feet apart, running in between. A concrete slab, on permanent metal decking, spans between floor beams and acts with the beams to maximize the efficiency of the system. Structural stability is provided by cross bracing, concealed in the solid walls of the galleries. Lateral forces are transferred back to a braced steel core that runs along the east side of the building.

The structure for the outer glass facade of the museum has been developed to maximize its transparency. Corner point-supported glazing is adopted, leaving the facade free of mullions. The glass is hung from the sixth level, and propped off the primary structure, which provides lateral support. The system minimizes the structure of the facade, creating a pure glass plane. Above the sixth level, the facade spans between floor slabs, assisted as necessary by vertical glass stabilizing fins.

Mechanical Principle:
Climate Zones and the Double Skin

Air Distribution:

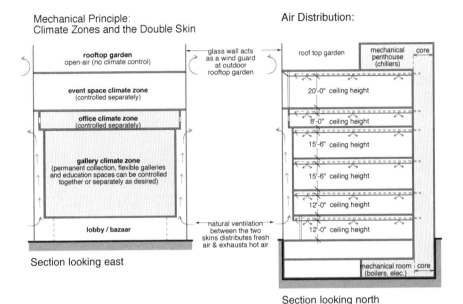

Section looking east

Section looking north

Mechanical Systems

The museum building will be fed from a floor-by-floor air-handling unit supported by central heating and cooling equipment located on the rooftop. This minimizes shaft space and duct sizes and allows several microclimates to function separately. All ducts are concealed above the ceiling, and discreet linear diffusers are used in all public spaces.

The outer glass wall forms a protective shroud around the inner building of the museum, reducing the solar radiant gain and internal cooling loads to the inner space as well as improving the acoustic isolation of the interior spaces from external traffic noise. The void is naturally ventilated in the summer to reduce the build-up of heat, while in the winter, the glass traps the heat behind it, acting as an additional layer of insulation. Covered, air-conditioned rampways run through the interstitial space between the glazing and the wall of the museum, providing climate-controlled transitional spaces throughout the void at various levels. The use of glass for the building, at once visually striking and technologically advanced, thus solves many ecological and functional concerns.

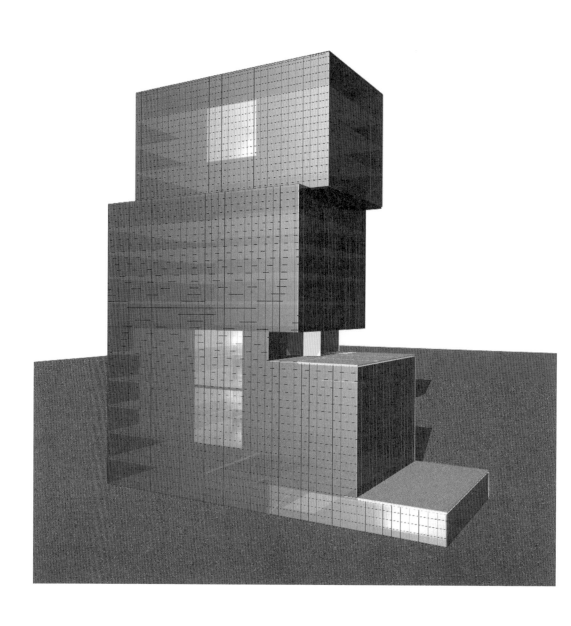

Designing the Adjacent Site: The School and Headquarters

As is common in New York real estate, the museum intended to share the site with a development partner—a national educational organization. We were asked to design a proposal for a building adjacent to the museum that would accommodate the educational organization's national headquarters, together with a new type of school. The resulting proposal exploited the tight zoning constraints of the site through a provocative architectural strategy for addressing the relationship between the museum and school. In contrast to the museum's transparent glass-and-wood cube, the school and headquarters would be housed in a rectangular translucent tower with three visible and colorful inner courts. In this cityscape—an urban still life—the museum would appear as an object poised against the larger background of the tower. The translucent volume, given texture by colored shades, would satisfy all the needs of an office complex while adapting to the requirements of a progressive school. In contrast, the visual effect of the museum is of a darkly mysterious object within a transparent vitrine.

In the case of the educational tower, the zoning code permits a cantilever containing executive suites with grand views toward the park on its upper levels. The glass tower proposed for the school and headquarters does not follow the traditional model of the red-brick schoolhouse, but instead, suggests a contemporary presence for the age of the Internet, encouraging new social thinking and invention. The emblems of the school and headquarters are four large double-height communal inner courts with wide crossing stairs linking two floors each.

A double-height lobby beyond the main entrance provides an overview of the activities of the school. To the right, visitors can look through transparent glass windows onto the capacious double-height gymnasium occupying part of the basement and ground-floor levels. Also visible from the lobby are the cafetorium and main library.

Above the school are 74,000 square feet per floor of generic office space. The top three floors accommodate the library, teacher training rooms, dining facilities, executive offices, and a double-height board room, all with striking views of Central Park.

Note: In 2002, shifts in the economic climate led to a change of investment partners for the museum. The program for the school and headquarters was replaced by one for a residential tower, which in turn led to an entirely new scheme.

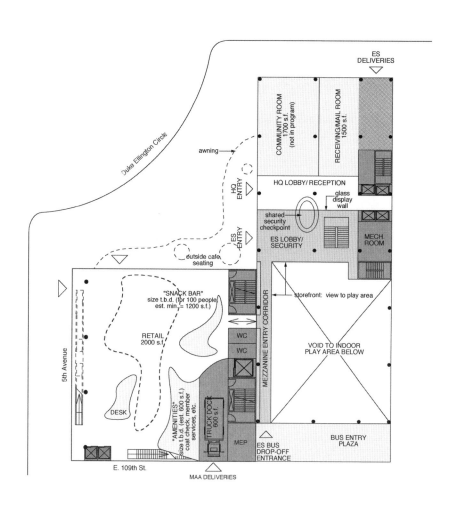

Museum and tower, ground-floor level

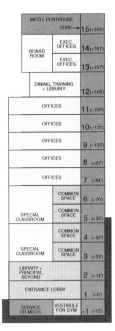

Cross-section looking north

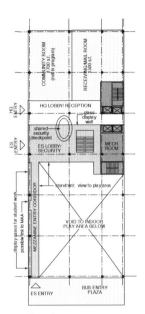

Level 1

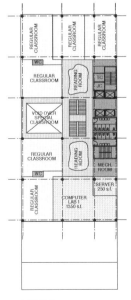

Level 4

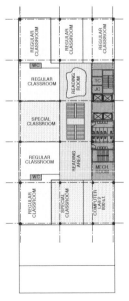

Level 5

School tower

New York, Museum for African Art,
Version 2, 2003–04

The Tower vs. the Museum

Museum / Residential Massing Options

As-of-right

Museum:
Presence on Fifth Ave. and Circle +
Expensive facade development -

Residential:
Presence on Fifth Ave. +
Wedding-cake top -

All:
Convoluted layout,
High coordination required -

Variance "Original"

Museum:
Presence on Fifth Ave. and Circle +
Views of park +

Residential:
Recessed from Fifth Ave. -

All:
Clear concept +
Simple structure and ductwork +

Variance "Earth"

Museum:
Limited park views -
Simple circulation +

Residential:
Penthouses -
No entrance on Fifth Ave. -

All:
Clear concept +
Simple ductwork, extra structure =

Variance "Sky"

Museum:
Exciting views, phasing option
(auditorium) +
Extra stairs and elevators -

Residential:
Entrance and full presence on Fifth Ave. -

All:
Clear concept +
Simple structure, extra ductwork =

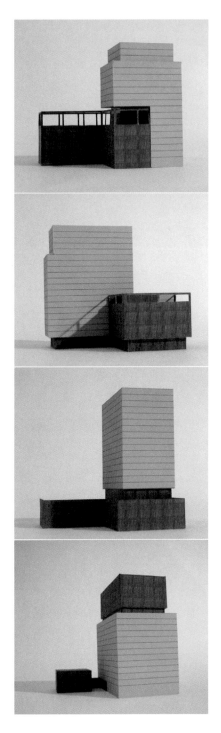

Building in New York means contending with not only stringent zoning and planning constraints but also economic restrictions. By 2003, the partnership between the Museum for African Art and its intended development partner and neighbor, an educational organization, had dissolved. We were asked to prepare the ground for an entirely different project on the same site: instead of accommodating a tall office building next to the museum, the design now had to locate a residential one on top of it.

Alternative hypotheses were first tested—for instance, a tower with a museum on top—but prospective private residential developers favored the more traditional solution of a museum base surmounted by a tower.

The initial agreement established that we would be the architects for the museum and the design architects for the massing and facade of the tower above. As negotiations between the museum and the residential developers drew to a close, however, the developers insisted on separating the design of the tower from that of the museum, and imposed aesthetic decisions that we found incompatible with the museum base. It was the first time we felt compelled to withdraw from a project and to part ways with an esteemed client.

The following pages contain excerpts from our preliminary sketches and diagrams.

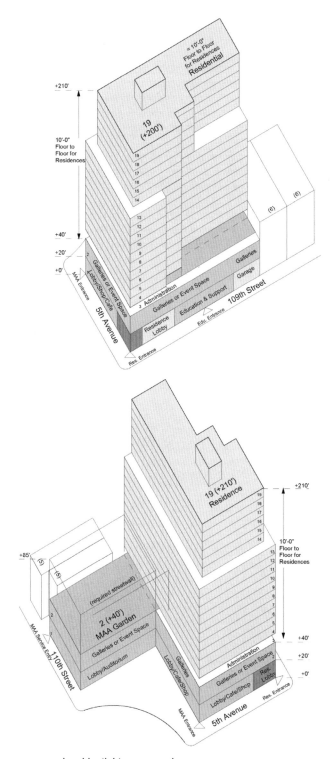

As-of-right scheme: museum and residential tower massing

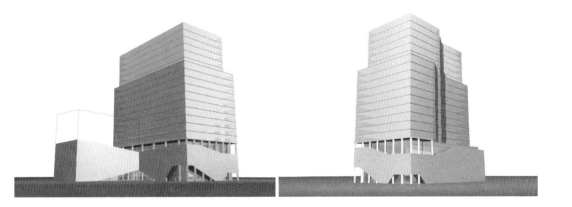

As-of-right scheme (as per zoning regulations)

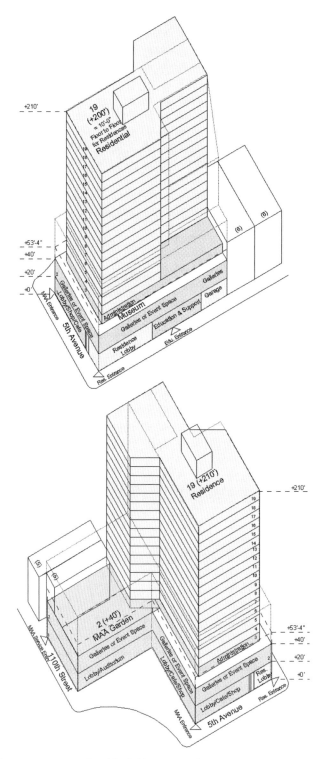

Variance "Earth" scheme: museum and residential tower massing

Residence Levels 4–19

Museum Level 2

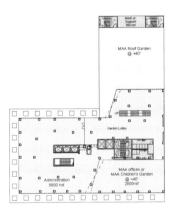

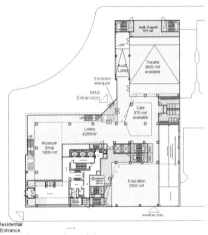

Museum Level 3

Museum Level 1

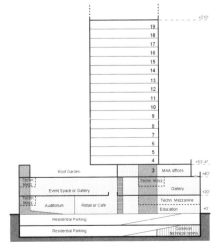

Museum and residential tower section

Variance "Earth" scheme (selected by the Museum and developer)

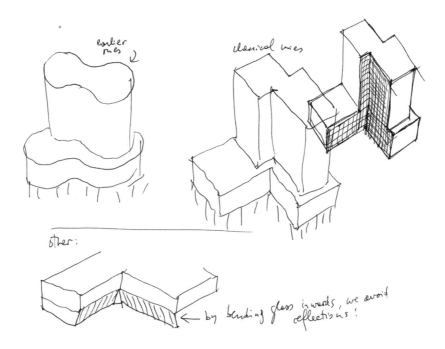

earlier
ones

classical ones

other:

← by bending glass inwards, we avoid reflections!

Variance "Earth" scheme: historical parallels

15 oct 03

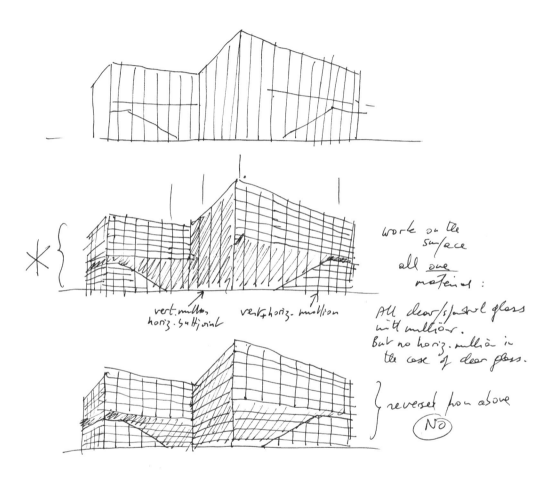

work on the
surface
all _one_
material :

All clear/spandrel glass
with mullion.
But no horiz. mullion in
the case of clear glass.

} reversed from above
(No)

vert. mullion
horiz. buttjoint

vert.+horiz. mullion

✳ = suggests that 3rd stairs in _inside_, the other two along the façades.

Curtain wall studies for the museum

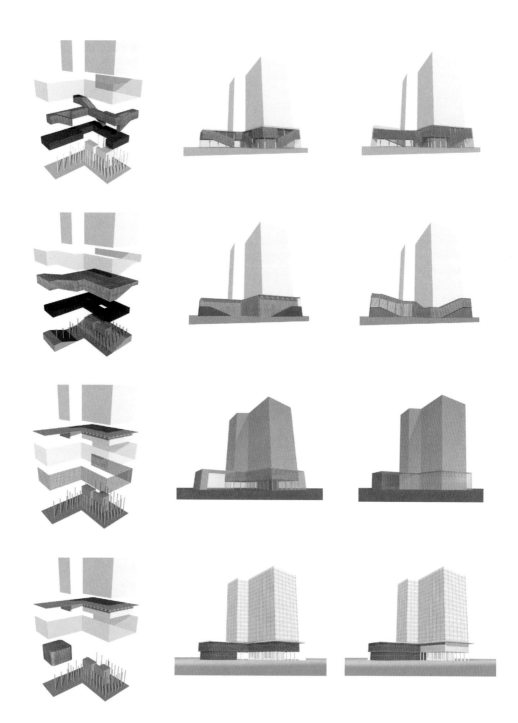

Four families of museum massing options

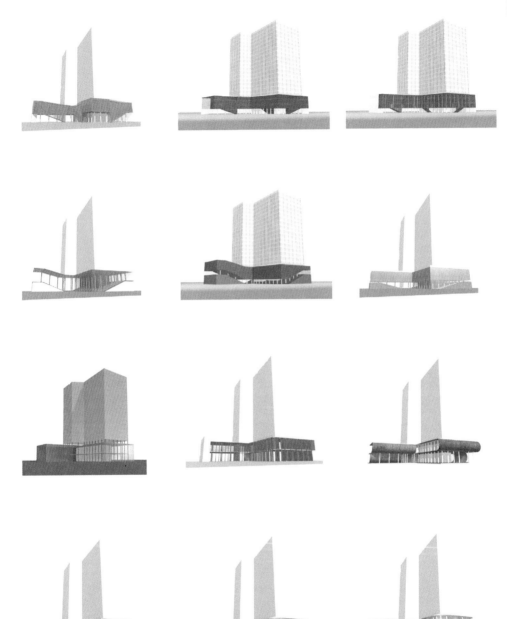

AF 005
26 oct 03

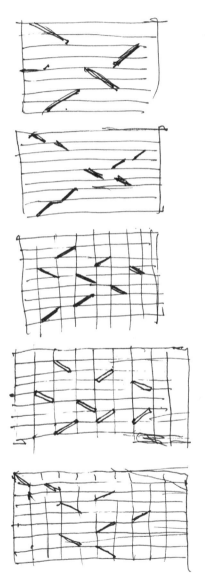

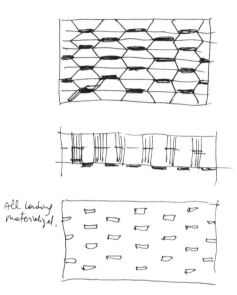

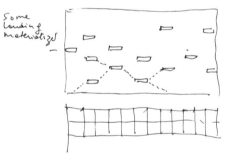

All loading materialized.

Some loading materialized

Color studies

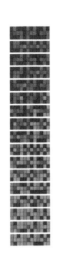
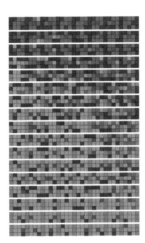
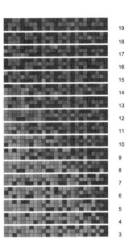

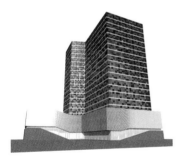

Pixelated tower facade

Alternate envelope with wood fins

The staircase concept allows multiple routes to the upper floors.

Preliminary rendering done for fundraising

Cincinnati, Athletic Center, 2001–

Contextual Free Form

glass envelope
with wood
or brick
chambers

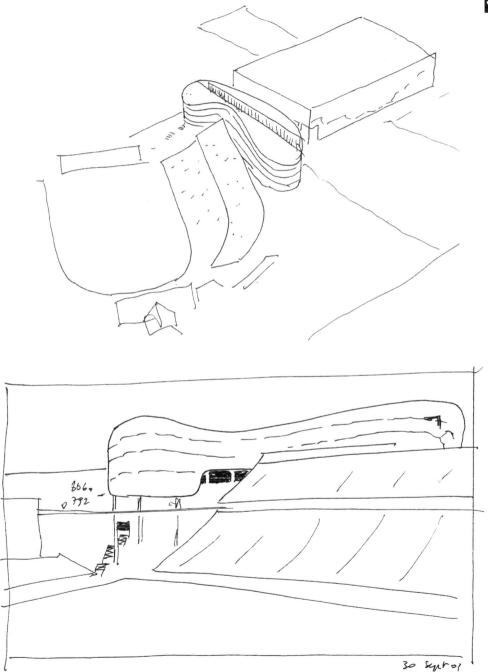

306
792

30 sept 01

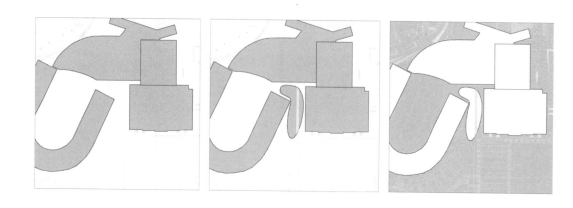

Site, freestanding infill, contextual free form

The Athletic Center at the University of Cincinnati can be described as either a free-standing infill or a contextual free-form structure. The university originally had stated that the center could be located at any place within the sports complex, provided we put everything back within the same general confines. While a truly freestanding building was a feasible option, we decided to locate the Athletic Center—intended to be an epicenter of athletic and academic activities—literally at the heart of the campus, in a narrow gap between a stadium and a large indoor arena. Its unusual curvilinear shape is designed to take advantage of the tight constraints of the site, resulting in dynamic residual spaces between the proposed building and the existing stadium, sports fields, and recreation center.

The new five-story Athletic Center links the north and south entrances of the university campus, and acts as a unifying hub for the complex array of adjacent existing buildings. Consequently, the atrium at the core of the Athletic Center becomes a central terminal for athletic events, housing a centralized ticket office and acting as a filter for students, coaches, and administrators. The building also contains offices on the top floors, an auditorium, museum, gift shop, practice gymnasium, sports medicine facilities, training rooms, and locker rooms below ground. Although the building will be used mainly by athletes, the new auditorium, classrooms, faculty club, tennis courts, and soccer fields will be shared by the greater university community.

Materialization of Concept: A Structural Envelope

Several other contextual constraints contributed to the architectural concept, including an existing below-ground mechanical area that had to be column-free, and a requirement for access to the adjacent buildings' loading docks. In order to provide the clear spans dictated by these site conditions, the design called for a stiff perimeter, an "exoskeleton" that allows the envelope to act as a continuous truss bridging the spaces below. A diagonal grid frame, or "diagrid," was developed: a highly efficient structural system in which column elements are laid out in a diagonal pattern at relatively close spacing. These elements not only form a diagonalized truss but also serve as the facade's mullion structure, resulting in a cost-effective solution overall. The envelope's triangulated expression reinforces the concept of the contextual free form and the building's "athletic" character.

In selecting the material for the diagrid, exposed steel and heavy timber were ruled out because of fire regulations. Structural precast concrete was also considered. It became apparent, however, that the extreme freeze-thaw cycles in Ohio created numerous problems with thermal movements and condensation. These problems would exist at the points at which the perimeter diagonal grid structure interfaced with the interior floor framing. Studies were conducted to design all of the floor systems on rollers to allow for these thermal movements. In the end, it was decided to insulate the perimeter frame in order to keep it at a constant temperature. The final design was an insulated structural steel frame with precast concrete cladding.

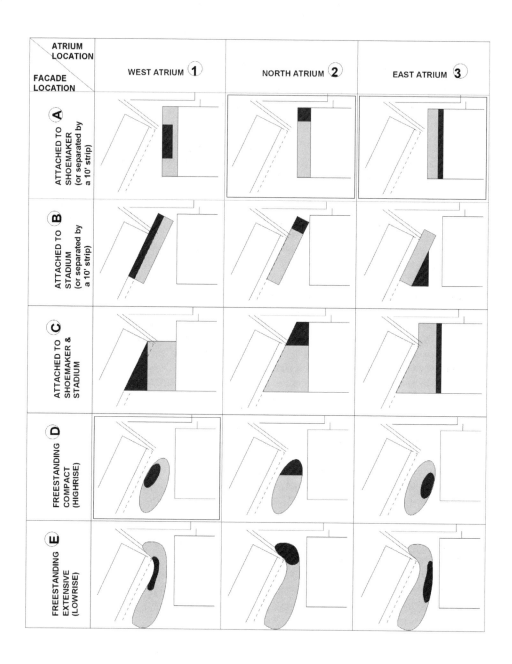

Free-standing infill or contextual free form: building and atrium siting studies

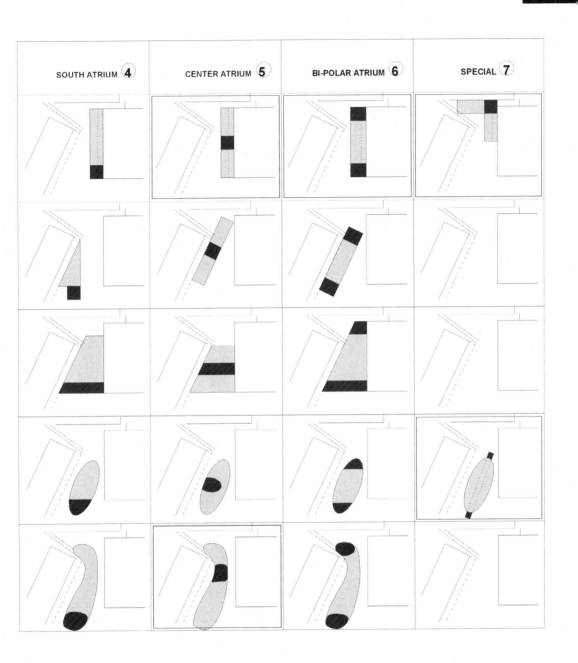

SOUTH ATRIUM ④   CENTER ATRIUM ⑤   BI-POLAR ATRIUM ⑥   SPECIAL ⑦

freestanding in-fill
or
contextual freeform?

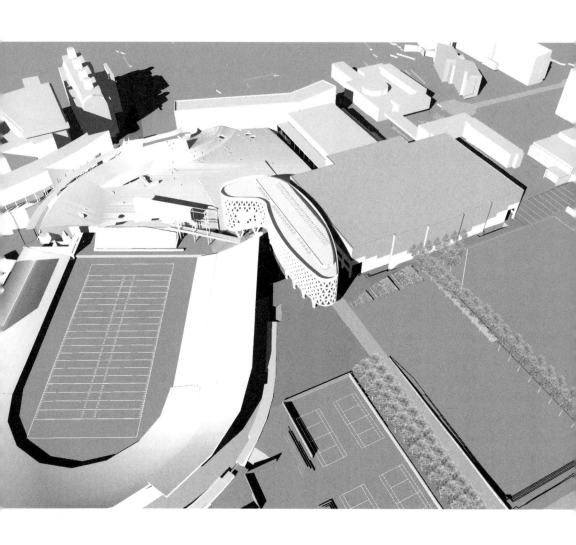

Contextual free form or free-standing infill

Materialization of a concept: facade as truss, so as to cantilever or bridge over site constraints

Main entrance from the south

View from the stadium

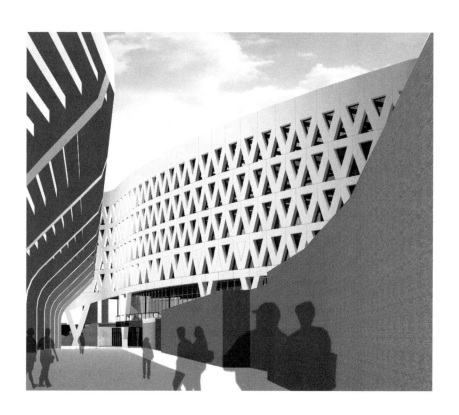

Interstitial spaces: between the stadium and athletic center

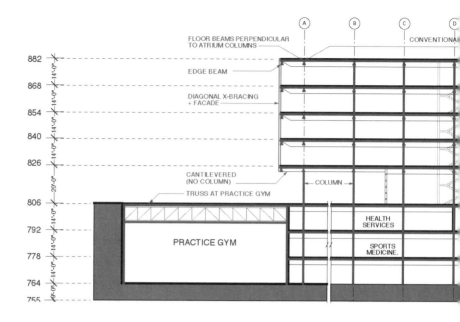

FLOOR BEAMS PERPENDICULAR
TO ATRIUM COLUMNS

EDGE BEAM

DIAGONAL X-BRACING
+ FACADE

CANTILEVERED
(NO COLUMN)

TRUSS AT PRACTICE GYM

COLUMN

CONVENTIONA

HEALTH
SERVICES

SPORTS
MEDICINE.

PRACTICE GYM

882
868
854
840
826
806
792
778
764
755

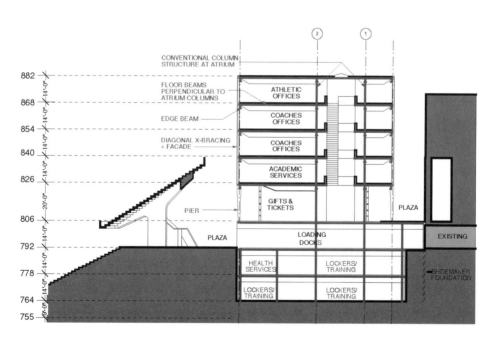

CONVENTIONAL COLUMN
STRUCTURE AT ATRIUM

FLOOR BEAMS
PERPENDICULAR TO
ATRIUM COLUMNS

EDGE BEAM

DIAGONAL X-BRACING
+ FACADE

PIER

PLAZA

ATHLETIC
OFFICES

COACHES
OFFICES

COACHES
OFFICES

ACADEMIC
SERVICES

GIFTS &
TICKETS

PLAZA

LOADING
DOCKS

EXISTING

HEALTH
SERVICES

LOCKERS/
TRAINING

SHOEMAKER
FOUNDATION

LOCKERS/
TRAINING

LOCKERS/
TRAINING

882
868
854
840
826
806
792
778
764
755

Longitudinal section showing MEP distribution
Structural cross-sections through south athletic wing and north public wing

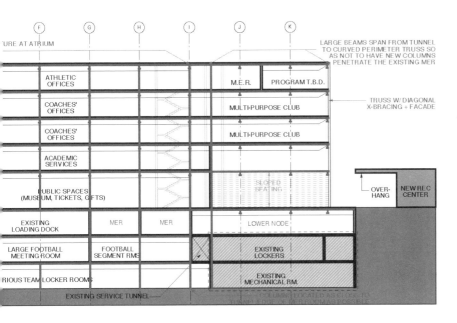

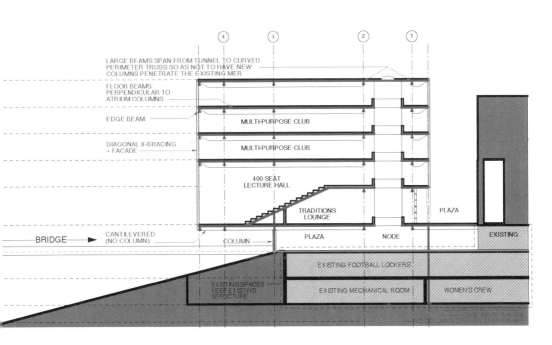

Existing campus mechanical rooms and the need for column-free access to nearby loading docks led to the use of large cantilevers and long spans. Using the periphery of the building as a truss, we achieved the required structural spans and determined the building's architectural expression.

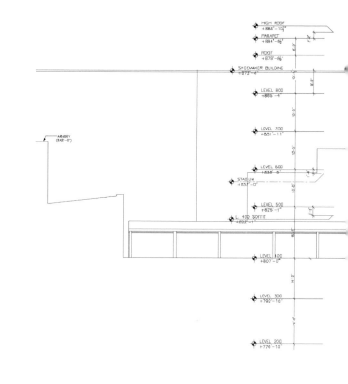

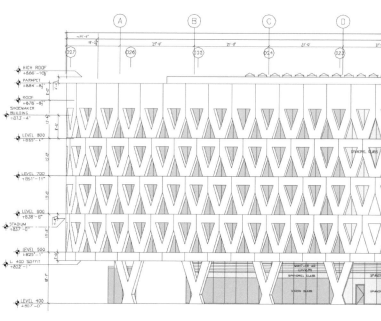

North and east elevations

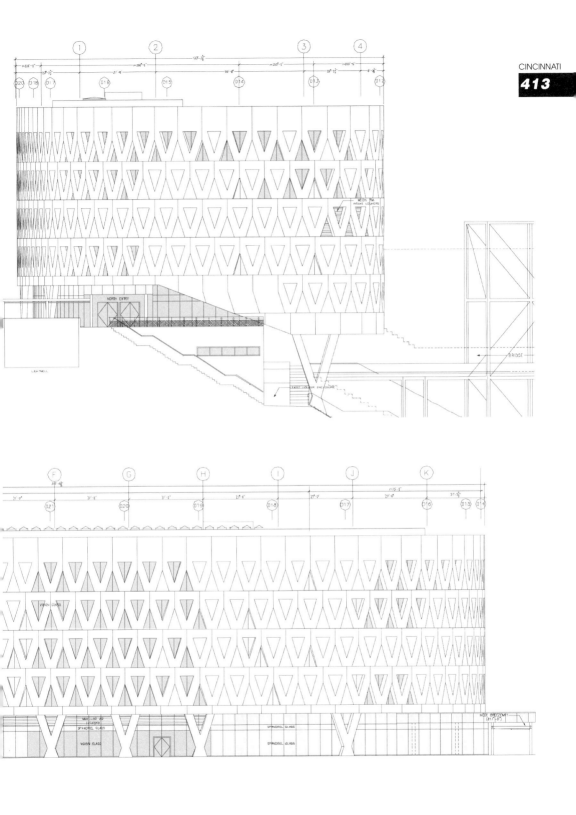

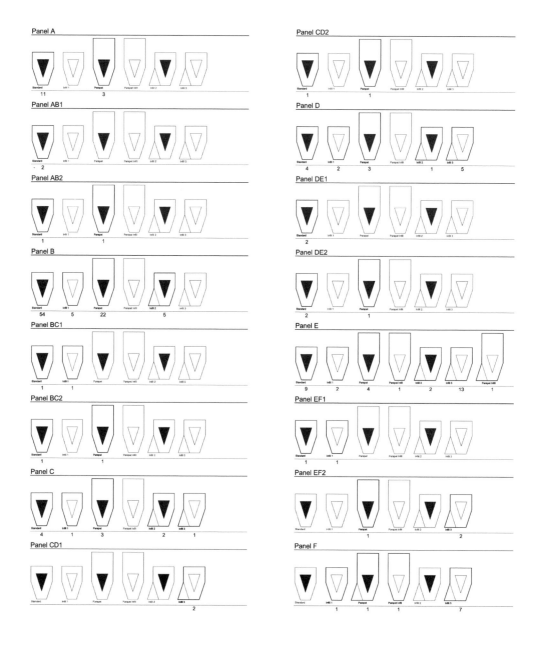

Panel A

Standard — 11
Infill 1
Parapet — 3
Parapet Infill
Infill 2
Infill 3

Panel AB1

Standard — 2
Infill 1
Parapet
Parapet Infill
Infill 2
Infill 3

Panel AB2

Standard — 1
Infill 1
Parapet — 1
Parapet Infill
Infill 2
Infill 3

Panel B

Standard — 54
Infill 1 — 5
Parapet — 22
Parapet Infill
Infill 2 — 5
Infill 3

Panel BC1

Standard — 1
Infill 1 — 1
Parapet
Parapet Infill
Infill 2 — 1
Infill 3

Panel BC2

Standard — 1
Infill 1
Parapet — 1
Parapet Infill
Infill 2
Infill 3

Panel C

Standard — 4
Infill 1 — 1
Parapet — 3
Parapet Infill
Infill 2 — 2
Infill 3 — 1

Panel CD1

Standard
Infill 1
Parapet
Parapet Infill
Infill 2 — 2
Infill 3

Panel CD2

Standard — 1
Infill 1
Parapet — 1
Parapet Infill
Infill 2
Infill 3

Panel D

Standard — 4
Infill 1 — 2
Parapet — 3
Parapet Infill
Infill 2 — 1
Infill 3 — 5

Panel DE1

Standard — 2
Infill 1
Parapet
Parapet Infill
Infill 2
Infill 3

Panel DE2

Standard — 2
Infill 1
Parapet — 1
Parapet Infill
Infill 2
Infill 3

Panel E

Standard — 9
Infill 1 — 2
Parapet — 4
Parapet Infill — 1
Infill 2 — 2
Infill 3 — 13
Parapet Infill — 1

Panel EF1

Standard — 1
Infill 1 — 1
Parapet
Parapet Infill
Infill 2
Infill 3

Panel EF2

Standard
Infill 1
Parapet — 1
Parapet Infill
Infill 2
Infill 3 — 2

Panel F

Standard — 1
Infill 1
Parapet — 1
Parapet Infill — 1
Infill 2
Infill 3 — 7

Catalog of precast concrete panels protecting the diagonal steel structure

Panel FG1

Panel FG2

Panel G

Panel GH1

Panel GH2

Panel H

Panel HA1

Panel HA2

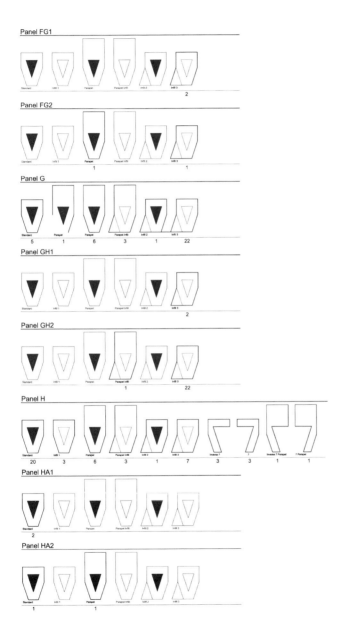

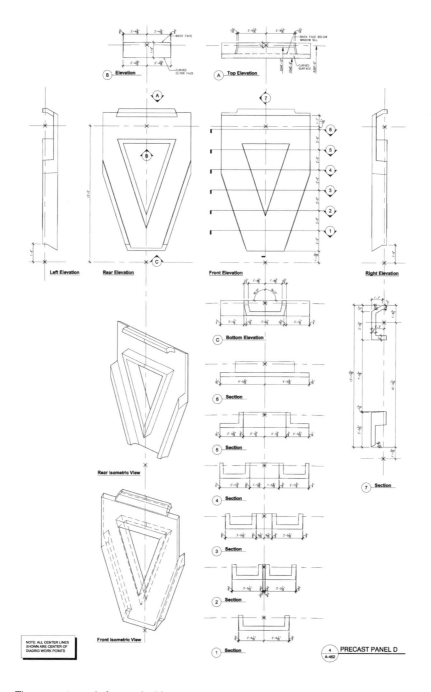

B Elevation

A Top Elevation

Left Elevation

Rear Elevation

Front Elevation

Right Elevation

C Bottom Elevation

Rear Isometric View

Front Isometric View

8 Section

5 Section

4 Section

3 Section

2 Section

1 Section

7 Section

4 PRECAST PANEL D
A-462

The precast panels form a double curve.

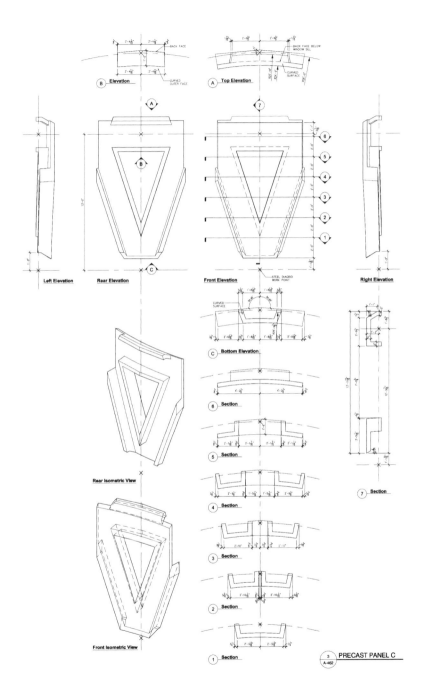

Elevation — B

Top Elevation — A

Left Elevation

Rear Elevation

Front Elevation

Right Elevation

Rear Isometric View

Front Isometric View

Bottom Elevation — C

Section — 6

Section — 5

Section — 4

Section — 3

Section — 2

Section — 1

Section — 7

PRECAST PANEL C
A-462

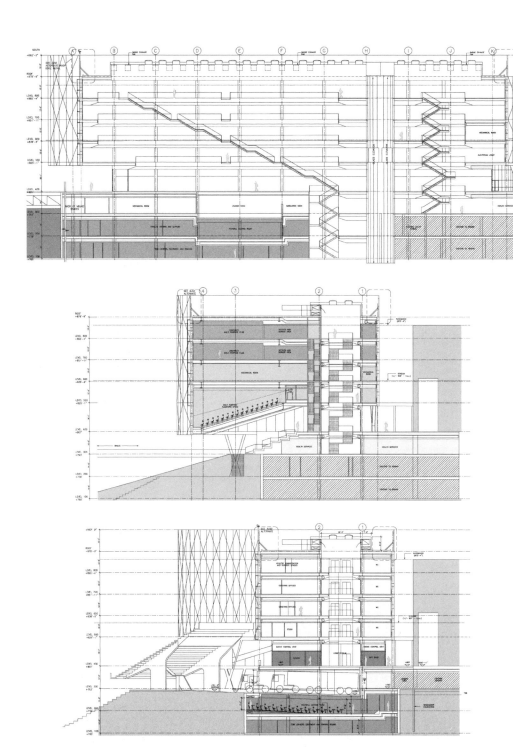

Longitudinal and transverse sections through the atrium: a straight slice through a free-form figure

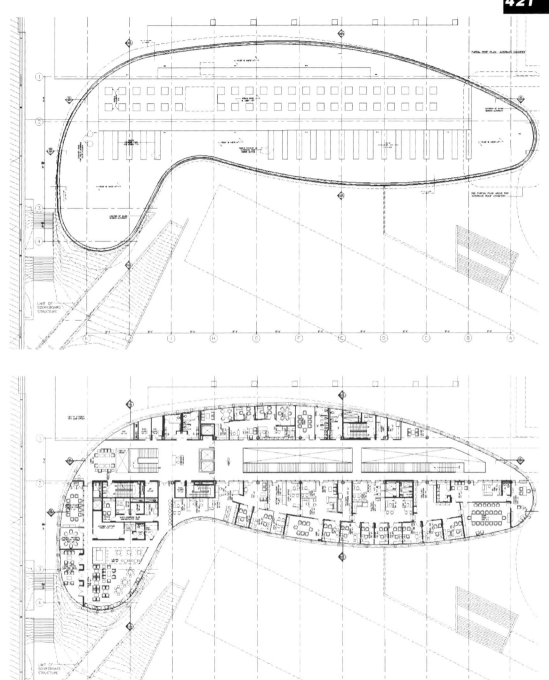

From top to bottom: Roof and level 800

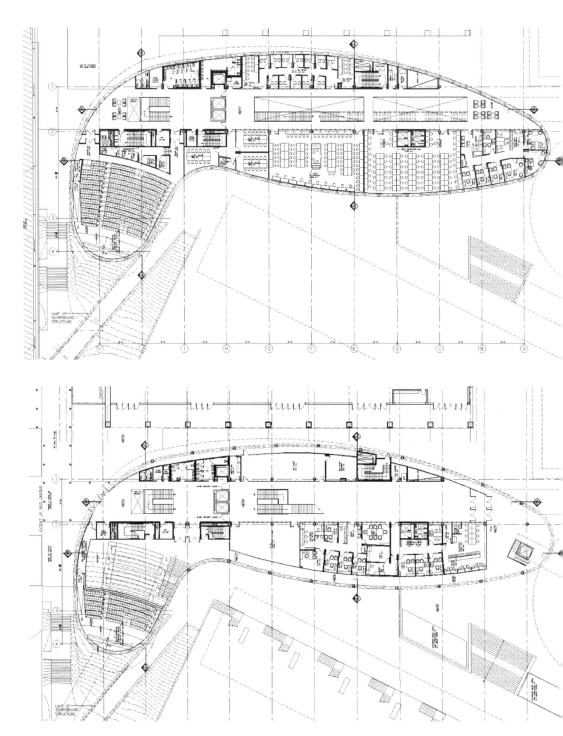

Levels 500 and 400

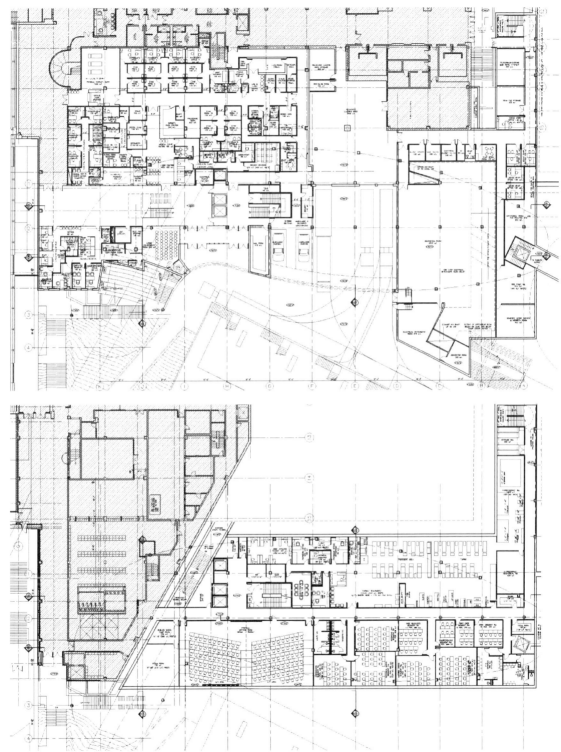

Levels 300 and 200: Inserting program into existing conditions

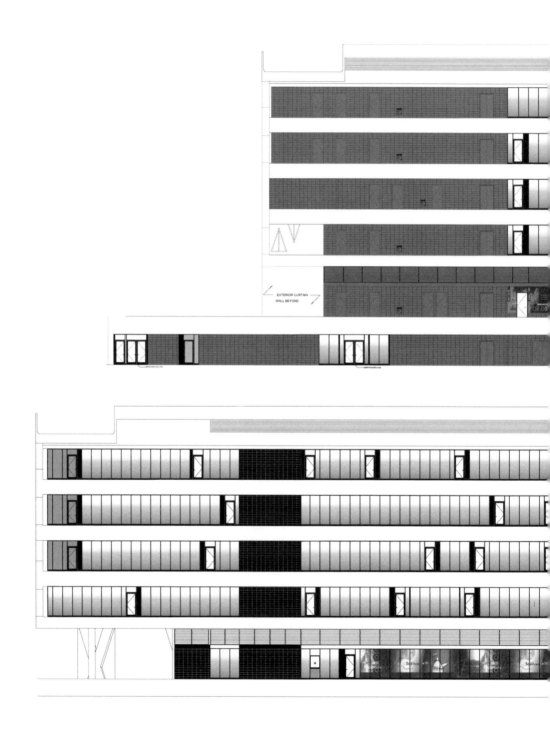

Atrium interior elevations

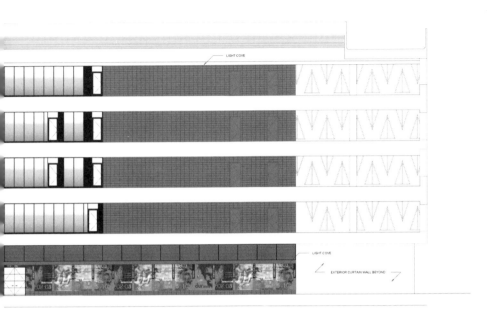

LIGHT COVE

LIGHT COVE

EXTERIOR CURTAIN WALL BEYOND

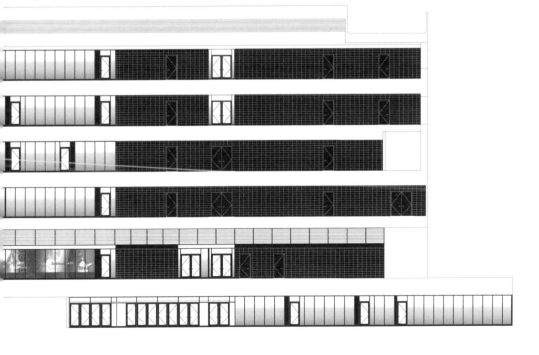

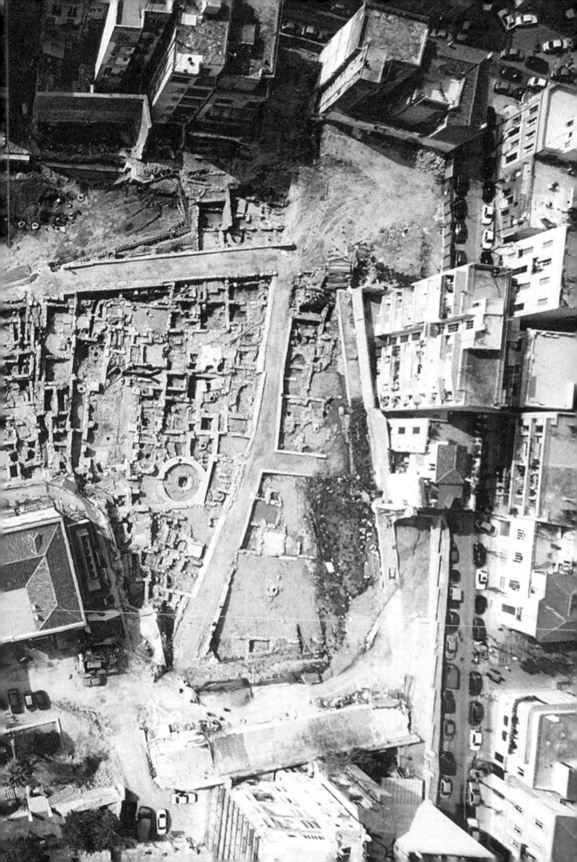

Athens, New Acropolis Museum, 2000–

Paradoxes, Paraboxes

conceptualizing context
or
contextualizing concept
?

A Triple Challenge

How to make an architectural statement at the foot of the Parthenon, arguably one of the most influential buildings of all time?

How to design a building on a site already occupied by extensive archaeological excavations, and in an earthquake-prone region?

How to design a museum to contain an important collection of classical Greek sculptures and a singular masterpiece, the Parthenon Frieze, currently still housed at the British Museum?

Contexts, Content

The site of the New Acropolis Museum lies immediately below the famed Acropolis hill, 300 meters from the Parthenon. It is filled with archaeological excavations containing valuable ruins that must remain untouched and yet be part of the museum visit. The task is all the more daunting given that Athens is subject to regular earthquakes, binding all new construction to strict structural constraints.

Moreover, the artifacts to be exhibited in the new museum are priceless and irreplaceable yet will be visited by tens of thousands of viewers every day. The plan of the museum must allow a chronological sequence that culminates in the famous frieze of the Parthenon Marbles. While direct visual contact with the original site of the Parthenon above should be established, the use of extensive glazing in a hot climate raises technical challenges. Last, nearly half of the frieze is currently at the British Museum in London, and its restitution is the object of major political struggles.

Concepts

At the outset, it was decided to play down the architectural approach and to address the evident dramatic complexities of the collection and the site with minimalist simplicity. The aim was maximum sobriety. If architecture can be described as the materialization of concepts, the building is about the clarity of an exhibition route expressed through three materials—marble, concrete, and glass. Within the unusual constraints of the site, the project ought to appear effortless and almost undesigned: a base of *pilotis* above the ruins, a middle section containing the main galleries, and a glass-enclosed space at the summit containing the Parthenon frieze. The goal of this orchestrated simplicity is to focus the viewers' emotions and intellect on the extraordinary works of art.

Three concepts turn the unusual constraints and circumstances of the museum into an architectural opportunity, resulting in a simple and precise museum context that aspires to echo the mathematical and conceptual clarity of ancient Greece.

Blue Sky: A Concept of Light

More than in any other type of museum, the conditions animating the New Acropolis Museum revolve around natural light. Much as the daylight in Athens differs from light in London, Berlin, or Bilbao, so light for the exhibition of sculpture differs from the light involved in the display of paintings or drawings. The museum not only begins from a specific collection but must also be preeminently a museum of ambient natural light, concerned with the presentation of sculptural objects within it.

People in Motion: A Concept of Circulation

The visitor's route through the museum forms a clear three-dimensional loop, an architectural promenade that provides a series of rich spatial experiences. Movement in and through time, always a crucial dimension of architecture, is an important aspect of this museum in particular. This movement sequence through the galleries follows a narrative that develops chronologically from the earliest archaeological findings through artifacts from the Archaic period to the Parthenon Marbles, ending with sculptures from the Roman Empire. The spatial narrative is arranged around an inner court, and combines linear movement through space with artistic and historical storytelling. With more than 10,000 visitors daily, the sequence of movement through the museum artifacts is designed to be of the utmost clarity.

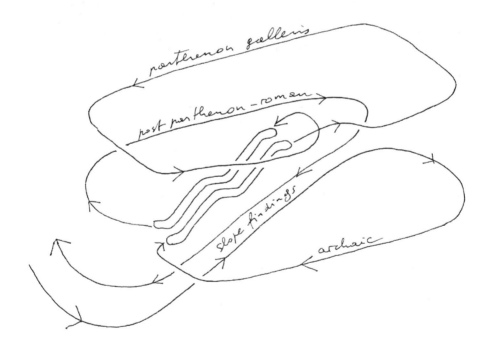

Base, Middle, and Top: A Programmatic Concept

The base of the museum hovers over the existing archaeological excavations on *pilotis*. This level contains the entrance lobby as well as temporary exhibition spaces, retail space, and all supporting facilities.

The middle is a large, double-height, trapezoidal plate that accommodates all the galleries. A mezzanine level includes a bar and restaurant with views toward the Acropolis and a multimedia auditorium.

The top is composed of the rectangular Parthenon Gallery, arranged around an indoor court. The glass enclosure of the gallery provides ideal light for viewing sculpture, with the historical reference point of the Acropolis directly visible in the background. In this gallery, the Parthenon Marbles will be visible from the Acropolis above. The enclosure is designed to protect both the sculptures and visitors from excessive heat and light, using the most contemporary glass technology. The orientation of the Marbles will be exactly as it was at the Parthenon centuries ago, providing an unprecedented context for understanding the accomplishments of the Parthenon complex itself.

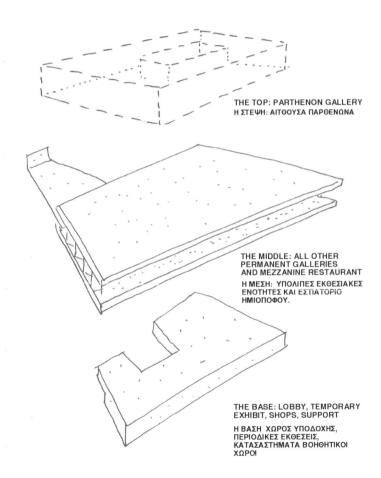

THE TOP: PARTHENON GALLERY
Η ΣΤΕΨΗ: ΑΙΤΘΟΥΣΑ ΠΑΡΘΕΝΩΝΑ

THE MIDDLE: ALL OTHER
PERMANENT GALLERIES
AND MEZZANINE RESTAURANT
Η ΜΕΣΗ: ΥΠΟΛΙΠΕΣ ΕΚΘΕΣΙΑΚΕΣ
ΕΝΟΤΗΤΕΣ ΚΑΙ ΕΣΤΙΑΤΟΡΙΟ
ΗΜΙΟΠΟΦΟΥ.

THE BASE: LOBBY, TEMPORARY
EXHIBIT, SHOPS, SUPPORT
Η ΒΑΣΗ ΧΩΡΟΣ ΥΠΟΔΟΧΗΣ,
ΠΕΡΙΟΔΙΚΕΣ ΕΚΘΕΣΕΙΣ,
ΚΑΤΑΣΑΣΤΗΜΑΤΑ ΒΟΗΘΗΤΙΚΟΙ
ΧΩΡΟΙ

A vigorous debate over the fate of the Parthenon Marbles has taken place internationally in news-papers and Web sites. More than one hundred lawsuits disputing the museum's location, its archae-ological content, the fate of neighboring buildings, or the contemporary expression of its architecture have been filed and eventually cleared by the Greek Supreme Court. After two years of delays, a question is raised: will the new museum ever house its intended inhabitants? Or will it find another raison d'être? Does the justification for architecture extend beyond a narrowly defined program?

THE NEW YORK TIMES EDITORIALS/LETTERS SATURDAY, FEBRUARY 2, 2002

Return the Parthenon Marbles

By the time Lord Elgin obtained the authority to remove "pieces of stone with old inscriptions and figures" from the Greek Parthenon, that remark-able building was already more than 2,200 years old. The year was 1801, and Lord Elgin's authority came from the Turks, who occupied Greece. For the next decade, workmen in Athens removed enormous sections of architectural sculpture from the build-ings on the Acropolis, including friezes from the Parthenon.

The irreplaceable friezes were lowered to the ground, sometimes cut into pieces to make them easier to handle, and loaded on ships bound ulti-mately for England, one of which sank in the Mediterranean. In 1816 Parliament authorized the purchase of the Parthenon marbles, and they were given to the British Museum, where they still reside. At the time, Lord Elgin's exploit was already widely regarded, by the English as well as the Greeks, as an act of cultural depredation if not outright theft. In a sense, what persuaded Parliament and the nation to hang onto the sculptures anyway was their shat-tering beauty. People who saw them wanted to protect them.

Throughout their history, the Parthenon friezes have been hostages to Christianity, to Islam, to the diplomatic tensions between France and England during the Napoleonic era. But they have also become hostages of affection, of a profound love for their dynamism and grace, for the clarity of vision they embody. And hostages they remain.

Most of the old arguments used to justify British possession of the Parthenon marbles have long since eroded, if they were ever true. The British originally vowed to give them "an honour-able shelter" and keep them "safe from ignorance and degradation." Those are the terms of a cultural imperialism that sounded plausible in 1816. But no one now argues that the Greeks are incapable of protecting their own artistic treasures. The ratio-nale in England has dwindled to mere legalities, with much quoting by the British Museum of the provisions of the British Museum Act, which gives it the collection "in perpetuity."

It is time for perpetuity to have an end, at least where these sculptures are concerned. Greece has most modestly asked to borrow the Parthenon marbles for the 2004 Athens Olympics, with almost prostrate guarantees of their safe return. Despite strong popular support in England for giving up the marbles, even this loan has been denied.

Instead of lending them, the British Museum should find, in Parliament, the legal authority to return them outright. Museums around the world fear establishing a precedent that would cause a broad new look at the legal status of their own antiquities. But that look has already begun.

And there can be few instances where the case for repatriation seems so reasonable as this one. The building from which these sculptures were stripped still stands. The people from whom they were taken can preserve them and display them with just as much care as the British Museum can, and with real, untainted honor.

NEW YORK TIMES **INTERNATIONAL** WEDNESDAY, DEC

A frieze from the Parthenon marbles at the British Museum in London, which Greece has long demanded should be returned to Athens.

Jonathan Player for The New York Times

Major Museums Affirm Right To Keep Long-Held Antiquities

By CELESTINE BOHLEN

Directors of major European and American museums have issued a strongly worded statement affirming their right to keep long-held antiquities that countries like Greece and Egypt, with increasing insistence, have demanded be repatriated.

The statement, signed by directors of 18 museums, including Philippe de Montebello of the Metropolitan Museum of Art and the heads of nine other American institutions, was released last week to a newspaper in London, where the British Museum has resisted Greek demands for the return — even on temporary loan — of the marble sculptures and friezes removed from the Parthenon by Lord Elgin in 1801.

That statement acknowledges that illegal traffic in ancient and ethnic artwork should now be "firmly discouraged." But it argues that objects acquired in the past should be "viewed in the light of different sensitivities and values, reflective of that earlier era."

Those objects "have become part of the museums that have cared for them, and by extension part of the heritage of the nations which house them," the statement says.

Nonetheless, the statement notes that each repatriation case should be judged individually. "The point of the statement was not to take clear-cut positions on any individual case," said James N. Wood, director of the Art Institute of Chicago and one of the signatories, "but really to understand the history, the contribution and the importance of the universal museum as a concept."

Mr. de Montebello, in an interview yesterday, said that the statement was first discussed at an international meeting of museum directors held in Munich last October. He said it began as a largely European initiative; another museum director, speaking on condition of anonymity, said it began as a "call for help" from Neil MacGregor, director of the British Museum.

Greece has been lobbying hard to [have] the Parthenon marbles returned to Athens for the 2004 Summer Olympic Games, where they would be the centerpiece of a new museum being built at the Acropolis.

A Greek campaign began in earnest some 20 years ago when Melina Mercouri, then minister of culture, made the return of the marbles a cause of national pride. "The marbles were martyred by an Englishman to decorate his house," said the actress. "It was an act of barbarism. For Greeks the Parthenon is a sacred monument, it's the sun... It represents our soul."

Not surprisingly, neither the British Museum nor any other museum in London listed among the signatories to the statement, which was circulated electronically as directors added names to the text. The statement first appeared on Sunday in

Mr. MacGregor is quoted as supporting the statement.

Many major works of art over the centuries have ended up in museums far from their place of origin, and disputes over ownership surface periodically. There are other unresolved restitution cases besides the Parthenon marbles, including the Pergamon Altar, claimed by Turkey, now at the Pergamon Museum of the state museums of Berlin — among the signatories, along with the Louvre, the Prado in Madrid and the State Hermitage Museum in St. Petersburg — and the Benin Bronzes from Nigeria, now held at the Royal Academy of Arts in London.

Lord Elgin obtained Turkish permission to remove the marbles when he was ambassador to the Ottoman Empire, of which Greece was then a part. They were later sold to the British government, which insists to this day that the marbles were legally obtained.

"Today museums would not condone what people did 200 years ago," Mr. de Montebello said. "But you cannot rewrite history. Those were

Viewing artworks acquired in another era differently.

different times, with different ethics and different mores," Mr. de Montebello insisted that the statement did not refer to any recent acquisitions, which are governed by international conventions, including one adopted by Unesco in 1970, and by an increasingly strict interpretations of United States law on stolen property.

In recent years the art world has been rocked by a series of ownership disputes. Heirs of Holocaust victims have laid claim to artwork that was looted by the Nazis, and later improperly sold to collectors and museums. Art-rich countries in Europe, but also Latin America, have become more protective about their cultural patrimony, passing laws that declared anything found abroad the ground to be national property.

Given the perplexing tangle of law, diplomacy and moral claims now facing museums, some directors at the Munich meeting tried to expand the statement to include guidelines for future acquisitions. But that effort failed for lack of a consensus, said one museum director, speaking on condition of anonymity.

"Museums feel that they ought to remind people that they are not private collections, that the great works of antiquities are not kept behind closed doors, but that they are out there — to be admired, studied, and viewed," Mr. de Montebello said. "They are there to be seen in the

---

Greece Affirms Limits To Elgin Marble Claim

By CELESTINE BOHLEN

Greece's case for the return of the so-called Elgin Marbles — fragments of the Parthenon frieze now housed in the British Museum — has nothing to do with claims for the repatriation of other cultural assets, Evangelos Venizelos, the Greek culture minister, said yesterday.

He was responding to a recent statement signed by 18 museum directors representing most of the major museums of the United States and Europe (except those in Britain and most of those in Italy). The statement affirmed the museums' right to hold on to artworks that have long been in their collections.

"We do not intend to claim other fragments of friezes on display in other museums and which are not linked with programs like the one we have for the Acropolis Museum and the Parthenon," Mr. Venizelos said in a statement that linked Greece's current campaign for the return of the Parthenon frieze to the 2004 Summer Olympic Games to be held in Athens.

This claim is different, he argued. "The Parthenon Marbles are part of a standing monument," he explained. He added that a special museum was being built to house what Greek officials hope will be a display of all the surviving remnants of the original fifth-century B.C. frieze. (Some are now in Athens.) Lord Elgin removed a part of the frieze in 1801, when he was ambassador to the Ottoman Empire, and sold it to the British Museum in 1811.

The museums' statement, which never mentioned the Parthenon Marbles, was meant as a collective defense of collections that were put together in another era, before countries like Greece became more protective of their cultural patrimony. The statement argued that museums, as the guardians of artifacts from civilizations around the world, had become international institutions with missions that transcended national boundaries.

Andrew Hamilton, a spokesman

Two countries, each with a piece of the same treasure.

for the British Museum, said that Neil MacGregor, the museum's director, purposely did not sign the statement so as not to detract from its larger purpose. "It was felt this initiative would be more valuable as a movement by museums in Europe and the United States that have not yet made their position on restitution clear," Mr. Hamilton said.

But the Greek government, which has been lobbying the British Museum for the return of the marbles for more than two decades, has argued that a combined display of the Parthenon's frieze would not challenge the roles and functions of major museums. "On the contrary," Mr. Venizelos said, it "affirms them."

As construction of the new Athens museum proceeds, the Greeks have been pressing their case with increasing intensity. The subject was raised last month at a meeting between Prime Minister Costas Simitis of Greece and Britain's prime minister, Tony Blair.

But the British government and the British Museum, a national institution, have not budged. "Neil MacGregor has made clear our position," Mr. Hamilton said, "which is that the British Museum is the best place for the marbles, and they are part of a select group of objects that are the core of the museum's collection, which cannot be loaned."

The Italian government has taken a different stance, and this week returned to Greece a small piece of the Parthenon frieze, depicting the foot of the goddess Peitho. A gift of a British diplomat in the 19th century, it had been in a museum in Palermo, Sicily. Mr. Venizelos, who received the fragment on Wednesday, said its return was a gesture of "great symbolic significance."

Evangelos Venizelos, Greek culture minister, visiting the British Museum, which owns the contested Elgin Marbles (some in background).

Agence France-Presse

Greece's Colossal

Diplomacy Couldn't Win Back the Elg

man Turks,
those who
world's m
far, all the
back to A
many re
the man

By FRED A. BERNSTEIN

ies of frustration, Greece
2004 Summer
world

ew Guilt Trip

bles. Can Modern Architecture?

Courtesy of Bernard Tschumi Architects

A museum designed by Bernard Tschumi will sit below the Acropolis and, Greece hopes, someday hold the Elgin Marbles.

...d as the Parthenon Marbles by ...re stolen, they have become the ...y contested works of art. But so ...has not succeeded in getting them ...for a short-term loan. Among the ...n officials give for not relinquishing ...e doesn't even have a suitable mu...em.

...overnment sponsored an internation-...h Bernard Tschumi, the cele-...hosen to build a new ...e start of the

Olympics, every television set in the world would broadcast its image, and announce the triumphant return of Greece's lost icons. And if they weren't returned, the building would stand as a gleaming reproach to Britain's intransigence.

But the structure intended to settle a controversy has become an object of controversy itself. The design clashes with the setting, some critics say. It jeopardizes an archaeological site, others claim. And perhaps most dispiritingly, the Olympic deadline is hopelessly out of reach. Like an athlete who trains for a lifetime and then

Continued on Page 28

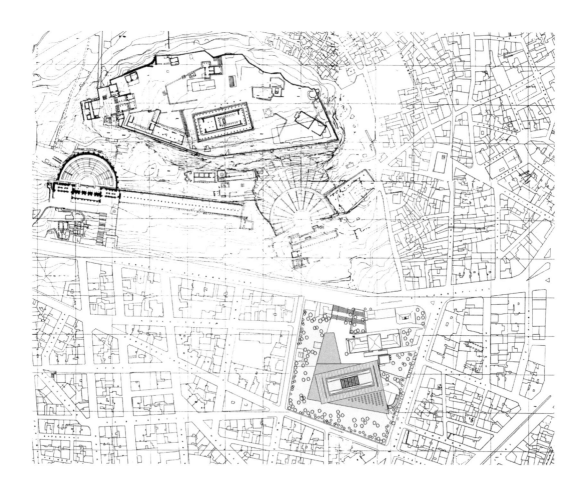

Context: Stringent local zoning rules, the Parthenon 300 meters away, major archaeological ruins on the ground, a subway station below, a 19th-century armory to preserve, and a maximum height restriction
Content: Prominent antiquities, including sculptures currently at the British Museum in London

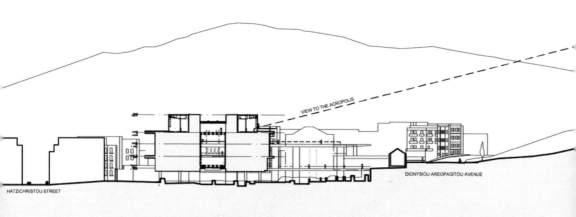

HATZICHRISTOU STREET

VIEW TO THE ACROPOLIS

DIONYSIOU AREOPAGITOU AVENUE

Athens, between the pagan and the sacred: a museum hovering over archeological ruins, in paradoxical dialogue with the Parthenon

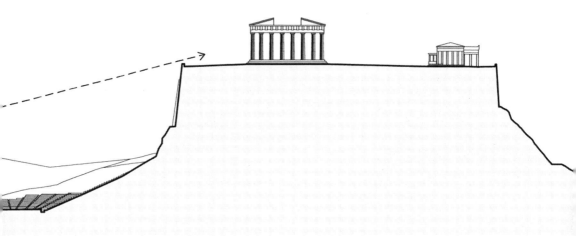

Studies

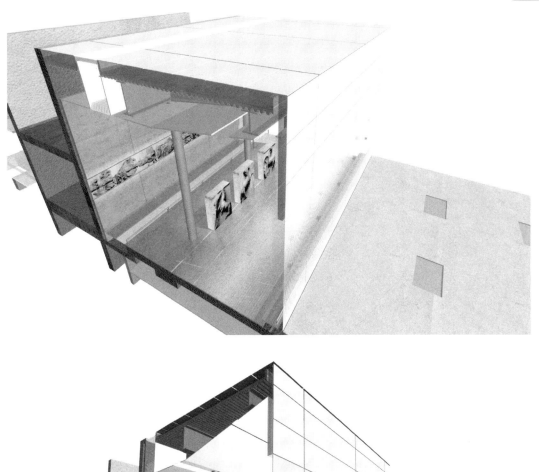

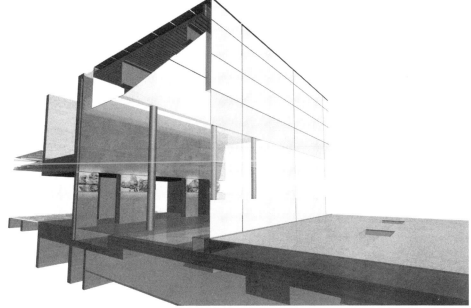

Sections through gallery

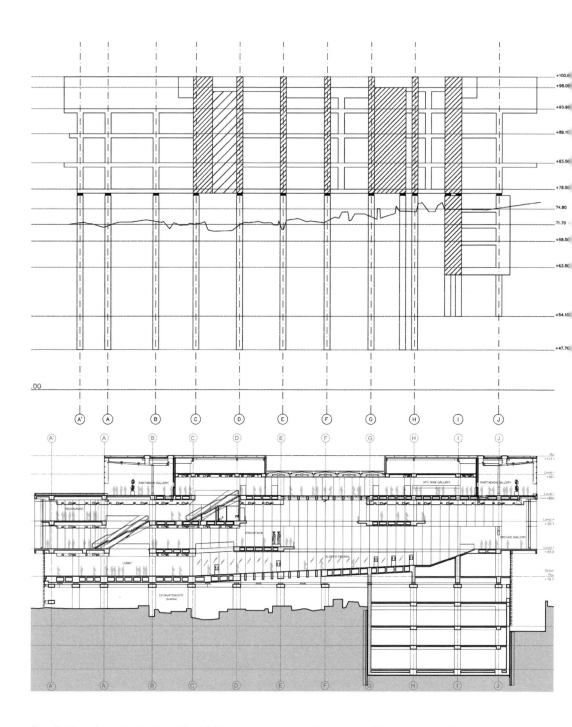

Top: Earthquake protection is achieved through a base insulation system. A large structure floats
over piles anchored in the ground.
Bottom: Longitudinal and transverse sections

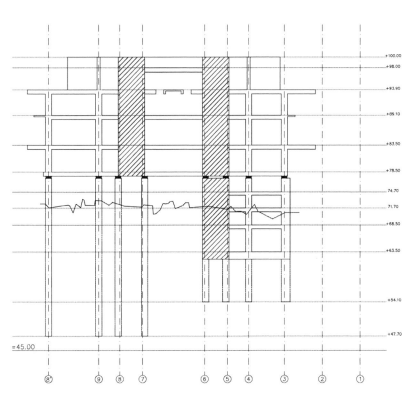

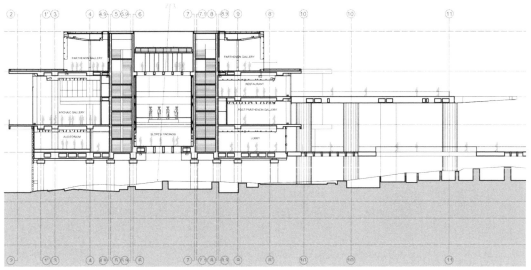

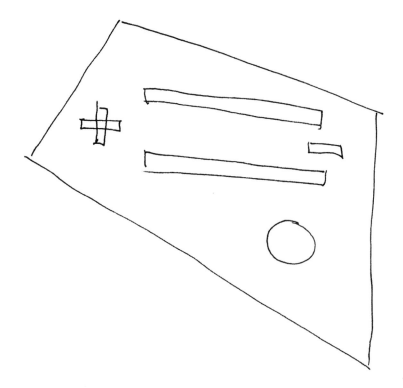

Final diagrammatic study

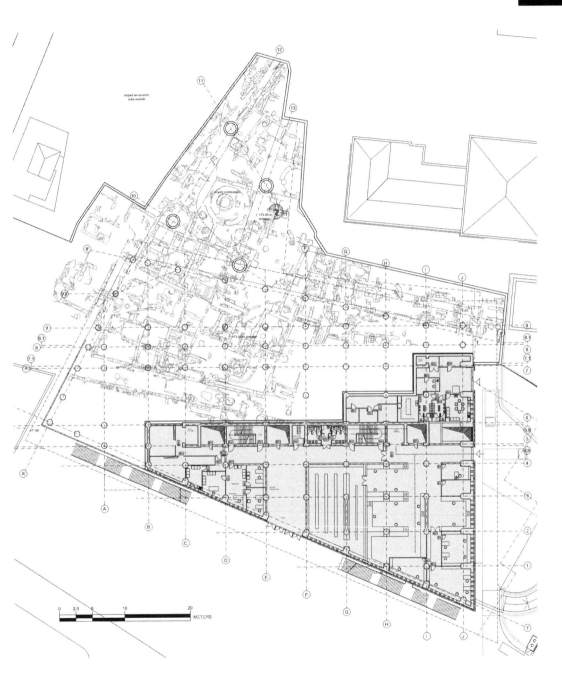

Lower level: Administration and archeological storage
The location of each column set in the ruins was negotiated with archaeologists.

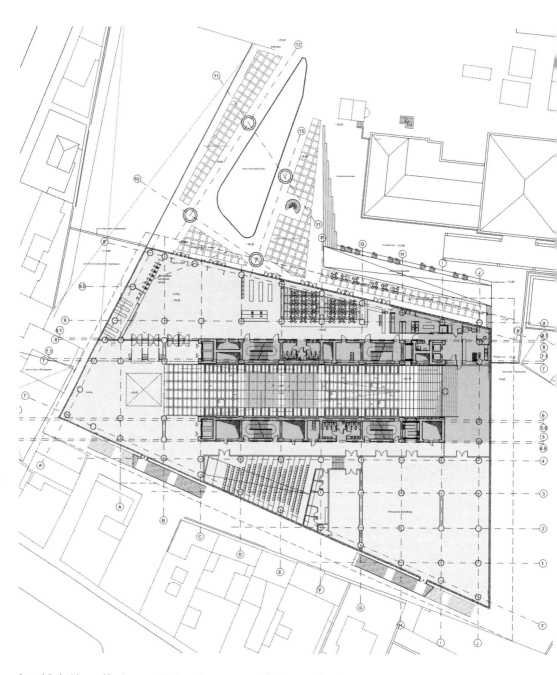

Level 0: Lobby, café, shop, auditorium, temporary exhibitions, and a glass ramp overlooking
archaeological findings and leading to the main galleries above

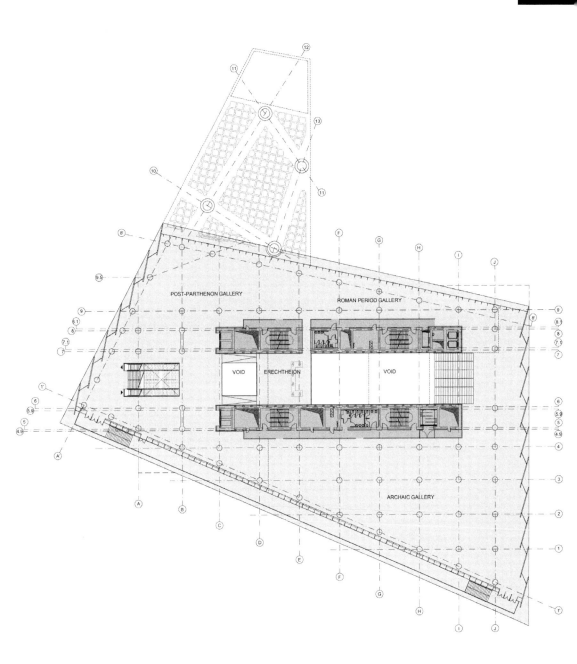

POST-PARTHENON GALLERY

ROMAN PERIOD GALLERY

VOID

ERECHTHEION

VOID

ARCHAIC GALLERY

Level +1: Main gallery level

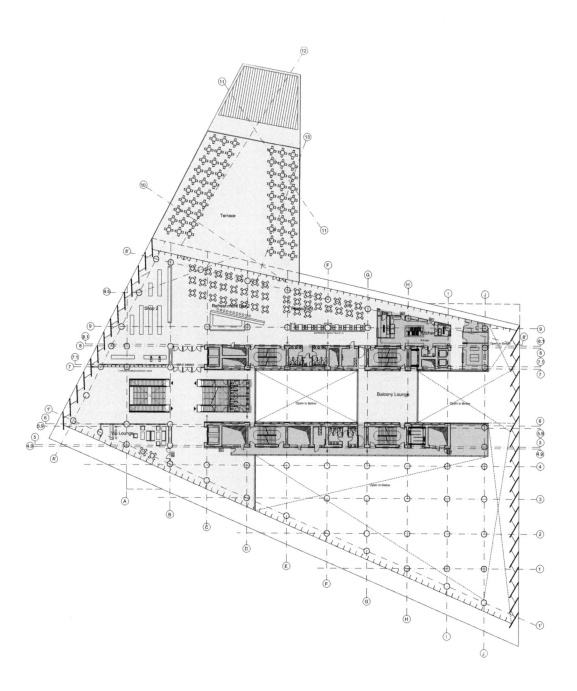

Level +2 Mezzanine: Restaurant, shops, VIP lounge

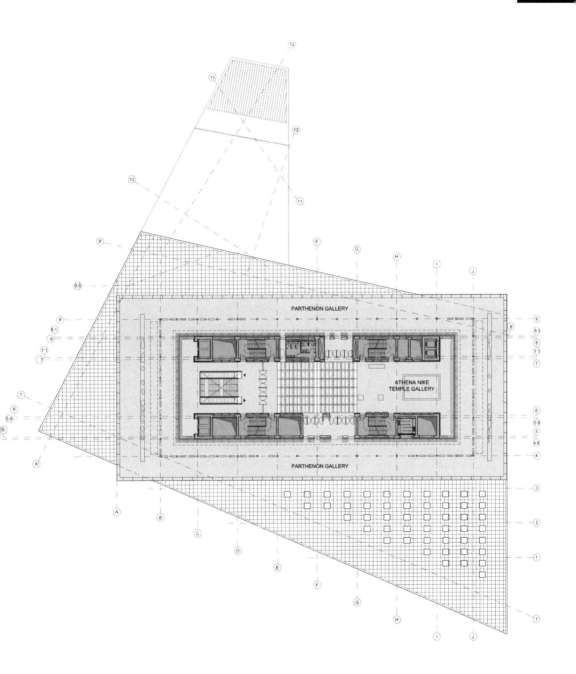

Level +3: Parthenon and Athena Nike Temple galleries

E.
Contexts Becoming Concept

It is not unusual for clients to make contradictory demands, so when we were asked to design a university campus master plan that simultaneously would provide a bold symbolic presence and blend into a wooded natural landscape, we responded by finding an equally paradoxical solution. Camouflage, a technique developed by the French army during World War I, relies on a combination of extreme similarity (blending) and extreme difference (dazzle). It provided the ultimate strategy, allowing a clear spatial idea—that of a centrally networked campus plan—to be concealed without being diluted. The context therefore defined the concept of the project. Or was it the other way around?

Nice, Sophia-Antipolis Campus, 2004

Camouflage

Nature and Communication

The project began with an existing campus of a technological institute that needed to expand. As is often the case today, the client wanted the new campus both to have a specific identity and to be fully integrated into the lush French Mediterranean surroundings; the mandate was to be simultaneously visible and invisible.

Located near Nice, the original campus was part of a large development initiated in the 1970s with the goal of becoming France's Silicon Valley. It suffered, however, from neglect and lack of ambition. The competition's aim was not only to produce facilities for research and education in media and computer technologies, but also to generate a new image, albeit on a low budget. Also implicit in the program was the idea of communication. The institute sought cross-fertilization between the different buildings to be located on the site, which included a reception and research center, a building containing offices and laboratories, computer science center, sports center, and library.

The project posed multiple challenges. Despite the site's steep slope (a nearly 20-percent grade), a strict zoning code required that no roof exceed a height of 12 meters. Nearly one thousand parking spaces had to be accommodated. Last, each building required its own identity.

Concept

In response to the need for communication, all institutions were organized around a pivot in the heart of the site, directly accessible through glazed covered walkways. The majority of the parking spaces were placed under the individual buildings, so as to preserve the natural wooded landscape as much as possible.

Finally, a new image was considered—one that both fit with the natural surroundings and was also distinctive. Parallels were made with Cézanne's unfinished paintings depicting this very area in the south of France, and also with the fragmentation of photographs of nature achieved through computer pixelization. Our earlier research into means of bypassing the compositional clichés of architectural history naturally led to a closer look at the techniques of camouflage.

Camouflage allows a functional object to look like something else without altering what it does. Using computer technology, the building envelopes of the proposed design were made to mimic nature and the colors of its seasons: spring, summer, autumn, and winter, giving each building a unique identity.

ROUTE DES LUCIOLES

ROND POINT
SAINT-PHILIPPE

IUT

IUT

IUT

RU

GALERIE
COUVERTE

TRANCHE 2

BIBLIOTHÈQUE

POUR RENDRE LA LECTURE PLUS
FACILE, NOUS AVONS DISTINGUÉ SUR
LE PLAN 1:1000 LES CIRCUITS DES
UTILISATEURS (À GAUCHE) ET LES
CIRCUITS DES SERVICES ET PARKING (À DROITE)

INRIA

EPU

EPU

ACCUEIL /
RECHERCHE

PROMENADE

DÉTENTE

GALERIE
COUVERTE

CENTRE
SPORTIF

COMPAQ

TRANCHE 2 -
80 PL PARKING
SOUS-TERRAIN

PROMENADE

GALERIE COUVERTE

TRANCHE 2 -
25 PL PARKING

DÉTENTE

GET

AA

VOIE DE SERVICE

TRANCHE 2 -
75 PL PARKING

BASSIN DE
RETENTION
(450 M2)

TRANCHE 2 -
260 PL PARKING
SOUS-TERRAIN

TRANCHE 2 -
12 PL PARKING

VOIE D'ACCÈS

UTILISATEURS:

ÉTUDIANTS / ENSEIGNANTS -

CHERCHEURS -

VISITEURS -

CLOTURE -

ACCÈS CONTROLES -

Site plan: organization around a pivot

The site is a tree-covered landscape.

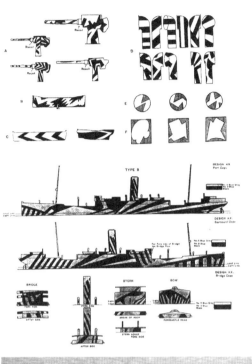

Camouflage combines extreme similarity with extreme difference.

Paul Cézanne's palette

Pixelated nature: spring, summer, autumn, winter, and the four seasons

Nature, communication, technology, urbanism, landscape

Reception and Research Center (The Four Seasons)
The Reception and Research Center is the hub of the project. Located an equal distance from each of the other facilities, and connected to them by colorful glass-covered walkways, the center offers a panoramic view of the surrounding hills, Alps, and Mediterranean Sea. Surrounded by conference rooms, a triple-height atrium serves as a large meeting hall, with the research areas on the higher floors.

EPU/Polytech Sophia (Spring)
The EPU is both a new building and the extension of an existing facility. Organized around a spine that connects the whole, two wings perpendicular to the slope accommodate offices and laboratories.

GET Computer Science Building (Summer)
The Computer Science Center is organized in two parallel wings with auditoriums at their eastern
extremities.

Sports Center (Autumn)
The roof of the Sports Center is flush with the higher end of the slope and can be used as an athletic field. Users enter from above and walk down to the locker rooms and gymnasium.

Library (Winter)
The Library had to be located within the massing of the old campus and yet is made to participate in the logic of the new. Access is provided mid-slope, so as to improve communication between the upper and lower campuses. Two reading rooms provide a panoramic view. A system of book shelves perforated at varied intervals simultaneously allows light in and offers readers shade from the sun.

Concepts may be indifferent,
reciprocal or conflictual
in relation to context(s)

F.
Concepts Becoming Context

Urban design historically has oscillated between the treacherous poles of social control and manipulation, on one hand, and the banal orchestration and management of urban services, on the other. The scale of urban projects presents a challenge: Is it possible to impose a single plan on a large tract without trampling on the intricacy and peculiarities that mark the city? All of the projects in this last section approach urban design not as occasions to realize grand visions at a large scale, but as opportunities to question the nature of the city of the future. From Paris to Toronto to New York to Beijing, what kinds of urban concepts can both preserve and advance the way we live in the city?

Paris, Expo 2004, 2001

Virtual City of Images

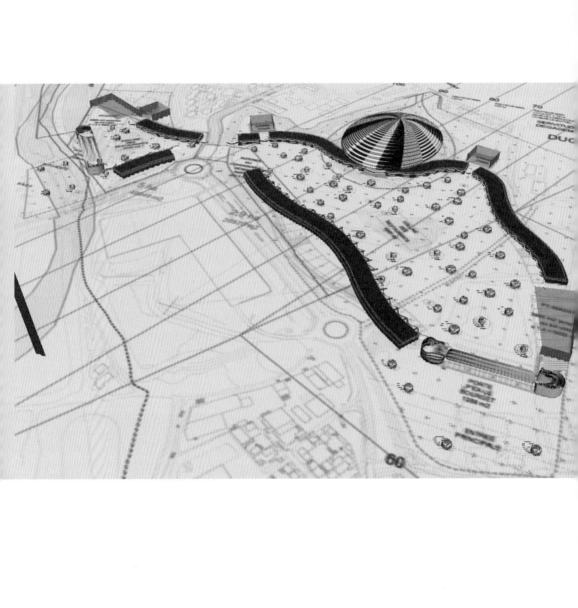

The Imaginary Image

The theme for the Paris International Exposition 2004 (Expo 2004) was the image in all its manifestations. The unifying spatial concept of the exposition, which includes pavilions from multiple nations, is thus the juxtaposition of different kinds of images—moving versus surface images, the image of the part versus the image of the whole, and images that shock versus smoothly continuous filmic images. These images in turn can be broken down into composite elements—namely, points, lines, grids, frames, and pixels—that have architectural analogs in the master plan of the exhibition. The plan includes a central court, gates, bridges, national pavilions, kiosks, and an auditorium, all located on a 51-hectare site in Seine-St.-Denis, a community just north of Paris.

The proposed master plan design for Expo 2004 (the fair was later canceled in 2002 after a national election ushered in a new French government) therefore attempted to create a setting that transcends the static, pictorial characteristics of the image by addressing the realm of the imaginary. We seek to invent a coherent and precise device to transport the public toward a new dimension—the meeting point between real and virtual worlds. The goal is not to immerse the spectator in a world of images, but instead, to enable him or her to become an active mediator in the displacement between the real and virtual.

The Gates, Long Court, Cultural Kiosks, and Auditorium

Visitors first encounter the gates, which serve to filter the crowd into the Expo site. Constantly changing messages and textures are projected onto curvilinear screens embedded in the gates.

The "long court" is a common space that functions both as a city square and as a route linking the exposition's two proposed entrance rotundas. (After the conclusion of Expo 2004, the Long Court is intended to connect the Parc de la Courneuve to the existing Exhibitions Center of Le Bourget, with a route branching off toward the city of Dugny.)

As a central gathering space, the long court unifies the exposition's circulation systems. Instead of emphasizing the autonomy of individual national pavilions, the national buildings are organized according to a repetitive matrix and all contribute to the common goal of defining an ideal space for assembly—facilitating a community of nations. The long court also serves as a unifying space for images. Projections on the canopies of the national pavilions animate the court, resulting in a kaleidoscope of cultural representations.

The long court is interspersed by cultural kiosks or small, circular, thematic buildings that function as programmatic devices in the middle of the circulation space.

Other major buildings include the bulbous VIP pavilion with its appended bridges and the large 70,000-spectator-capacity auditorium, intended to become permanent and to accommodate major events both during Expo 2004 and after.

Color Scheme: Global Structure versus Singularities

Using the analogy of the black-and-white versus the color image, the global components of the project (ground, infrastructure, furniture, and signage) form the "black-and-white layer," recognizable as a distinct entity. Superimposed on this stratum are the "colored layers," which are the singular interventions of the various nations or events of the exposition.

Entrance to the exposition grounds

The long court, with the VIP building flanked by the national pavilions

A repetitive matrix unifies and links the national pavilions.

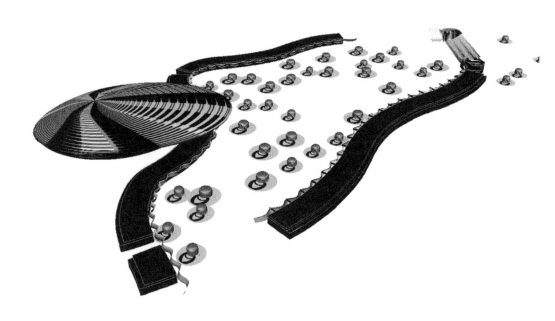

Two curvilinear strips composed of repetitive pavilions define a central court interspersed with individual cultural kiosks.

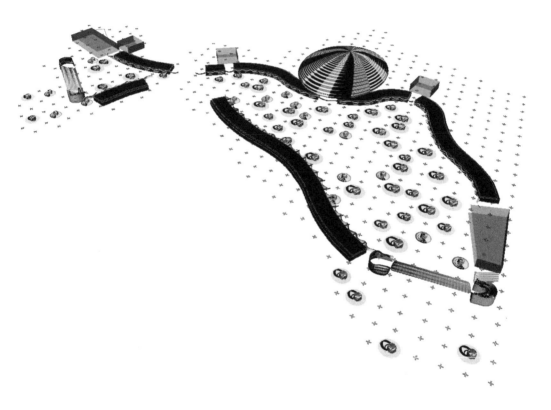

The long court acts as a route between the east and west entrance gates.

Curvilinear configuration

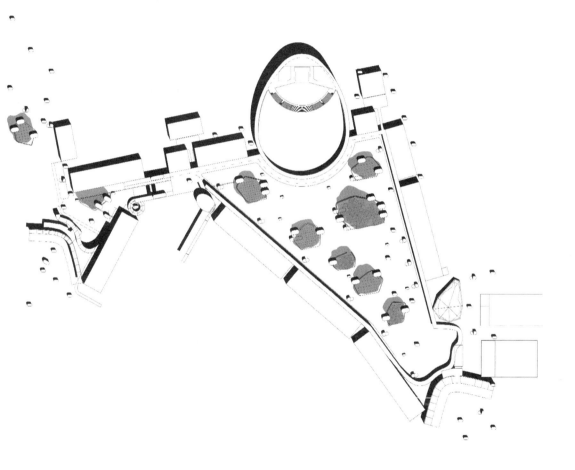

Alternative linear configuration

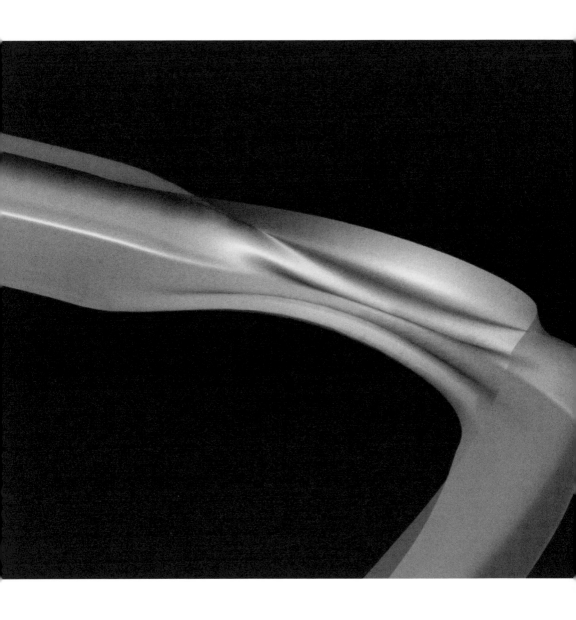

Studies of the entrance gates

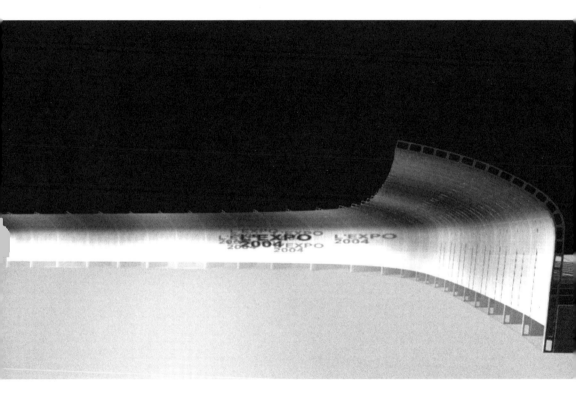

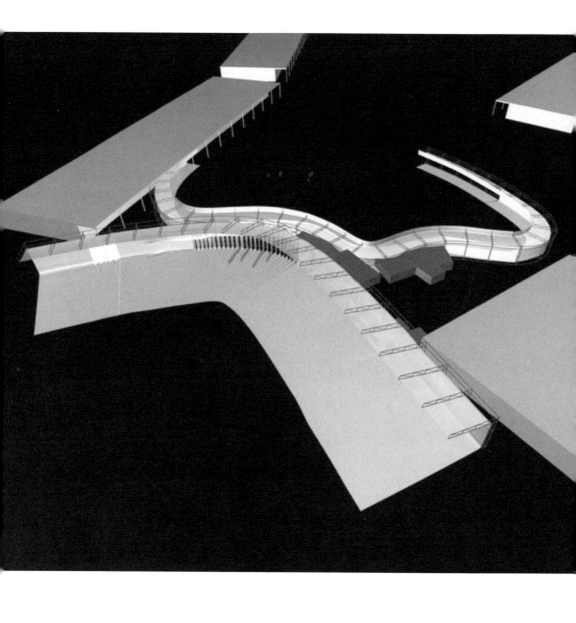

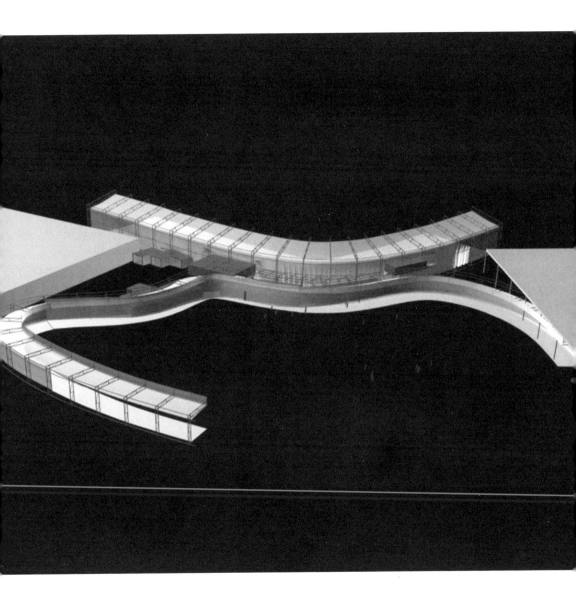

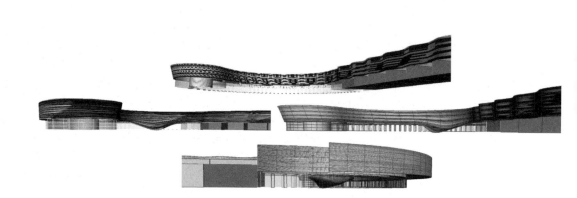

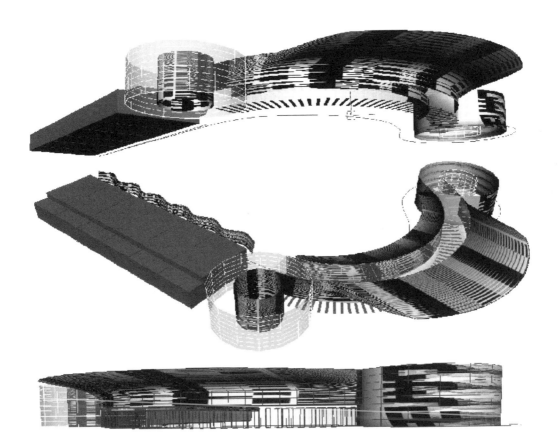

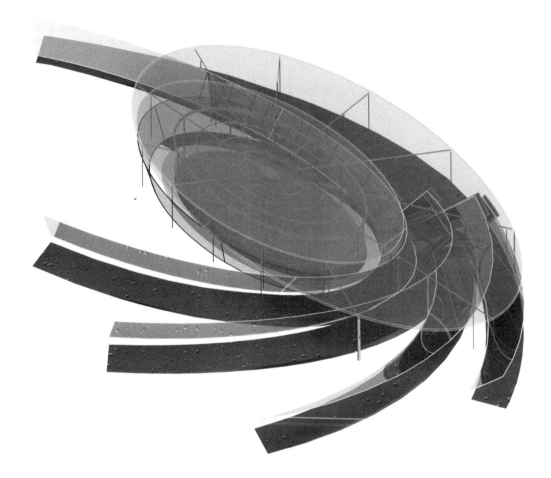

Multiple accesses to the information center

Cultural kiosks: programmatic devices that activate the site

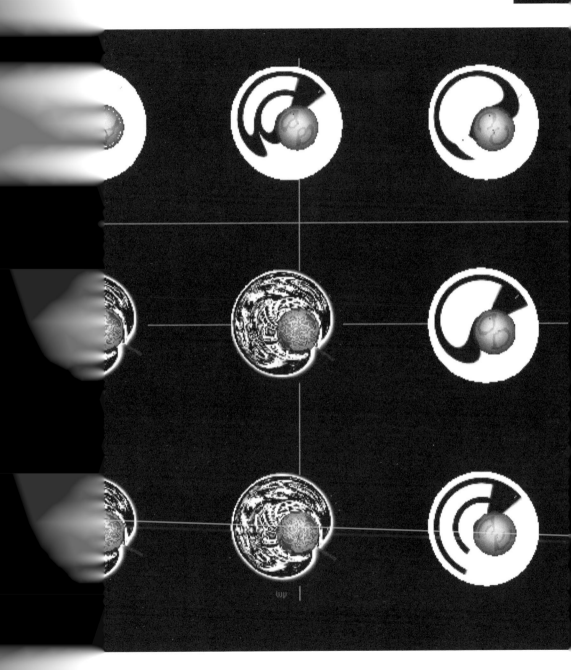

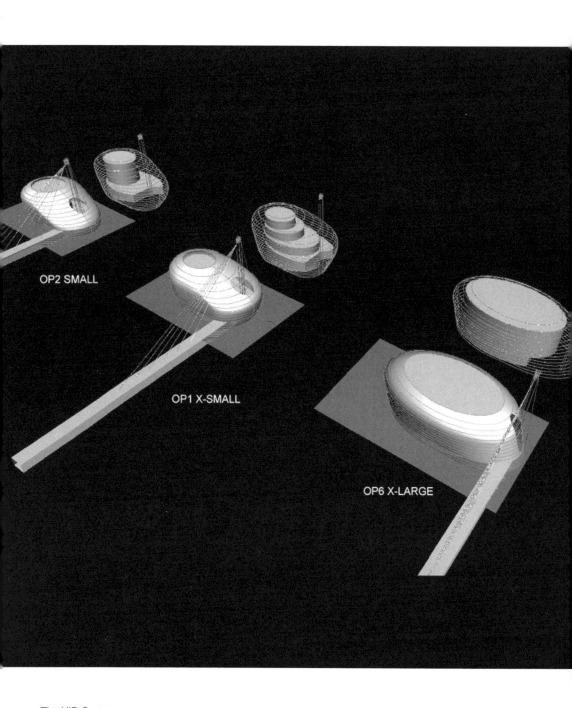

OP2 SMALL

OP1 X-SMALL

OP6 X-LARGE

The VIP Center

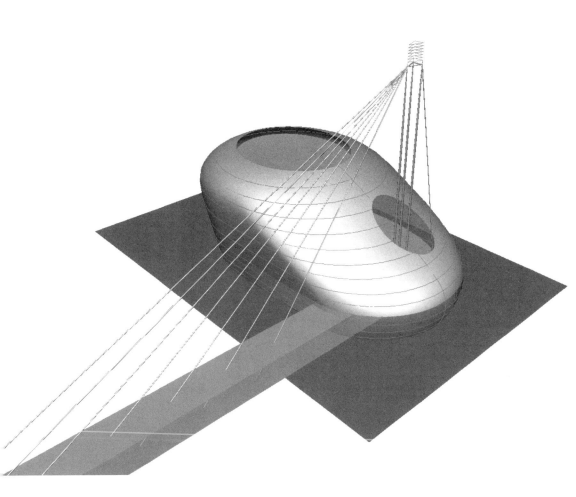

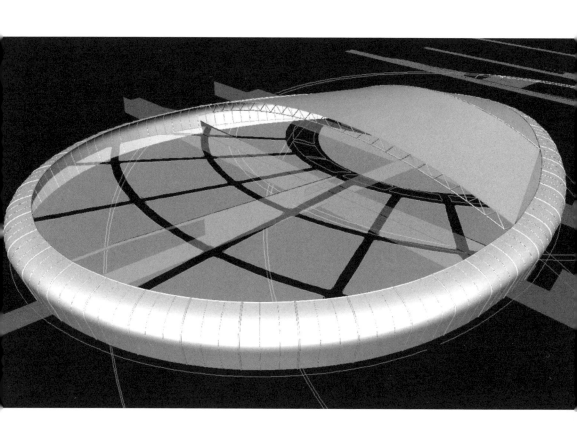

The 75,000-seat Agora

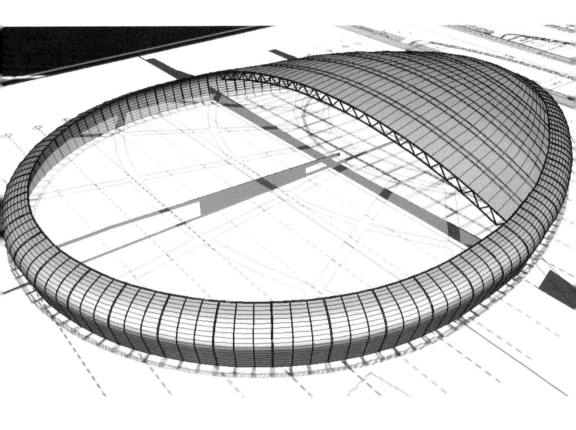

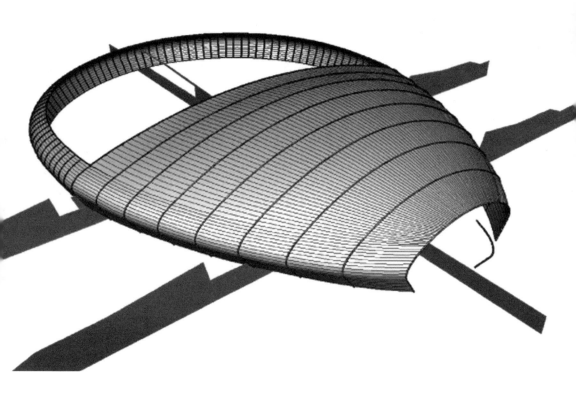

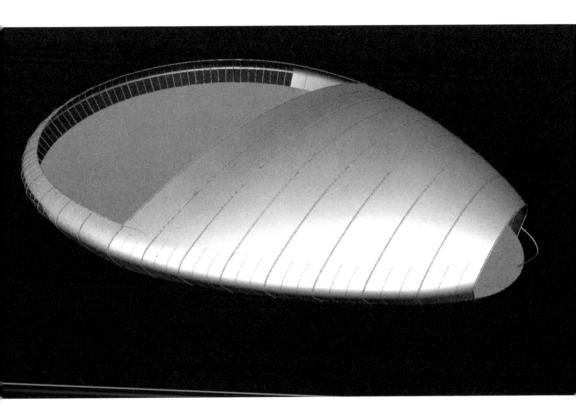

Toronto, Downsview Park, 2000

Natural Artifice

The coyote at the edge of digital mass culture

In 2000, we led a team in a competition to design Downsview Park, Canada's first national urban park, on the site of a former military base in Toronto. We felt challenged to create something radically different from another urban park, the Parc de La Villette, produced nearly 20 years earlier. The following chart was drawn up, highlighting the differences between the two projects:

1982 La Villette	**2000 Downsview**
19th-century archaeology	20th-century archaeology
slaughterhouses	airport landing strips
urban	suburban
Europe	America

Then we looked at the design potentialities of these differences:

discontinuous	continuous
superimpositions	contaminations
points, lines, surfaces	flows, ebbs, fields, zones
follies and galleries	spools and digits
solids	liquids
analog	digital
hardware	software
dead cows	live coyotes
tabula rasa	genius loci
critical mass	viscous, fingering
refraction	absorption
articulated	amorphous
common denominator	multiplier
dialectics	uncertainty principle
generators	attractors/basins of attraction
clocks	clouds
critical density	cross entropy
difference	self-similarity
specificity	hybrid
vectors	drifts
acceleration	duration
fixed points	fluctuation, relativity
certainty	probability
algebra	statistics
fractures	fractals
cubes	holes
spine	sponge
points	perimeters

The list in the right-hand column became our program.

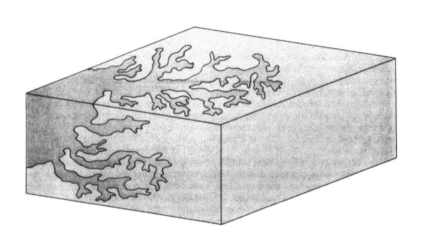

Fluidity of digits

The Digital and the Coyote

The aim of the design competition for Downsview Park was to develop a new landscape combining public use with a strong ecological dimension. Simultaneously a recreational space and a green space, it would mix "culture" with "nature." Yet culture and nature are elusive concepts today, when much culture leans toward entertainment and much nature towards the artificial.

On one hand, the park is to be located on the site of an obsolete military air base, part of which is still being used by Bombardier/de Havilland to test airplanes. It must integrate the airstrip as well as existing military sheds that are to be converted to cultural, recreational, and community uses. On the other hand, it is situated on a topographical divide between two large watersheds in an area where the logic of water flows informs much of the site design. Neither theme park nor wildlife preserve, the Downsview proposal does not seek renewal according to the conventions of traditional park compositions such as those of Calvert Vaux or Frederick Law Olmsted. The combination of advanced military technologies with water courses, flows, and streams suggests another fluid, liquid, digital sensibility. Airstrips, information centers, public performance spaces, Internet and World Wide Web access all point to a redefinition of received ideas about parks, nature, and recreation in a 21st-century setting where everything is "urban," even in the middle of the wilderness.

In short, the project confronts two realities—the digital and the wild—or (in homage to a creature encountered on an early-morning visit to the site), the digital and the coyote. The proposal mixes the two terms of the equation, so that, far from being in opposition, they permeate each other in a remarkably positive and fluid manner.

Digits, Spools, and Screens

Conceiving of any large spatial organization begins with a strategy, rather than a form. At Downsview, the strategy is to maximize, attract, and seduce. First, the presence and length of the perimeter is maximized. (Downsview is large—but not necessarily large enough to qualify as the largest urban park in Canada. Minus the corporate business area, the park is about the size of the Parc de la Villette in Paris, or five times smaller than Central Park in New York.) Digits—or fingers of nature—are added to maximize the perimeter, to serve both as a boundary and an extended definition, and to increase the interface between natural artifacts and cultural ones. This can be compared to the fractal phenomenon of viscous fingering, observed at the interface of two liquids between two glass plates, as one liquid invades the other.

The fractal dimension of all edges and interfaces in the park is a crucial element of our strategy. Semi-circular clearings—the "spools"—are located throughout the park and accommodate activities ranging from sports to education to mass events.

To give a common identity to the former industrial and military buildings on the site, large screens made of photographic fabric or electronic devices are attached to the building facades at various intervals. These digits, spools, and screens are the major physical and spatial means for defining and activating the park.

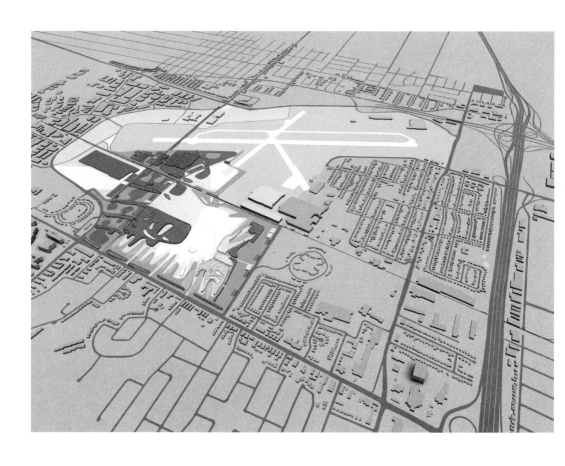

Aerial view from the southwest: Digital mass culture is juxtaposed with the emerging ecology of the wild where the folded cultural field meets the perimeter landscape of the coyote.

Screens, spools and digits: The perimeter landscape of earthworks, trees, and wild gardens
interlocks with the fingers at the edges. At their intersections are "pools" of wetland.

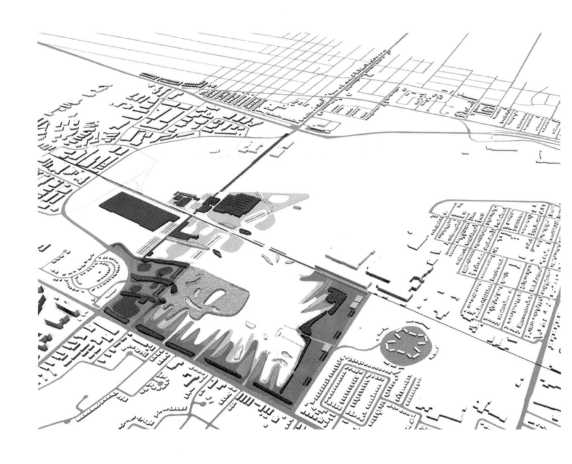

Digits, digital (defining edges)

Linking the edge to the center

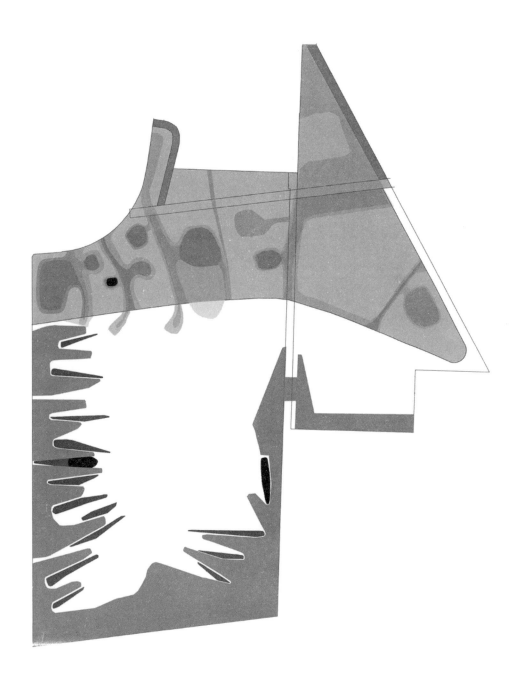

Earthwork system

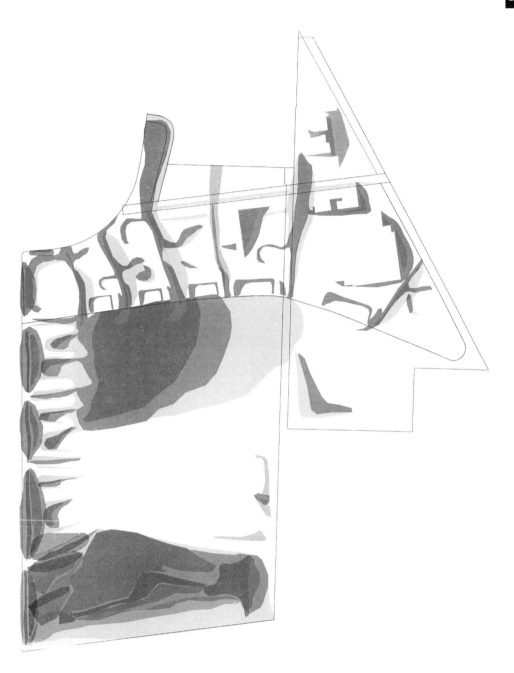

Microclimates

New York, Tri-Towers of Babel:
Questioning Ground Zero, 2002

Whose Context?

World Trade Center site: mid-1960s, 1973, 2002

September 11, 2001 was an attack not only on the World Trade Center or even America, but on the city itself. To address 9/11 required that we interrogate the very idea of the future city, rather than simply try to rebuild memories of the past or reconcile the demands of local interest groups and parties with financial stakes in the site. With this in mind, we began working in 2002 on a "counter-project" for Ground Zero. The aim was not to propose yet another plan for the site but, instead, to pose a set of critical questions that had gone unaddressed in the reconstruction debate, namely: What is this place for, and what role does it play in the future of New York and in the development of the cosmopolitan city? Should a new architecture for Ground Zero be specific to its circumstance and site, that is, deeply rooted in the events of 9/11? Or should it have a global reach and be a model for the evolving city of tomorrow?

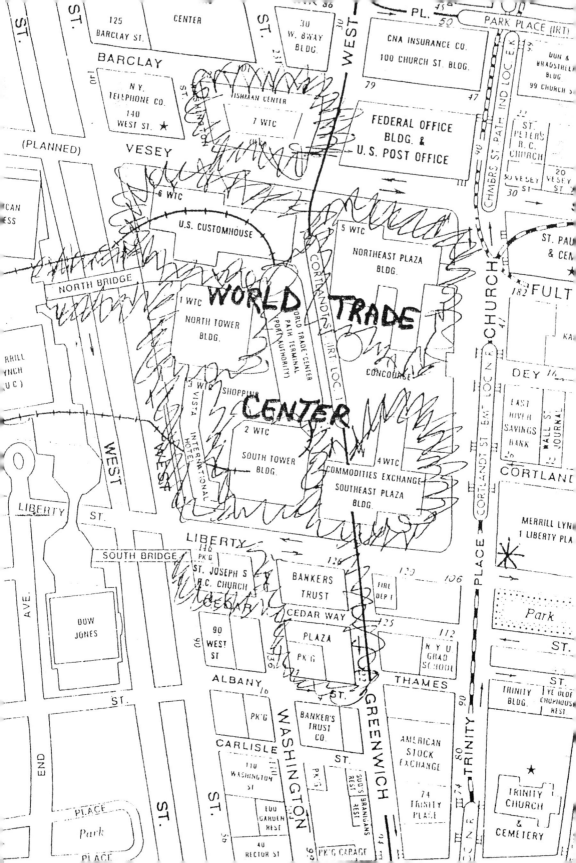

	YES	NO
Should the plan for Ground Zero be:		
A set piece, for example, a composition à la Rockefeller Center?	☐	☐
A "volumetric strategy," defining only zoning and bulk?	☐	☐
A skyline beacon, visible from a distance like the World Trade Center in 1973 or the Eiffel Tower?	☐	☐
A sacred void?	☐	☐
A new typology, not specific to the site but adaptable to it (including symbolically)—a generic or "ideal" type?	☐	☐
Something specific to the site and its recent tragic history?	☐	☐
Programmatically determinate—a project in which most activities are defined ahead of time?	☐	☐
Programmatically indeterminate—a plan that allows a variety of contents?	☐	☐
Does the downtown area as a whole play a role in the definition of the Ground Zero proposal? (Fragments throughout downtown, or taking down West Street?)	☐	☐
Is Ground Zero an autonomous piece with its own logic, while the rest of downtown has another logic of its own?	☐	☐
Is the site meant to be split—one part sacred, the other profane?	☐	☐

How to start?
How not to start?

This project is not about providing images or "designs."

Architects must first determine the context in which they operate.

Matrix

We began analytically, in an objective or rational way, with a matrix of possibilities extending from void to solid, from small to extra-large.

Whatever the size or configuration, each scheme inevitably confronts the idea of density. Whether low or high, density is an unavoidable dimension of the city.

The matrix does not express value judgments, only scenarios or typological permutations. The alternatives represented in the matrix, however, are not neutral. Many have strong ideological connotations. Moreover, no typological configuration has much relevance unless it is complemented by a program. Without excluding the viability of any of the other options, we eventually decided to focus on the Tri-Towers model, in the belief that the typology of the skyscraper might be a pertinent object of investigation. As a building type, the skyscraper had been stagnant for some time. Could we perhaps take it a step forward?

We decided not to do a project in the conventional sense, but rather, to attempt to generate a set of questions.

The fact that several months ahead of time, a number of these scenarios prefigured subsequent designs by others (09=SOM, 11 and 12=Libeskind, 14=Foster) is entirely coincidental.

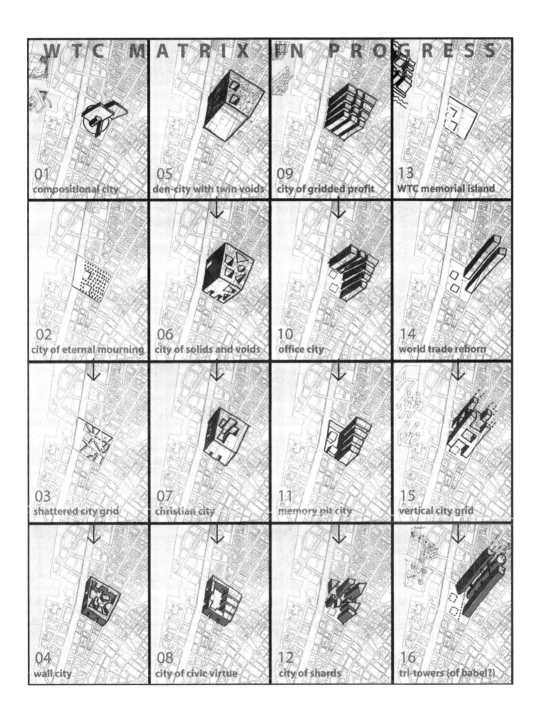

WTC MATRIX IN PROGRESS

01 compositional city

02 city of eternal mourning

03 shattered city grid

04 wall city

05 den-city with twin voids

06 city of solids and voids

07 christian city

08 city of civic virtue

09 city of gridded profit

10 office city

11 memory pit city

12 city of shards

13 WTC memorial island

14 world trade reborn

15 vertical city grid

16 tri-towers (of babel?)

Ground

The next step was to focus on the idea of the ground.

What is "ground"?
The opposite of "figure"?
The bedrock? Street level? (If so, which street?)
Which one of the above is Ground Zero?
Is "ground" continuous or discontinuous?
Is "ground" pedestrian or vehicular?
Is "ground" horizontal or oblique?

Endgeschoss? Parterre? Ground floor? *Rez-de-chaussée?*
In America, "first floor" means the ground floor. In all other cultures, it means the next floor above the ground. In the 21st century, is "ground" purely a mental construction? We eventually located the ground horizontally at the level of Church Street and extended it partially over the highway-like West Street, providing a new urban continuity between east and west.

We arbitrarily decided that in this project, "ground" meant public urban space, and that the "ground" was anywhere that could be accessed freely by all. Would we also have ground in the air?

Program

We next asked about program (namely, the set of planned activities to take place in a building or on a given site).

Who determines the program?

Market forces? Banks? Architects? Social planners? Community groups? Local residents? Insurance companies? Security forces? Tabloids? The governor? The mayor? The president? Major public institutions? Tourist demand? The owner? The leaseholder? The retailer? The tenant? Zoning resolutions? Multinational corporations? Artists and intellectuals? Trusted social and cultural voices? All of the above? None of the above?

We concluded that the program would be urban, characterized by a dense multiplicity of heterogeneous activities. Together, density and "mixity" define the urban condition. We proposed, polemically, that the site would contain spaces for working, living, and the arts, all mixing together above a transit node. The Tri-Towers of Babel would be a microcosm of the city itself.

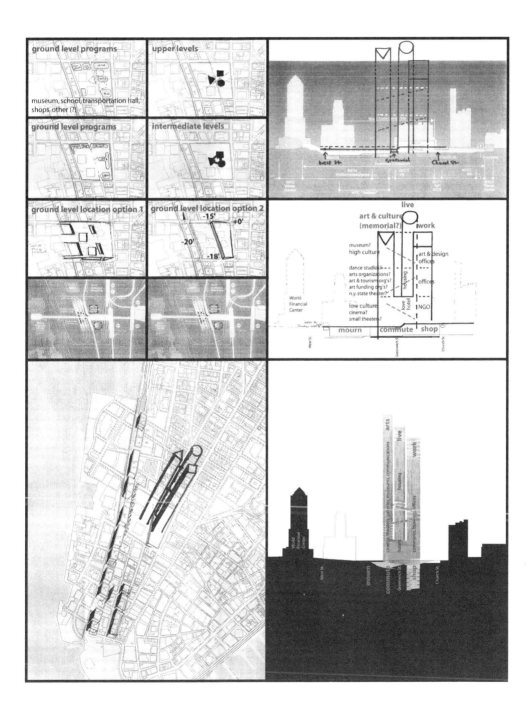

ground level programs

museum, school, transportation hall, shops, other (?)

ground level programs

ground level location option 1

ground level location option 2

upper levels

intermediate levels

-15' +0'
-20'
-18'

live
art & culture
(memorial?) work

museum?
high culture

art & design
offices

dance studios?
arts organizations?
art & tourism org's?
art funding org's?
n.y. state theater?

offices

low culture
cinema?
small theaters?

NGO

World
Financial
Center

mourn commute shop

arts
live
work

A project about movement: movement vectors within the proposed transit hub

Movement vectors on West Street

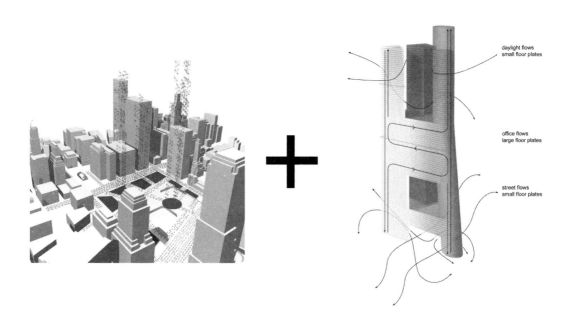

daylight flows
small floor plates

office flows
large floor plates

street flows
small floor plates

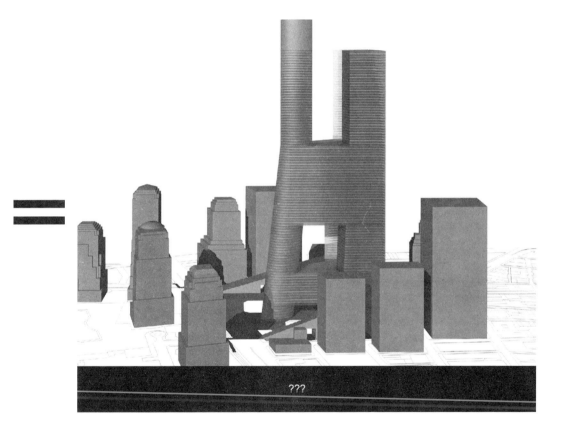

???

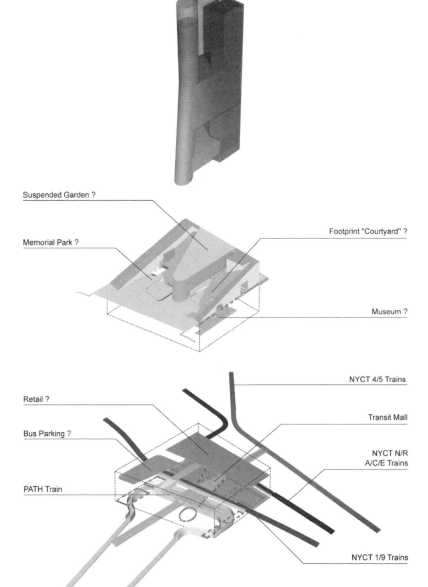

Suspended Garden ?

Footprint "Courtyard" ?

Memorial Park ?

Museum ?

NYCT 4/5 Trains

Retail ?

Transit Mall

Bus Parking ?

NYCT N/R
A/C/E Trains

PATH Train

NYCT 1/9 Trains

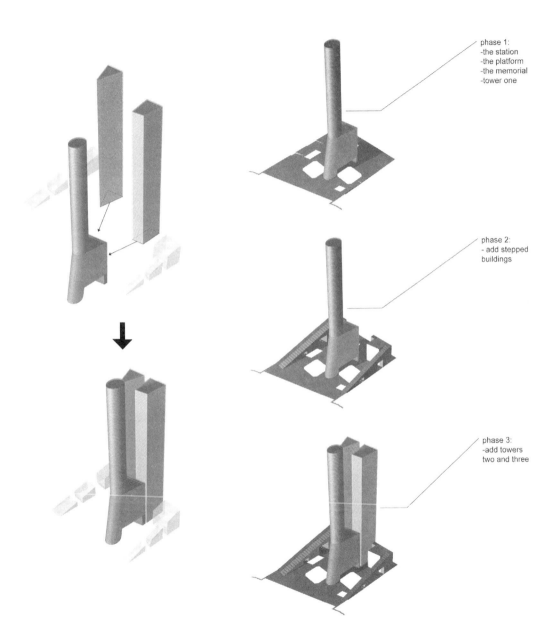

phase 1:
-the station
-the platform
-the memorial
-tower one

phase 2:
- add stepped
buildings

phase 3:
-add towers
two and three

Phasing

**Questioning Program:
A Multitude of Possible Answers**

Below is a list of programs that have been proposed by various architects, planners, government officials, civic organizations, and other interested parties for the Ground Zero site:

Arts (housing, studios, and exhibition spaces for artists and writers)
Aviary
Broadcast tower
Cafés
Cathedral
Chapel
Cinemas
Classrooms
Community/senior center
Conference centers
Cultural center
Forest
Gardens
Hotel
Housing
Information center
Infrastructure
Labyrinths
Library
Mausoleum
Meditation space
Memorial
Monument (for example, obelisk)
Museum
Museum of the Family of Man

Museum of Freedom and Tolerance
Offices
Planetarium
Playground
Pools
Restaurants
Retail
Observation tower/decks
Opera house for New York State Opera
Park
School
Stock exchange
Theater
Transit hub
University
Windmills and water turbines
World Citizens Conference Center
World Cultural Center
World Peace Center

Why not include them all?

Regardless of which programs are eventually selected, density and "mixity" make up the city.

What if...?

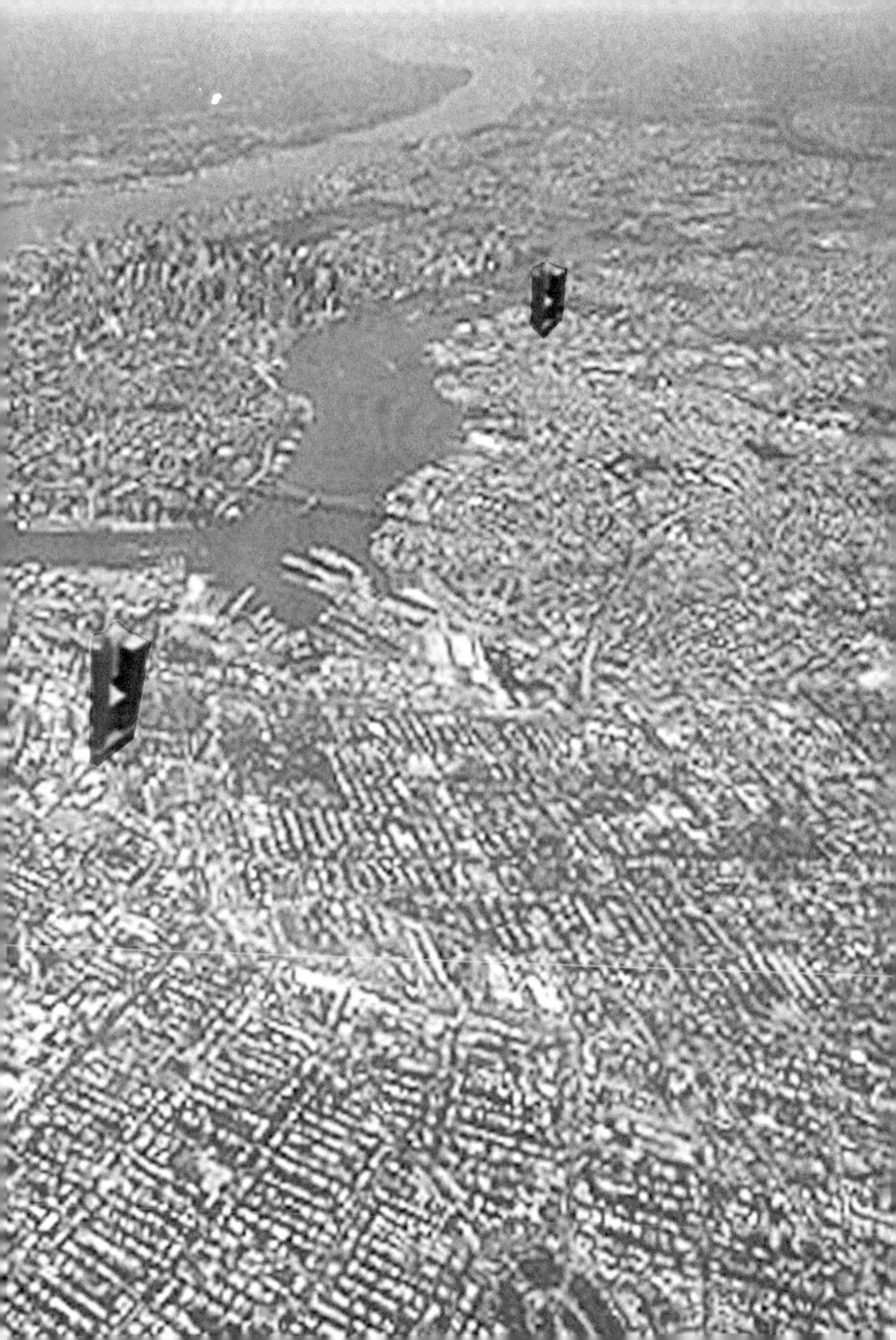

Questioning Singularity

	YES	NO
No design should be prisoner of its own context. There should be no cult of the unique.	☐	☐
After being tested throughout the world for years, the Tri-Towers finally reached Manhattan.	☐	☐
First conceived for Ground Zero, the Tri-Towers proved so successful that they were exported throughout the world.	☐	☐

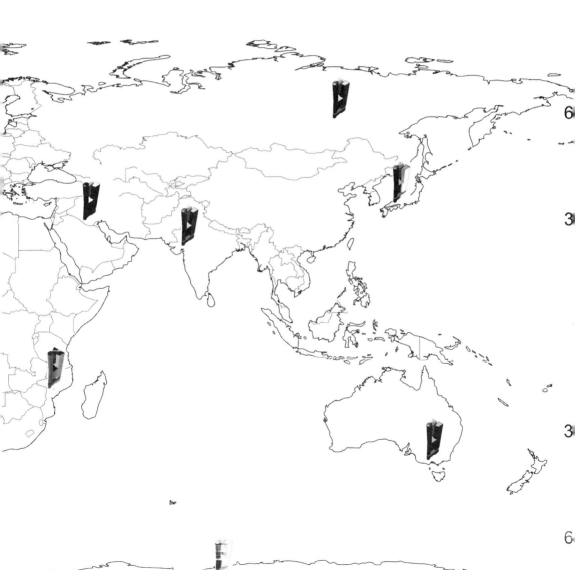

Questioning Context

Whatever their functions, objects and designs do not operate in a vacuum. Buildings are located not only in New York, Paris, or Tokyo but also in a larger cultural context that gives them sense. The early Russian filmmaker Lev Kuleshov illustrated this point nearly one hundred years ago. Kuleshov placed images of the motionless face of an actor in a variety of backgrounds—a stormy night, a crowded railway station, a sunny pasture. He then asked the audience to read the emotions of the actor from these juxtapositions. Although the actor's expression never changed, the audience interpreted his emotions differently with each change of scenery. Similarly, in architecture, context and frame are as important as the inhabited object itself.

21st-Century City of Eternal Memory

21st-Century City of Spectacle

21st-Century City of Patriots

21st-Century City of Friendship and Brotherhood

Beijing, Factory 798, 2003–

Superposition

At the beginning of the 21st century, China is witness to one of the most rapid developments of any civilization in history. Unleashing extraordinary resources, it has simultaneously generated substantial destruction of traditional Chinese cities, with their low-rise *hutong* alleys, replaced almost overnight by high-rise residential blocks, at the cost of disappearing public space and communal life.

Numerous Western architects, eager to participate in the new building boom, have helped to plan these developments, oblivious to the social consequences of the new cityscape. The project for Factory 798 in China's capital city presented a first opportunity to explore some alternative strategies.

Program

In recent years, a vibrant art community has emerged in a mixed-use and industrial neighborhood in northeastern Beijing. Artists' studios, lofts, galleries, and bookstores have taken over the spaces of Factory 798, an old manufacturing facility built in the 1950s. Now developers have proposed that Factory 798 and its surrounding fabric be demolished and the site developed into one million square meters of residential towers, threatening the livelihood of the existing community. Although the site's current residents have protested the new plan, the fate of Factory 798 lies with the Chinese government, which ultimately will decide whether to authorize the developers' proposal.

According to the developers' program, of the one million square meters of new construction, 70 percent will be usable space, with 30 percent going to circulation and infrastructure. This may yield 5,600 units of housing in addition to various commercial spaces.

The question is whether it is possible to fulfill the massive requirement for new housing and at the same time preserve the existing fabric of small art galleries, artists' studios, and local community life. It is at this juncture that we venture the thesis presented in this project. We suggest that alternative developers be sought who are ready explore new forms of urbanism.

In-between(s)

Acknowledging the inevitable confrontation of old and new, the following proposal is intended as an alternative to the wholesale demolition of the existing arts facilities. Instead, the existing buildings are allowed to remain at ground level. Over these is superimposed a new high-density residential quarter, a horizontal city hovering 25 meters above the ground, with light courts open to the galleries below. The project, thus, is about a strategy of in-betweens: spaces between the old and the new, below and above, east and west.

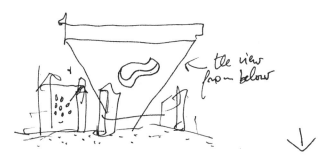

the view from below

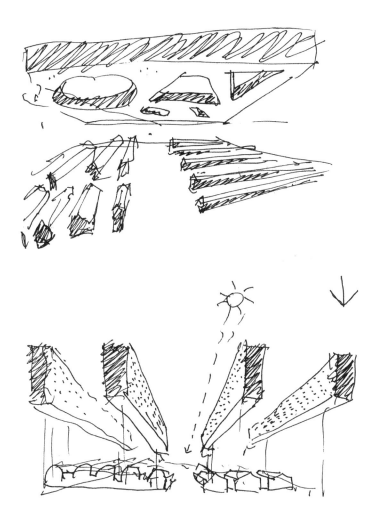

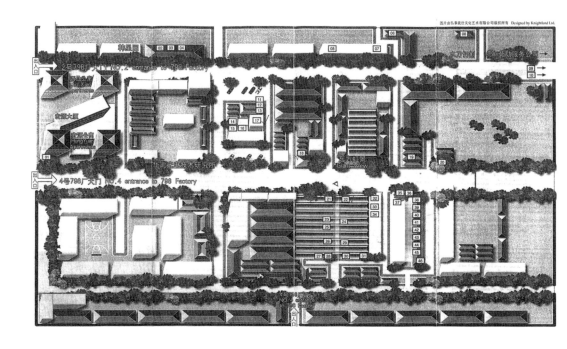

Plan and photographs of existing facilities

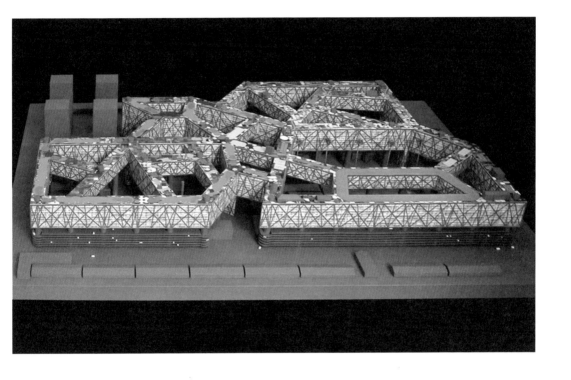

The required one million square meters of residential space hover 25 meters over the existing facilities.

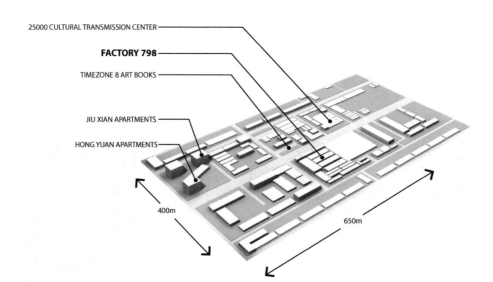

25000 CULTURAL TRANSMISSION CENTER

FACTORY 798

TIMEZONE 8 ART BOOKS

JIU XIAN APARTMENTS

HONG YUAN APARTMENTS

400m

650m

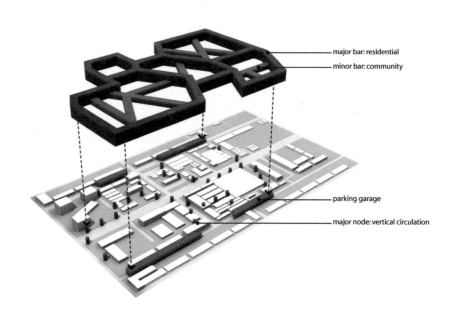

major bar: residential
minor bar: community

parking garage

major node: vertical circulation

Views from the street

Massing studies: How to distribute one million square meters of housing? Variations on a grid 25 meters above ground were explored.

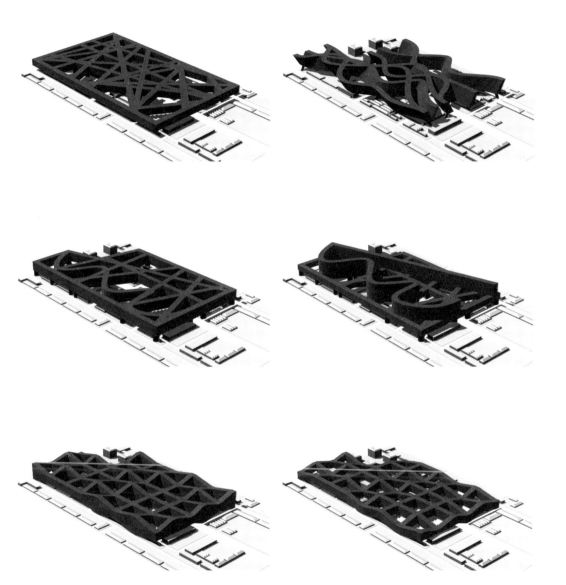

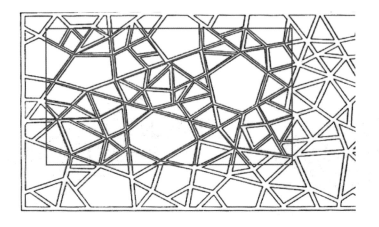

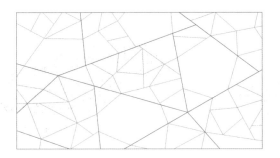

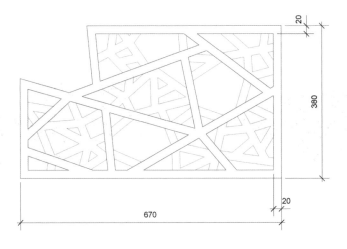

The lattice presented an ideal arrangement.

Concept of the Lattice

lattice

1a. An open framework made of strips of metal, wood, or similar material overlapped or overlaid in a regular, usually crisscross pattern.

1b. A structure, such as a window, screen, or trellis, made of or containing such a framework.

2. Something, such as a decorative motif or heraldic bearing, that resembles an open, patterned framework.

Physics

3a. A regular, periodic configuration of points, particles, or objects throughout an area or a space, especially the arrangement of ions or molecules in a crystalline solid.

3b. The spatial arrangement of fissionable and nonfissionable materials in a nuclear reactor.[1]

The lattice is a well-known decorative motif in classical Chinese architecture. However, it is also an important concept in the fields of physics, mathematics, cryptography, and the military. Defined as a partially ordered set of objects, the lattice is a system that is simultaneously ordered and flexible.

In the project for the Factory 798 site, the concept of the lattice arises out of two constraints: first, the need for a structural grid and a regular system of vertical circulation/egress, and second, the requirement that the new structure touch down at points that interfere minimally with the existing fabric. One constraint is orderly—a maximum egress span of 50 meters—and the other is disorderly, that is, dictated by the vagaries of existing circumstances. The lattice is the ideal structure for mediating between these two constraints.

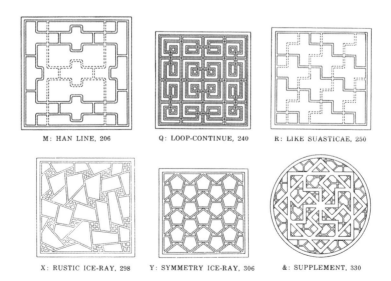

M: HAN LINE, 206   Q: LOOP-CONTINUE, 240   R: LIKE SUASTICAE, 250

X: RUSTIC ICE-RAY, 298   Y: SYMMETRY ICE-RAY, 306   &: SUPPLEMENT, 330

1. *Merriam-Webster's Collegiate Dictionary*, 10th ed. (Springfield, Mass.: Merriam-Webster, Incorporated, 1993).

我们可以同时共有新和旧！

拯救工厂798！

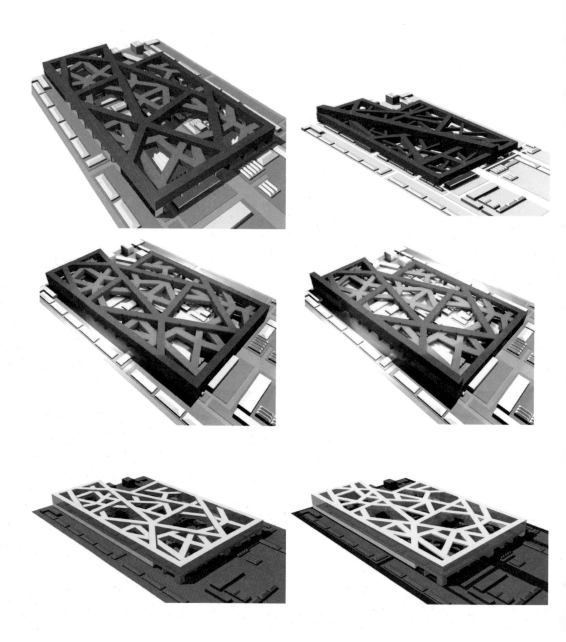

The lattice permitted complete freedom to adjust housing densities in relation to ground-level activities.

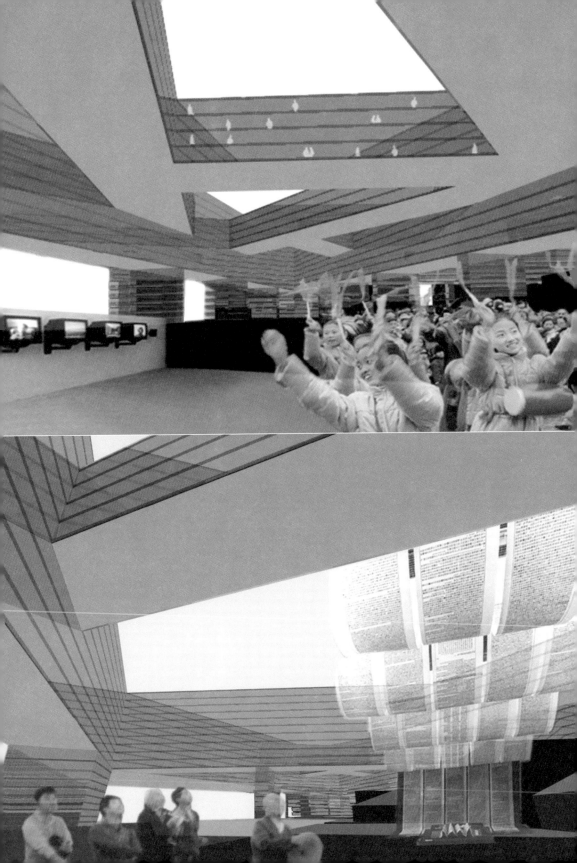

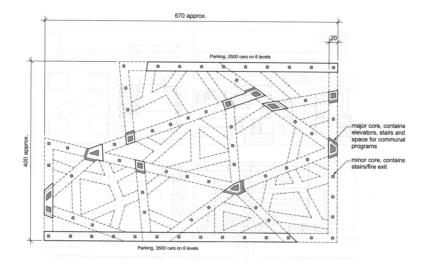

670 approx.

20

400 approx.

Parking, 2500 cars on 6 levels

major core, contains
elevators, stairs and
space for communal
programs

minor core, contains
stairs/fire exit

Parking, 3500 cars on 6 levels

Street level

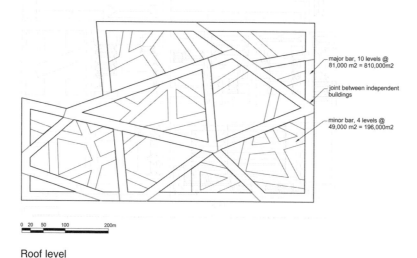

major bar, 10 levels @
81,000 m2 = 810,000m2

joint between independent
buildings

minor bar, 4 levels @
49,000 m2 = 196,000m2

0 20 50 100   200m

Roof level

The lattice also offered full flexibility in bringing vertical connections to the ground wherever
needed, without destroying the existing buildings.

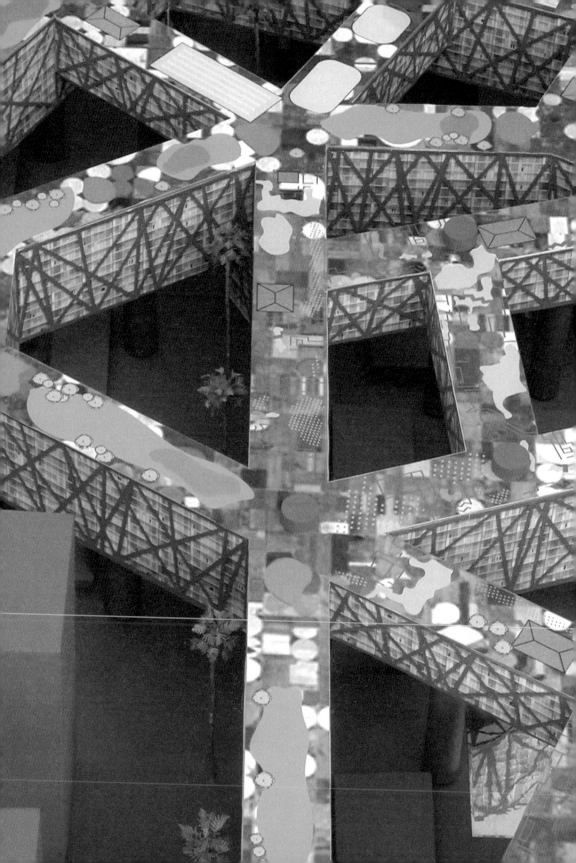

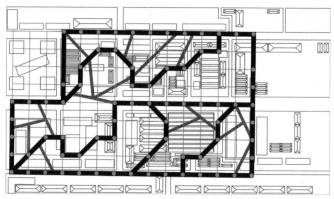

Orthogonal 50 m x 50 m grid

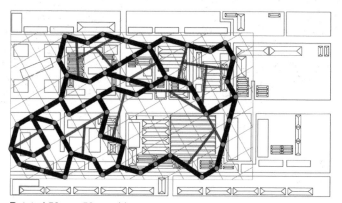

Rotated 50 m x 50 m grid

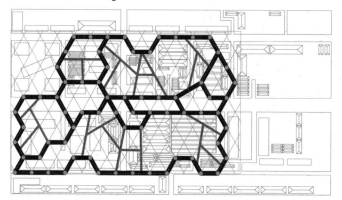

Parallelogram 50 m x 50 m grid

Lattice studies: The lattice can be shaped in many possible ways.

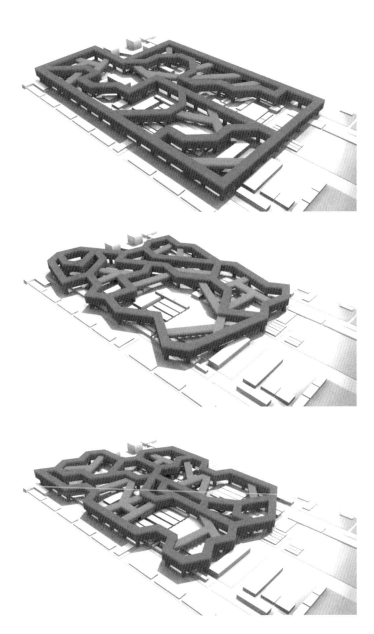

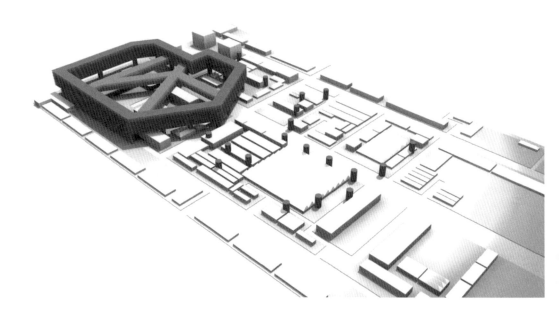

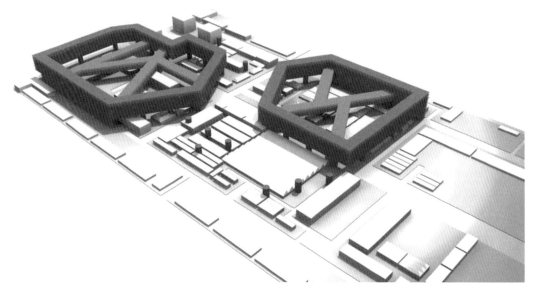

Construction sequence: one possible scenario

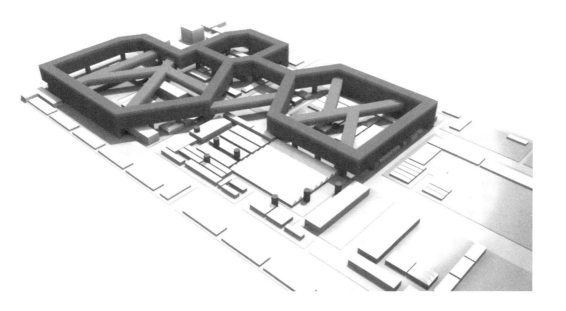

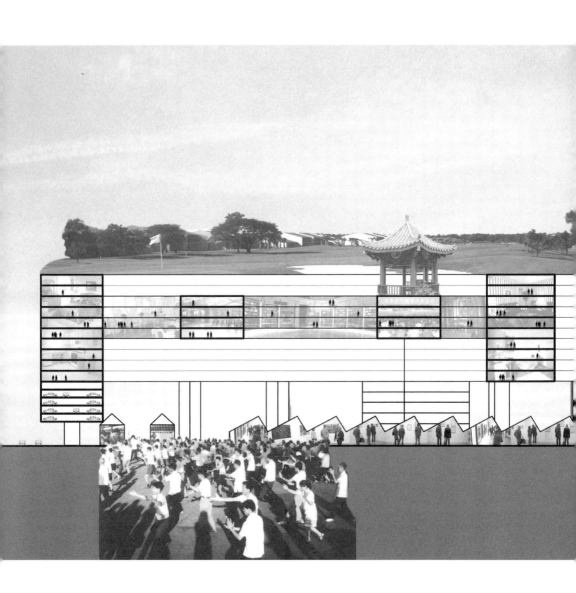

Locating the program of activities: private spaces in the air, gardens on the roofs, public spaces on the ground

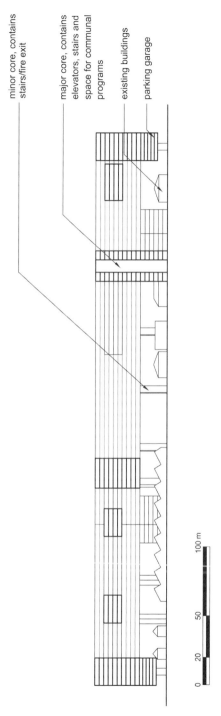

minor core, contains stairs/fire exit

major core, contains elevators, stairs and space for communal programs

existing buildings

parking garage

0 20 50 100 m

The building contains one million square meters of space for over 10,000 inhabitants. Major (ten-story) and minor (four-story) bars are supported by pylons and hover 25 meters above the ground.

古典的?	共产主义的?	资本主义的?
鸟类饲养场	人民公园	草地
庙宇	游泳池	瑜伽
假山水	共同锻炼	私有艺廊
园林	人民文化堂	墓园
竹林	陵墓	餐厅
映水池	共同厨房	办公室
太极	工厂	电视塔
京剧院	毛主席铜像	健身俱乐部
坟墓	运动场	电影院
茶室	电影院	游戏场
农地		高尔夫球场
宝塔		零售商
		迪斯科
		会议中心

Classical?
Aviary
Temple
Rock garden
Scholar's garden
Bamboo grove
Reflecting pool
Tai chi
Traditional opera house
Tea house
Farm
Pagoda

Communist?
People's park
Swimming pool
Communal exercise
People's culture palace
Mausoleum
Communal kitchen
Factory
Mao statue
Gymnasium
Cinema

Capitalist?
Lawn
Jacuzzi
Yoga
Private art gallery
Restaurant
Office
TV tower
Health club
Cinema
Playground
Golf course
Retail
Disco
Conference center

Programs

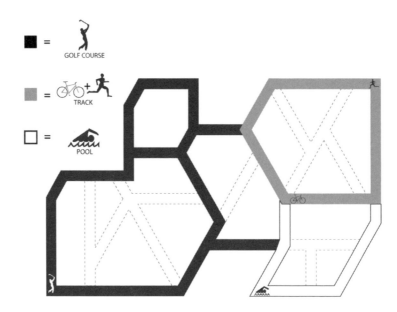

= GOLF COURSE

= TRACK

= POOL

FACTORY 798 : ROOF LATTICE
LEVEL: +55 m

0   20   100   200m

= RESIDENTIAL

= COMMUNITY

FITNESS CENTER · FOOD COURT

TEA HOUSE · BAR · DISCO · OPERA

CINEMA · THEATER

TEMPLE

MARKET

NURSING HOME

PUBLIC SCHOOL

DAY CARE

OFFICE

CONFERENCE CENTER

FACTORY 798 : PROGRAM LATTICE
LEVEL : +25m to +55m

0   20   100   200m

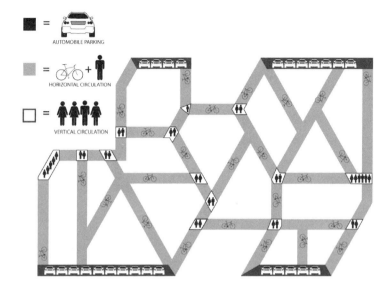

FACTORY 798 : CIRCULATION + NODE PLAN
LEVEL : +20m

0   20   100   200m

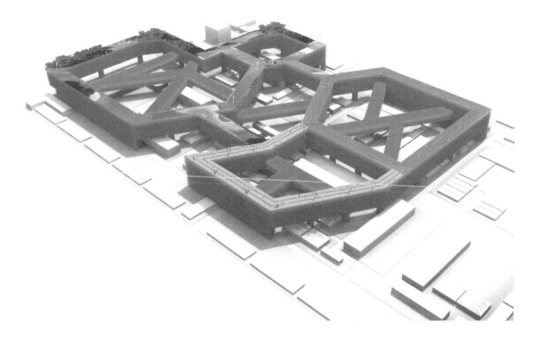

Gardens, swimming pools, golf courses, and a running track on the roof

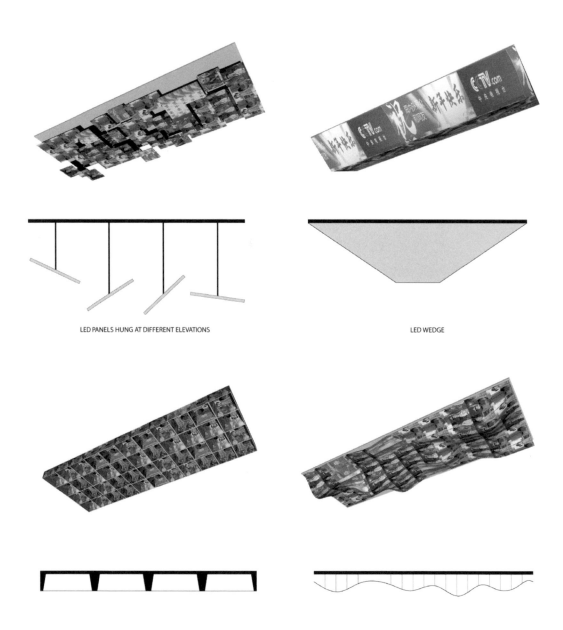

LED PANELS HUNG AT DIFFERENT ELEVATIONS

LED WEDGE

Underneath the lattice: surfaces for lights and graphics

Theory is a practice,
a practice of concepts
*
Practice is a theory,
a theory of contexts

New York, Urban Glass House
Bernard Tschumi, Andrew Vrana, Johanne Riegels Oestergaard, Philippos Photiadis

Angoulême, Exhibition Center
Bernard Tschumi, Véronique Descharrières, Kim Starr, Joel Rutten, Jonathan Chace, William Feuerman, Valentin Bontjes van Beek
Engineering and Cost Estimator: Technip TPS; *Acoustics:* Cabinet CIAL

Geneva, Vacheron Constantin Headquarters
Bernard Tschumi, Véronique Descharrières, Joel Rutten, Alex Reid, Matteo Vigano, Cristina Devizzi, Jean-Jacques Hubert, Antoine Santiard, Yann Brossier, Ludovic Ghirardi, Nicolas Martin, Phu Hoang, Jane Kim, Jonathan Chace, Adam Dayem, Robert Holton, Valentin Bontjes van Beek, Michaela Metcalfe, Justin Moore, Allis Chee, Joel Aviles, Liz Kim
Structural: ARUP (Matt King) and SGI; *HVAC:* Enerconom; *Electrical:* Scherler; *Facade:* BCS; *Landscape:* Michel Desvigne; *Mechanical:* ARUP (Nigel Tonks), *Wood:* Dic Dauner; *Construction Administration:* Ortech; *Bidding Documents:* EMA, Geneva

Strasbourg, Concert Hall
Bernard Tschumi, Anne Save de Beaurecueil, Véronique Descharrières, Jean-Jacques Hubert, Antoine Santiard, Dominic Leong, Sarrah Khan, Robert Holton
Engineering and Cost Estimator: Technip TPS; *Theater:* Scène; *Acoustic:* Cabinet CIAL

Pittsburgh, Carnegie Science Center
Bernard Tschumi, Kim Starr, Jonathan Chace, Anne Save de Beaurecueil, William Feuerman, Robert Holton, Valentin Bontjes van Beek, Joel Rutten, Kate Linker, Liz Kim
Structural: ARUP (Matt King); *Mechanical:* ARUP (Nigel Tonks)

Limoges, Concert Hall
Bernard Tschumi, Véronique Descharrières, Joel Rutten, Jean-Jacques Hubert, Antoine Santiard, Matthieu Gotz, Alex Reid, Dominic Leong, Sarrah Khan, Anne Save de Beaurecueil, Chong-zi Chen, Michaela Metcalfe, Alan Kusov
Construction Supervision and Local Architect: Atelier 4
Structural and Mechanical: Technip TPS, *Metal Structure:* Cabinet Jaillet Rouby, *Facades:* Hugh Dutton (HDA), Paris; *Wood Structure:* Natterer SA; *Theater:* Scène; *Landscape:* Michel Desvigne; *Cost Estimator:* Bureau Michel Forgue; *Security:* PCA, *Environmental:* Michel Raoust; *Acoustic:* Cabinet CIAL

Vendée, International Sports Center
Bernard Tschumi, Véronique Descharrières, Robert Holton, Jonathan Chace, William Feuerman, Jesse Seppi, Valentin Bontjes van Beek
Engineering and Cost Estimator: Technip TPS; *Acoustics:* Cabinet CIAL; *Theater:* Scène

Rome, Italian Space Agency
Bernard Tschumi, Kim Starr, Anne Save de Beaurecueil, Valentin Bontjes van Beek, Robert Holton, Johanne Riegels Oestergaard, Maia Small, Joel Rutten
Structural: ARUP (Matt King); *Mechanical:* ARUP (Nigel Tonks)

Antwerp, Museum aan de Stroom
Bernard Tschumi, Joel Rutten, Valentin Bontjes van Beek, Andrea Day, Robert Holton, Kate Linker, Johanne Riegels Oestergaard, Anne Save de Beaurecueil, Maia Small, Kim Starr
Consultant: ARUP (Matt King and Nigel Tonks)

São Paulo, Museum of Contemporary Art
Bernard Tschumi, Anne Save de Beaurecueil, Kim Starr, Jonathan Chace, William Feuerman, Joel Rutten, Robert Holton, Valentin Bontjes van Beek, Thomas Goodwill, Kate Linker, Liz Kim
Structural: ARUP (Matt King); *Mechanical:* ARUP (Nigel Tonks)

Troy, Electronic Media and Performing Arts Center
Bernard Tschumi, Anne Save de Beaurecueil, Kim Starr, Joel Rutten, Robert Holton, Valentin Bontjes van Beek, Jonathan Chace, Liz Kim, Thomas Goodwill, William Feuerman
Structural: ARUP (Matt King); *Mechanical:* ARUP (Nigel Tonks)

New York, Museum for African Art
Version 1
Bernard Tschumi, Kim Starr, Anne Save de Beaurecueil, Jonathan Chace, Valentin Bontjes van Beek, Johanne Riegels Oestergaard, Joel Rutten, Robert Holton, Andrea Day, Kate Linker, Liz Kim, Matt Kelley, Michaela Metcalfe, Georgia Papadavid
Structural: LERA; *MEP:* ARUP (Nigel Tonks); *Glass Structure:* ARUP (Matt King); *Facade:* Israel Berger; *Interiors:* J. Yolande Daniels

Version 2
Bernard Tschumi, Kim Starr, Adam Dayem, Matthew Hufft, William Feuerman, Jane Kim, Irene Cheng, Michaela Metcalfe, Chong-zi Chen, Phu Hoang, Sarrah Khan, Dominic Leong, Joel Rutten, Anne Save de Beaurecueil, Eva Sopeoglou

Cincinnati, Athletic Center
Bernard Tschumi, Kim Starr, Phu Hoang, Robert Holton, Jane Kim, Nicolas Martin, Eva Sopeoglou, Joel Aviles, Chong-zi Chen, Irene Cheng, Jonathan Chace, Adam Dayem, William Feuerman, Thomas Goodwill, Daniel Holguin, Matthew Hufft, Michaela Metcalfe, Valentin Bontjes van Beek, Allis Chee, Justin Moore
Associate Architects: Glaserworks (Art Hupp, Kevin Morris, Dave Zelman, and Mark Thurnauer)
Structural: THP and ARUP (Matt King and Ricardo Pittella); *MEP:* ARUP (Nigel Tonks and Brian Streby) and Heapy Engineering; *Landscape:* Human Nature; *Museum Design:* Eva Maddox

Athens, New Acropolis Museum

Bernard Tschumi Architects: Bernard Tschumi, Joel Rutten, Adam Dayem, Jane Kim, Aristotelis Dimitrakopoulos, Kim Starr, Anne Save de Beaurecueil, Joel Aviles, Valentin Bontjes van Beek, Jonathan Chace, Allis Chee, Thomas Goodwill, Robert Holton, Liz Kim, Kate Linker, Michaela Metcalfe, Justin Moore, Georgia Papadavid, Cristina Devizzi, Véronique Descharrières, Kriti Siderakis

Michael Photiadis Associates, Athens: Michael Photiadis, George Criparacos, Nikos Bakalbassis, Phillipos Photiadis

Structural: ARUP, New York (Leo Argiris) and ADK; *HVAC:* MMB; *Electrical:* Mechaniki Geostatiki; *Lighting:* ARUP, London

Nice, Sophia-Antipolis Campus

Bernard Tschumi, Phu Hoang, Irene Cheng, Adam Dayem, William Feuerman, Matthew Hufft, Jane Kim, Michaela Metcalfe, Antoine Santiard, Véronique Descharrières
Engineering and Cost Estimator: Technip TPS

Paris, Expo 2004

Bernard Tschumi, Véronique Descharrières, Luca Merlini, Anne Save de Beaurecueil, Jean-Jacques Hubert, Antoine Santiard, Cristina Devizzi, Matteo Vigano, Ido Avissar, Sami Tannoury, Yann Brossier, Sylviane Brossard, Daniel Holguin, Nicolas Martin, Lihi Gerstner, Michaela Metcalfe, Justin Moore, Jonathan Tremba
Master Plan: Luca Merlini; *Landscape:* Michel Desvigne; *Cost Estimator:* Cabinet Fouché; *Exhibition:* Scène; *Acoustic:* Cabinet CIAL; *Structural:* RFR; *Infrastructure:* Beture + JMI, Technip TPS

Toronto, Downsview Park

Bernard Tschumi, Robert Holton, Maia Small, Valentin Bontjes van Beek
Toronto: Dereck Revington Studio and Sterling Finlayson Architects
Landscape: Gunta Mackars

New York, Tri-Towers of Babel: Questioning Ground Zero

Bernard Tschumi, Irene Cheng, Adam Dayem, William Feuerman, Anne Save de Beaurecueil, Daniel Holguin, Michaela Metcalfe, Allis Chee, Jonathan Chace
Consultant: LERA (William Faschan)

Beijing, Factory 798

Bernard Tschumi, Irene Cheng, Adam Dayem, Matthew Hufft, Casey Crawmer, Adam Marcus, Amy Yang

The projects in Angoulême, Geneva, Strasbourg, Limoges, and Nice were coordinated by the Paris office, Bernard Tschumi urbanistes Architectes (BTuA), led by Véronique Descharrières, Architect, with Sylviane Brossard, Administrator. The projects in Pittsburgh, Rome, Antwerp, São Paulo, Troy, Cincinnati, Athens, Toronto, and Beijing were coordinated by the New York office, Bernard Tschumi Architects (BTA).

Project List

2004

- Renault, Ile Seguin, Facade Envelope, Paris, France *(competition)*
- Interactive Learning Center, Phase II, Alésia, France *(competition: first prize)*
- Sophia-Antipolis Campus Master Plan, Nice, France *(competition)*
- Residential Tower, Lower East Side, New York, New York
- *Biennale X International Exhibition*, International Pavilion, Venice, Italy *(exhibition)*
- *First Architectural Biennial Beijing,* International Architects Pavilion *(exhibition)*
- *The New Acropolis Museum,* Thessaloniki and Athens, Greece *(exhibition)*

2003

- Interface Flon, Phase II, Lausanne, Switzerland *(competition, 1988: first prize)*
- Museum for African Art, Phase II, New York, New York
- Concert Hall, Strasbourg, France *(competition)*
- Concert Hall, Limoges, France *(competition: first prize)*
- Concert Hall, Dijon, France *(competition)*
- OMC/WTO Headquarters, Geneva, Switzerland *(competition)*
- Museum of Contemporary Art, Yerevan, Armenia *(competition)*
- Factory 798, Beijing, China *(study)*
- *Concepts vs. Contexts,* Tyler Gallery, Philadelphia *(exhibition)*
- *The New Acropolis Museum,* The Onassis Foundation, New York *(exhibition)*

2002

- World Trade Center Design Diary *(study)*
- Interactive Learning Center, Phase I, Alésia, France *(feasibility study)*
- University Campus, Troyes, France
- Cultural and Administrative Center, Montreal, Canada
- *Biennale IX International Exhibition*, International Pavilion, Venice, Italy *(exhibition)*

2001

- Expo 2004, Paris, France *(competition: first place)*
- University of Cincinnati Athletic Center, Cincinnati, Ohio
- Museum of Contemporary Art, São Paulo, Brazil *(competition: first prize)*
- Vacheron Constantin Headquarters and Watch Factory, Geneva, Switzerland *(competition: first prize)*
- Palais du Sport, Ville d'Issy-les-Moulineaux, France *(competition)*
- Cité Europe-Méditerranée, Marseilles, France *(feasibility study)*
- Electronic Media and Performing Arts Center, Troy, New York *(competition)*
- American Museum of Natural History, New York, New York *(study)*
- FEIG, Geneva, Switzerland *(competition)*
- International Sports Center, Vendeé, France *(competition)*
- *Folds, Blobs + Boxes*, Carnegie Museum of Art, Pittsburgh, Pennsylvania *(exhibition)*

2000

- Exposition Center, Angoulême, France *(competition)*
- New Acropolis Museum, Athens, Greece *(competition: first prize)*
- Carnegie Science Center, Pittsburgh, Pennsylvania *(competition)*

- Museum for African Art, New York, New York *(competition: first prize)*
- *Biennale VIII International Exhibition*, International Pavilion, Venice, Italy *(exhibition)*
- Italian Space Agency, Rome, Italy *(competition)*
- Downsview Park, Toronto, Canada *(competition)*
- Museum aan de Stroom, Antwerp, Belgium *(competition)*
- Velodrome, Aulnay, France *(competition)*
- Cité Internationale, Lyon, France *(competition)*
- WIPO, Geneva, Switzerland *(competition)*
- Urban Glass House, New York, New York *(study)*

All projects and bibliographical information prior to 2000 are included in the first two volumes of *Event-Cities*.

Yerevan Museum of Contemporary Art, Armenia, 2003 *(competition)*

Books, Catalogs, and Selected Articles by Bernard Tschumi

2000

Event-Cities 2. Cambridge and London: The MIT Press, 2000.

"The City." *Time* (New York) 155, no. 7 (21 February 2000), pp. 86–87.

"Bodies from Outer Space." In Andreas Papadakis, ed. *New Architecture UK2K.* London: New Architecture Group Limited, January 2000, p. 17.

2001

Glass Ramps/Glass Walls: Deviations from the Normative. London: Architectural Association, 2001. (Coauthored with Hugh Dutton and Jesse Reiser)

"Passing Time in Space, Airports, and Urban Phenomena." In Cynthia C. Davidson, ed. *Anything.* New York and Cambridge: Anyone Corp. and The MIT Press, 2001, pp. 18–23.

2002

Bernard Tschumi, L'architettura della Disgiunzione. Michele Costanzo, ed. Rome: Testo e Immagine, 2002.

Virtuael. Barcelona: Actar, 2002.

2003

Bernard Tschumi. Giovanni Damiani, ed. Milan: Skira, 2003; London: Thames and Hudson, 2003. (Includes essays by K. Michael Hays and Giovanni Damiani, and an interview with Marco De Michelis)

"Bernard Tschumi: Vectors & Envelopes." Joohee Bong, ed. *Contemporary Architecture* (Seoul), November 2003 (special issue).

INDEX Architecture. Cambridge and London: MIT Press, 2003. (Coedited with Matthew Berman)

OSU Source Book In Architecture 3: Bernard Tschumi / Zenith de Rouen. Todd Gannon and Jeffrey Kipnis, eds. New York: The Monacelli Press, 2003.

The State of Architecture at the Beginning of the 21st Century. New York: The Monacelli Press, 2003. (Coedited with Irene Cheng)

Tri-Towers of Babel: Questioning Ground Zero. New York: Columbia Books of Architecture, 2003.

2000

"A Class Act for Columbia University." *Metals in Construction* (New York), Summer 2000, pp. 34–37.

Bevan, Robert. "All Things to All Men." *Building Design* (London), no. 1444 (9 June 2000), p. 8.

"Architecte: Bernard Tschumi." *Télérama Hors-série* (France), Summer 2000, pp. 34–35.

"Architektonische Verknüpfung von Stadtetagen." *Werk, Bauen, + Wohnen* (Germany), no. 12 (December 2000), pp. 54–57.

"Best of 2000." *Artforum International* (New York) 39, no. 4 (December 2000), p. 41.

Baldwin, Deborah. "Paris Blooms." *France Magazine* (Washington, D.C.), no. 53 (Spring 2000), pp. 20–21.

"Bernard Tschumi." *d'Architectures* (Paris), no. 102 (May 2000), pp. 24–29.

"Bernard Tschumi, Ove Arup et Hugh Dutton, Eiffel: Student Center, Lerner Hall, Université de Columbia, New York, Etats-Unis." *L'architecture d'aujourd'hui* (Paris), no. 329 (July–August 2000), pp. 60–65.

Cohl, Alan. "Interview with Architect Bernard Tschumi: Montage of Attractions." *Architecture of Israel* (Israel), no. 43 (Autumn 2000), pp. 2–13.

Cramer, Ned and Anne Guiney. "The Computer School." *Architecture* (New York) 89, no. 9 (September 2000), p. 94.

Deitz, Paula. "New Rhythm on Broadway." *ARTnews* (New York) 99, no. 2 (February 2000), pp. 108–110.

Deitz, Paula. "Tschumi Builds Columbia." *The Architectural Review* (London) 207, no. 1235 (January 2000), pp. 18–19.

Florence, Michel. "Clases desenclaustradas." *Arquitectura Viva* (Madrid), no. 74 (September–October 2000), pp. 90–94.

Forty, Adrian. *Words and Buildings: Vocabulary of Modern Architecture*. New York, NY: Thames and Hudson, 2000.

Fromonot, Francoise and David Leclerc. "Bernard Tschumi: Pour Quoi Faire?" *Le Visiteur* (France), no. 5 (Spring 2000), pp. 6–27.

Hower, Barbara. "Context is the Mother of Invention." *Interiors & Sources* (Northbrook, IL) 9, no. 1 (January/February 2000), pp. 102–106.

"Le Miami Che Sara." *Abitare* (Italy), no. 395 (May 2000), pp. 160–161.

Litt, Steven. "A Man in Motion." *The Plain Dealer* (Cleveland), 2 April 2000, p. 8-I.

"New York State of Mind." *World Architecture* (London), no. 83 (February 2000), p. 54.

Polo, Marco. "Environment as Process." *Canadian Architect* (Canada) 45, no. 10 (October 2000), pp. 14–19.

Porter, Tom and John Neale. *Architectural Supermodels*. Oxford: Architectural Press, 2000, pp. 114–115.

Richards, Ivor. *Manhattan Lofts*. Great Britain: Wiley-Academy, 2000, pp. 54–59.

"San Doute? Cents architectes parlent doctrine." *Les Cahiers de la recherche architecturale et urbaine* (Paris), no. 5–6 (October 2000), pp. 210–211.

Slessor, Catherine. "Containment Strategy." *Architecture* (New York) 89, no. 2 (February 2000), pp. 60–69.

Such, Robert. "Building Study: So Tschumi." *World Architecture* (London), no. 84 (March 2000), pp. 40–45.

Unali, Maurizio. "Bernard Tschumi: Alfred Lerner Hall." *Il Progetto* (Trieste), no. 6 (2000), cover, pp. 18–19.

"Urban Glass House of the 21st Century." *GA Document International* (Tokyo), no. 61 (April 2000), pp. 100–103.

"Visions 21: How We Will Live." *Time* (New York) 155, no. 7 (21 February 2000), pp. 86–87.

"Within the Politics of Place: United Nations World Intellectual Property Organization Competition in Geneva." *Competitions* (Louisville, Kentucky) 10, no. 2 (Summer 2000), pp. 36–39.

Zabalbeascoa, Anatxu and Javier Rodriguez Marcos. *Minimalisms*. Barcelona: Gustavo Gili, 2000, p. 98.

2001

Alberge, Dalya. "Greece to Build £29m Home for Elgin Marbles." *Times* (London), 26 October 2001, p. 17.

Arnaboldi, Mario Antonio. "Una poetica estrema." *L'Arca* (Italy), no. 164 (November 2001), pp. 26–37.

"Architecture and Animation." *Architectural Design* (London) 71, no. 2 (April 2001), pp. 17–19.

Bastea, Natasha. "You Respect Tradition, You Don't Imitate It." *Grand Larousse* (Greece), 3–4 November 2001, pp. 10–14.

"Bernard Tschumi, Escuela de Arquitectura/School of Architecture," *Metalocus* (Madrid), no. 8 (Winter 2001), pp.14–25.

"Bernard Tschumi, Architecte" *L'Hebdo* (Lausanne), 11 October 2001, p.39.

Booth, Robert. "Tschumi Plans Home for Elgin Marbles." *Building Design* (London), 19 October 2001, p. 5.

Borden, Iain. et al., eds. *The Unknown City: Contesting Architectural Space*. Cambridge, Mass.: The MIT Press, 2001, p. 371.

Campiotti, Alan. "Bernard Tschumi réfléchit, comme tous les New-Yorkais, à la renaissance de Manhattan." *Le Temps* (Paris), no. 1082 (3 October 2001), p. 43.

Czerniak, Julia, ed. *Case: Downsview Park Toronto*. Munich: Prestel Verlag and Cambridge: Harvard University Graduate School of Design, 2001.

"Desviación de la norma," *Arquitectura Viva* (Madrid), no. 76 (January–February 2001), pp. 42–45.

"Downsview Park," *Lotus International* (Milan), no. 109 (Summer 2001), pp. 34–63.

Doordan, Dennis P. *Twentieth-Century Architecture*. London: Laurence King, 2001, pp. 214, 236–9.

Giovannini, Joseph. "Lines of Desire." *Architecture* (New York) 90, no. 7 (July 2001), pp. 74–79.

"Interchanges: Interface Flon Railway and Bus Station." *Lotus International* (Milan), no. 108 (March 2001), pp. 92–95.

Illia, Tony. "Commission for Acropolis Museum, Intended as Home for Elgin Marbles, Goes to Tschumi." *Architectural Record* (New York) 189, no.12 (December 2001), p. 28.

Jodidio, Philip. "Tschumi fait son Zénith." *Connaissance des Arts* (Paris), no. 587 (October 2001), pp. 128–133.

Kipnis, Jeffrey. *Perfect Acts of Architecture*. New York: Harry N. Abrams, 2001, pp. 58–109.

"L'expo 2004 à La Courneuve, rendez-vous international de l'image," *Le Monde* (Paris), 23 November 2001, p. 30.

"Le Zénith Rouen." *L'architecture d'aujourd'hui* (Paris), no. 355 (July–August 2001), pp. 98–103.

Loriers, Marie-Christine. "Dé-familiarisation." *Techniques et Architecture* (Paris), no. 455 (September 2001), p. 90.

Mahler, Jonathan. "Gotham Rising." *Talk* (New York) 3, no. 4 (December 2001–January 2002), pp.120–125.

Merkel, Jayne. "Bernard Tschumi's *Event-Cities 2*." *Oculus* (New York) 63, no. 7 (March 2001), p. 11.

Michel, Florence. "Tschumi à Rouen." *Domus* (Milan), no. 838 (June 2001), pp. 56–67.

Morgan, William. "Melding the Arts with Technology: A New Arts Center at Rensselaer Polytechnic." *Competitions* 11, no. 4 (Winter 2001/2002), pp. 42–53.

"Neues Akropolismuseum." *StadtBauwelt* (Germany), no. 152 (December 2001), p. 9.

Orlandi, Alain. *Un Architecte/Une Oeuvre: Le Parc de La Villette de Bernard Tschumi.* Paris: Somogy éditions d'art, 2001.

Plaut, Jeannette. "Bernard Tschumi: Desde el language." *Ambientes* (Santiago), Summer 2001–2002, pp. 39–47, 66–67.

Polazzi, Giovanni. "Zenith Rock Arena, Rouen." *Area* (Milan), no. 59 (November/December 2001), pp. 40–53.

Rambert, Francis. "Rouen au Zénith de la forme." *d'Architectures* (Paris), no. 115 (November 2001), pp. 28–30.

Rattenbury, Kester. "Forms of Knowledge." *Building Design* (London), 2 November 2001, pp. 16–17.

Russell, James. "What About Blobs." *Details* 19, no. 6 (April 2001), pp. 88–90.

Ryan, Raymond. "Rouen's Zenith." *The Architectural Review* (London) 210, no. 1254 (August 2001), pp. 55–59.

Sowa, Axel. "Le Zénith." *Bauwelt* (Berlin), no. 38 (October 2001), pp. 24–27.

Sowa, Axel. "Le Zénith, Rouen." *L'architecture d'aujourd'hui* (Paris), no. 335 (July–August 2001), pp. 98–103.

Stephens, Suzanne. "Rouen Concert Hall." *Architectural Record* (New York), June 2001, cover, pp. 104–111.

Strickland, Carol. *The Annotated Arch: A Crash Course in the History of Architecture.* Kansas City: A John Boswell Associates Book, 2001, p. 153.

Tschumi, Bernard. "Carcasa Catedralica." *Architectura Viva* (Madrid), no. 81 (November/December 2001), p. 90.

Vernes, Michel. "Zenith: Rencontre de troisième type." *Architecture Intérieure Crée* (Paris), no. 299 (2001), pp. 96–101.

Xu, Jie and Wenjun Zhi. "The Old and New of Le Fresnoy National Contemporary Art Center, France." *Time and Architecture*, 2001, pp. 48–53.

2002
"Athens: Bernard Tschumi's Competition-Winning Scheme for the Acropolis Museum." *Architecture Today* (London), no. 125 (February 2002), p. 15.

Barmettler, Stefan. "Baumeister." *Facts* (Zurich), no. 25 (20 June 2002), p. 114.

"Bernard Tschumi: Urbi et Orbi." *Jalouse* (Paris), no. 47 (February 2002), pp. 100–101.

Bruno, Giuliana. *Atlas of Emotion: Journey in Art Architecture and Film.* New York: Verso, 2002, p. 57.

Campiotti, Alain. "Bernard Tschumi est sur les rangs pour combler le trou du WTC." *Le Temp* (Paris), 24 August 2002.

Capurso, Rossana. "Sala Concerti a Centro Espositivo a Rouen, France." *L'industria delle Costruzioni* (Rome), no. 365 (May/June 2002), pp. 52–61.

"Concert Hall and Exhibition Complex." *Space* (Seoul), no. 416 (July 2002), p. 118.

Dablis, Andy. "Athens Museum Awaits Disputed Marbles." *USA Today* (McLean, VA), 22 March 2002, p. 10.

"Demandez le programme!" *L'architecture d'aujourd'hui* (Paris), no. 339 (March–April 2002), pp. 38–43.

"De Vuelta a la Acropolis." *Pasajes* (Madrid), no. 36 (April 2002), p. 18.

Dufour, Nicolas. "Athènes dévoile son futur Musée de l' Acropole." *Le Temp* (Paris), no. 171, 21 February 2002.

"Fuegos artificiales del parquet de la Villette." *Oeste* (Madrid), no. 14 (July 2002), pp. 1–10.

Fuksas, Massimilliano. "Una stazione transparente." *L'Espresso* (Rome), 11 April 2002, p. 58.

Futagawa, Yoshio. "Bernard Tschumi." *StudioTalk*. Tokyo: A.D.A Edita, 2002, pp. 466–510 (interview).

Giovannini, Joseph. "In Brief." *New York Magazine* (New York), 21 October 2002, p. 55.

Glover, Michael. "Olympic Effort." *ArtNews* (New York) 101, no. 3 (March 2002), p. 60.

Huber, Joachim. *Urbane Topologie*. Germany: Verso, 2002, pp. 428–456.

Horn, Christian. "Zénith in Rouen." *Architektur* (Germany), February 2002, pp. 46–50.

"Interface Flon." *Werldstations*. Amsterdam: Centraal Museum, 2002, p. 64.

"Interface Flon Railway and Bus Station." *L'Industria della Costruzioni* (Rome), no. 367 (September–October 2002), p. 38.

International Architectural Yearbook 8/02. Australia: The Images Publishing Group, 2002, pp. 118–119.

"Intermodal Station in Lausanne." *L' Arca* (Milan), no. 171 (June 2002), pp. 9–13.

Jaunin, Francoise. "Un ecrin de verre pour la frise mythique." *24 Heures* (Paris), 11 March 2002.

Jodidio, Philip, ed. "Bernard Tschumi." *Architecture Now!* vol. 2. Cologne and Los Angeles: Taschen, 2002, pp. 480–488.

Kellogg, Craig. "Bilbao Backlash." *Oculus* (New York) 64, no. 7–8 (March/April 2002), p. 5.

"Lumineux Project." *24 Heures* (Paris), 20 February 2002.

"L'usine à rêves" *Telerama* (Paris), 19 June 2002.

Mattogno, Claudia. *Idee di spazio, lo spazio nelle idee.* Chartres: Franco Angeli/Urbanistica, 2002, p. 78.

Merkel, Jayne. "The Dean." *Versioning: Evolutionary Techniques in Architecture.* London: Architectural Design 72, no. 5 (September/October 2002), pp. 83–87.

"Museu de Arte Contemporanea." *GA Document International* (Tokyo), no. 70 (July 2002), pp. 66–69.

"The Museum for African Art." *Area* (Milan), no. 65 (December 2002), p. 110.

"The Museum for African Art." *Shtab-Kvartira* (Moscow), no. 4 (October 2002), p. 130.

Pellis, Marta. "Una Piazza da abitare." *Il Giorno* (Rome), 8 April 2002.

Rambert, Francis. "Musées: les très bon label France." *Le Figaro* (France), 5 February 2002.

"Rien ne se perd, rien ne se crée." *Architecture Intérieure Crée* (Paris), no. 304 (August 2002), p. 27.

"Rouen." *Nikkei* (Tokyo), no. 716 (April 2002), p. 20.

Trachtenberg, Marvin and Isabelle Hyman, eds. *Architecture from Prehistory to Postmodernity.* 2d ed. New York: Abrams, 2002, p. 564.

Wiesner, Anne. "Vektorielle Infrastruktur." *Archithese* (Switzerland), no. 2 (January/February 2002), pp. 26–31.

Yablonsky, Linda. "Harlem's New Renaissance." *ArtNews* (New York) 101, no. 4 (April 2002), p. 108.

2003
Aspden, Peter. "The Sharp Edge of Civilisation." *Financial Times* (London), 14–15 June 2003, p. W6.

Benjamin, Andrew. "Particular Spaces." *Monument* (Melbourne), August/September 2003, p. 104.

"Bernard Tschumi, Luca Merlini et Emmanuel Ventura: Gare d'interconnexion Lausanne." *AMC* (Paris), no. 123 (March 2003), pp. 41–46.

Blasi, Cesare and Padovano, Gariella ed. *La sfida della sostenibilità.* Italy: Foxwell and Davies, 2003, p. 154.

Bong, Joohee, "Bernard Tschumi." *Space* (Seoul), no. 428 (July 2003), pp. 109–157.

"Class Notes." *Metropolis* (New York) 23, no. 1 (August/September 2003), p.103–109.

Coates, Nigel. *Ecstacity.* London: Laurence King, 2003, pp. 36, 38, 295, 353.

"Contexto y concepto." *Arquitectura Viva* (Madrid), no. 92 (September/October 2003), p. 9.

Davidson, Cynthia. "Bernard Tschumi: The Exit Interview," *Log* (New York), no. 1 (Fall 2003), p. 141.

"Form and Formless." *Dialogue* (China), no. 70 (June 2003), p. 40.

Galpin, Richard. "Acropolis Building Site Stirs Up Storm." *BBC News On-Line World Edition*, www.bbc.co.uk, 18 August 2003.

"Historic Preservation and Architectural Renewal." *Dialogue* (China), no. 69 (May 2003), p.123.

Ho, Cathy Lang. "Looking for a Leader." *The Architect's Newspaper* (New York), no. 1 (10 November 2003), p. 16.

"Interplay of Light and Shadow." *Intelligent Build and Design Innovations* (London), no. 5 (2003/2004), p. 52.

Lubow, Arthur. "How Architecture Rediscovered the Future." *The New York Times Magazine* (New York), 18 May 2003, p. 42.

Muschamp, Herbert. "Miami's Juicy New Lesson Plan." *The New York Times* (New York), 6 April 2003, Arts and Leisure sec. 2, p. 34.

Pearson, Clifford. "FIU School of Architecture." *Architectural Record* (New York) 191, no. 10 (October 2003), p. 103.

Picadas, Costas. "Bernard Tschumi." *Status* (Athens), no. 180 (March 2003), p. 102.

Rattenbury, Kester. "The Main Event." *Building Design* (London), 10 January 2003, pp. 12–15.

Rosenbaum, Lee. "Meeting of the Marbles?" *Art in America* (New York), no. 5 (May 2003), p. 41.

"Rouen Concert Hall." *Shtab-Kvartira* (Moscow), no. 8 (April 2003), p. 117.

Santiard, A. and J. Cadilhac. *E2: Exploring the Urban Condition*. Barcelona: Actar, 2003, pp. 100–111 (interview).

Stephens, Suzanne. "Strangely Familiar." *Architectural Record* (New York) 191, no. 7 (July 2003), p. 93.

"Un cofre de crystal para las joyas de la Acrópolis." *GEO* (Madrid), no. 201 (October 2003), p. 14.

"University of Cincinnati Athletic Center." *GA Document International* (Tokyo), no. 73 (April 2003), p. 74.

Ungoed-Thomas, Jon. "Museum in Secret Talks to Return Elgin Marbles." *The Sunday Times* (London), 2 August 2003, p. 1.

Van Gelder, Lawrence. "Greece: Approval for a Museum." *New York Times* (New York), 29 July 2003, sec. E, p. 2.

Vidler, Anthony. "Deconstructivist Architecture." *Artforum* (New York), no. 8 (April 2003), p. 99.

Vossoughian, Nader. "Interview with Bernard Tschumi: On Designing an Architectural Education." *Agglutinations* (New York) 1, no. 8 (21 May 2003), p. 1.

Walker, Enrique. "Interview with Bernard Tschumi." *Summa+* (Buenos Aires), no. 57 (January 2003), p. 36.

Weiss, Lois. "Deal to Rescue Harlem Museum." *New York Post* (New York), 26 June 2003, p. 36.

2004
"Acropolémiques." *Libération* (Paris), 12 March 2004, Culture sec., p. 35.

Bernstein, Fred. "Greece's Colossal New Guilt Trip." *The New York Times* (New York), 18 January 2004, Arts and Leisure sec. 2, p. 1. Reprinted in French in *La Presse* (Montreal), 28 January 2004.

Fei, Qing and Gang Fu. "Interview with Bernard Tschumi." *World Architecture* (Beijing), no. 166 (April 2004), pp. 20, 36–39.

"Greece Builds a Museum for Missing Statues." *The Week* (New York) 4, no. 143 (February 13, 2004), p. 25.

Hosch, Alexander. "Das Lock-Museum." *Architectural Digest Germany* (Munich), no. 45 (January 2004), p. 48.

Lobell, Jarrett. "Acropolis Museum Back on Track and Wants the Parthenon Marbles to Come Home." *Archaeology* (New York) 57, no. 4 (July/August 2004), pp. 10–12.

"In-Jury." *Area* (Milan), no. 73 (March/April 2004), p. 24.

Last, Nana. "Conceptualism's (Con)quests." *Harvard Design Magazine* (Cambridge, MA), no.19 (Fall 2003/Winter 2004), pp. 14–21.

"The New Acropolis Museum." *GA Document International* (Tokyo), no. 79 (April 2004), p. 64.

Way, James and Deborah Grossman. "Polyphonic Monologues." *The Architect's Newspaper* (New York), no. 9 (25 May 2004), p. 16.

Photography Credits

p. 16–17 Richard Berenholtz   **p. 72/73/76–77/78/79/80/81/82/83** Peter Mauss/Esto
p. 84–85 City of Strasbourg   **p. 112–113** Darrell Sapp   **p. 138-139** City of Limoges
p. 174 Encino Velodrome   **p. 175** Greater Houston Convention and Visitors Bureau
p. 192–193 State Photographic Archive of Italy   **p. 334–335** Museum for African Art
p. 390–391 THP Limited, Inc.   **p. 430–431** OANMA   **p. 487** Norman Wilkinson
p. 488 The Phillips Collection   **p. 502–503/506–507/508–509/510–511** Arte Factory
p. 556 Peter Skinner, *The World Trade Center*   **p. 582–583** Zhu Yan   **p. 638–639** Ma
Han, *Flying Machine*, 2002

DATE DUE
